# Perl 6 and Parrot Essentials

# Other Perl resources from O'Reilly

**Related titles**

Programming Perl
Learning Perl
Perl Cookbook
Perl Template Toolkit
Perl Debugger Pocket
   Reference
Perl Pocket Reference

Learning Perl Objects,
   References, and
   Modules
Perl in a Nutshell
Practical mod_perl
Regular Expression Pocket
   Reference

**Perl Books
Resource Center**

*perl.oreilly.com* is a complete catalog of O'Reilly's books on Perl and related technologies, including sample chapters and code examples.

*Perl.com* is the central web site for the Perl community. It is the perfect starting place for finding out everything there is to know about Perl.

**Conferences**

O'Reilly brings diverse innovators together to nurture the ideas that spark revolutionary industries. We specialize in documenting the latest tools and systems, translating the innovator's knowledge into useful skills for those in the trenches. Visit *conferences.oreilly.com* for our upcoming events.

Safari Bookshelf (*safari.oreilly.com*) is the premier online reference library for programmers and IT professionals. Conduct searches across more than 1,000 books. Subscribers can zero in on answers to time-critical questions in a matter of seconds. Read the books on your Bookshelf from cover to cover or simply flip to the page you need. Try it today with a free trial.

SECOND EDITION

# Perl 6 and Parrot Essentials

*Allison Randal, Dan Sugalski,*
*and Leopold Tötsch*

O'REILLY®

Beijing · Cambridge · Farnham · Köln · Paris · Sebastopol · Taipei · Tokyo

**Perl 6 and Parrot Essentials, Second Edition**
by Allison Randal, Dan Sugalski, and Leopold Tötsch

Published by O'Reilly Media, Inc., 1005 Gravenstein Highway North, Sebastopol, CA 95472.

O'Reilly books may be purchased for educational, business, or sales promotional use. Online editions are also available for most titles (*safari.oreilly.com*). For more information, contact our corporate/institutional sales department: (800) 998-9938 or *corporate@oreilly.com*.

**Editor:**              Tatiana Apandi Diaz

**Production Editor:**    Matt Hutchinson

**Production Services:**  Octal Publishing, Inc.

**Cover Designer:**      Ellie Volckhausen

**Interior Designer:**   David Futato

**Printing History:**

June 2003:      First Edition. Originally published as *Perl 6 Essentials*.

June 2004:      Second Edition.

 This book uses RepKover™, a durable and flexible lay-flat binding.

ISBN: 0-596-00737-X

[M]

# Table of Contents

# Preface

There is nothing as scary to the average programmer (to the average human, really) as the single word "change." Change means taking the time to learn a new way of doing things. Changes can be annoying: moving to a new home, finding the shelves reorganized at your neighborhood computer store, or ordering your favorite beer at your favorite pub only to be told they don't make it anymore. But changes can also be good: a vacation on the beach, a promotion, a raise, finding the perfect shortcut to work that shaves 20 minutes off your commute. This book is all about change...the good kind.

Perl 6 isn't far enough along to support a book on the level of *Programming Perl*. However, as development goes on, we've found that the accumulated lore of the past few years is quite an entry barrier for new people. This book is a snapshot of the current status, designed to ease that first step. It covers the project through Apocalypse 12 and the 0.1.0 release of Parrot. We expect that this will be the last edition of the book, but we will publish updates as needed.

## How This Book Is Organized

This book has 11 chapters:

Chapter 1 is a high-level overview of the project, with some history of how and why the project was started.

Chapter 2 provides more detail on life cycles within the project and how to get involved.

Chapter 3 explains some of the principles behind Perl 6 design work.

Chapters 4–7 are an introduction to Perl 6 syntax.

Chapter 8 explains the overall architecture of Parrot (the virtual machine that runs Perl 6).

Chapter 9 is an introduction to Parrot assembly language.

Chapter 10 is an introduction to Parrot intermediate representation.

Chapter 11 is a reference for Parrot assembly language, Parrot intermediate representation, and command-line options for the Parrot interpreter.

If you're a Perl programmer who is completely new to Perl 6, you'll be interested in this book to get an idea of what it'll be like to work with Perl 6, why we're making the changes we're making, and how the project is going. You'll want to read the first seven chapters. If you think you might be interested in getting involved in implementation, read the rest as well.

If you're already involved in the Perl 6 project, you'll be interested in this book to see how all the pieces fit together, and you may want to use it as a reference while you're working. If you've been involved only on the language side or the internals side, you'll also get a chance to see what the other half is doing. In this way, the entire book is relevant to you.

If you're interested in implementing another language on top of Parrot, you'll want to skim through the Parrot information in Chapter 2, and then skip straight to Chapter 8 and go from there.

If you're not involved in Perl but just want to see what the "Perl 6" buzz is all about, you'll want to read Chapters 1, 3, and 8. You'll get an overview of what we're doing and why, without all the nitty-gritty details.

# Font Conventions

The following font conventions are used in this book:

*Italic*
> Used for filenames, URLs, and email addresses

`Constant width`
> Used in code listings and for function names, variable names, and other literal text

`Constant width italic`
> Shows text that should be replaced with user-supplied values

# Using Code Examples

This book is here to help you get your job done. In general, you may use the code in this book in your programs and documentation. You do not need to contact us for permission unless you're reproducing a significant portion of the code. For example, writing a program that uses several chunks of code from this book does not require permission. Selling or distributing a CD-ROM of examples from O'Reilly books *does* require permission. Answering a question by citing this book and quoting example code does not require permission. Incorporating a significant amount of example code from this book into your product's documentation *does* require permission.

We appreciate, but do not require, attribution. An attribution usually includes the title, author, publisher, and ISBN. For example: *"Perl 6 and Parrot Essentials*, Second Edition, by Allison Randal, Dan Sugalski, and Leopold Tötsch. Copyright 2004 O'Reilly Media, Inc., 0-596-00737-X."

If you feel your use of code examples falls outside fair use or the permission given above, feel free to contact us at *permissions@oreilly.com*.

## We'd Like to Hear from You

Please address comments and questions concerning this book to the publisher:

O'Reilly Media, Inc.
1005 Gravenstein Highway North
Sebastopol, CA 95472
(800) 998-9938 (in the United States or Canada)
(707) 829-0515 (international or local)
(707) 829-0104 (fax)

We have a web page for this book, where we list errata, examples, or any additional information. You can access this page at:

*http://www.oreilly.com/catalog/059600737X/*

To comment or ask technical questions about this book, send email to:

*bookquestions@oreilly.com*

For more information about our books, conferences, Resource Centers, and the O'Reilly Network, see our web site at:

*http://www.oreilly.com*

## Acknowledgments

Many thanks to our reviewers for this edition of the book: Leon Brocard, Piers Cawley, Damian Conway, chromatic, Jeffrey Dik, Simon Glover, Garrett Goebel, Trey Harris, Gregor Purdy, Jérôme Quelin, Jens Rieks, Brent Royal-Gordon, Joseph Ryan, Hugo van der Sanden, and Melvin Smith.

This book is dedicated to the Perl community, because it wouldn't exist without them.

# CHAPTER 1

# Project Overview

Perl 6 is the next major version of Perl. It's a complete rewrite of the interpreter, and a significant update of the language itself. The goal of Perl 6 is to add support for much-needed new features, and still be cleaner, faster, and easier to use.

The Perl 6 project is vast and complex, but it isn't complicated. The project runs on a simple structure with very little management overhead. That's really the only way it could run. The project doesn't have huge cash or time resources. Its only resource is the people who believe in the project enough to spend their off-hours—their "relaxation" time—working to see it completed. This chapter is as much about people as it is about Perl.

## The Birth of Perl 6

Back on July 18, 2000, the second day of the fourth Perl Conference (TPC 4), a small band of Perl geeks gathered to prepare for a meeting of the Perl 5 Porters later that day. The topic at hand was the current state of the Perl community. Four months had passed since the 5.6.0 release of Perl, and although it introduced some important features, none were revolutionary.

There had been very little forward movement in the previous year. It was generally acknowledged that the Perl 5 codebase had grown difficult to maintain. At the same time, infighting on the *perl5-porters* list had grown so intense that some of the best developers decided to leave. It was time for a change, but no one was quite sure what to do. They started conservatively with plans to change the organization of Perl development.

An hour into the discussion, around the time most people nod off in any meeting, Jon Orwant (the reserved, universally respected editor of the Perl Journal) stepped quietly into the room and snapped everyone to attention with an entirely uncharacteristic and well-planned gesture. *Smash!* A coffee mug hit the wall. "We are *@$!-ed (*Crash!*) unless we can come up with something that will excite the community (*Pow!*), because everyone's getting bored and going off and doing other things! (*Bam!*)" (At least, that's basically how Larry tells it. As is usually the case with events like this, no one remembers exactly what Jon said.)

Awakened by this display, the group started to search for a real solution. The language needed room to grow. It needed the freedom to evaluate new features without the obscuring weight of legacy code. The community needed something to believe in, something to get excited about.

Within a few hours the group settled on Perl 6, a complete rewrite of Perl. The plan wasn't just a language change, just an implementation change, or just a social change. It was a paradigm shift. Perl 6 would be the community's rewrite of Perl, and the community's rewrite of itself.

Would Perl 6, particularly Perl 6 as a complete rewrite, have happened without this meeting? Almost certainly. The signs appeared on the lists, in conferences, and in journals months in advance. If it hadn't started that day, it would have happened a week later, or perhaps a few months later, but it would have happened. It was a step the community needed to take.

# In the Beginning...

Let's pause and consider Perl development up to that fateful meeting. Perl 6 is just another link in the chain. The motivations behind it and the directions it will take are partially guided by history.

Perl was first developed in 1987 by Larry Wall while he was working as a programmer for Unisys. After creating a configuration and monitoring system for a network that spanned the two American coasts, he was faced with the task of assembling usable reports from log files scattered across the network. The available tools simply weren't up to the job. A linguist at heart, Larry set out to create his own programming language, which he called *perl*. He released the first version of Perl on December 18, 1987. He made it freely available on Usenet (this was before the Internet took over the world, remember), and quickly a community of Perl programmers grew.

The early adopters of Perl were system administrators who had hit the wall with shell scripting, *awk*, and *sed*. However, in the mid-1990s Perl's audience exploded with the advent of the Web, as Perl was tailor-made for CGI scripting and other web-related programming.

Meantime, the Perl language itself kept growing, as Larry and others kept adding new features. Probably the most revolutionary change in Perl (until Perl 6, of course) was the addition of modules and object-oriented programming with Perl 5. Although this made the transition period from Perl 4 to Perl 5 unusually long, it breathed new life into the language by providing a modern, modular interface. Before Perl 5, Perl was considered simply a scripting language; after Perl 5, it was considered a full-fledged programming language.

Larry, meanwhile, started taking a back seat to Perl development and allowed others to take responsibility for adding new features and fixing bugs in Perl. The Perl 5 Porters (p5p) mailing list became the central clearing-house for bug reports and proposed changes to the Perl language, with the "pumpkin holder" (also known as the "pumpking") being the programmer responsible for integrating the patches and distributing them to the rest of the list for review. Larry continued to follow Perl development, but like a parent determined not to smother his children, he stayed out of the day-to-day development, limiting his involvement to situations in which he was truly needed.

Although you might think that the birth of the Perl 6 project would be the first nail in the coffin for Perl 5, that's far from the case. If anything, Perl 5 has had a huge resurgence of development, with Perl 5.7.0 released only two weeks after the initial decision to go ahead with Perl 6. Perl 5.8.0, a July 2002 release by pumpking Jarkko Hietaniemi, includes usable Unicode support, a working threads interface, safe signals, and a significant improvement of the internals with code cleanup, bug fixes, better documentation, and more than quadrupled test coverage. 5.8 has quarterly maintenance releases thanks to pumpking Nicholas Clark. The 5.9–5.10 releases have Hugo van der Sanden as architect and Rafaël Garcia-Suarez as pumpking. Plans for those releases include enhancements to the regular expression engine, further internals cleanup and a "use perl6ish" pragma that will integrate many of the features of Perl 6. Perl 5 is active and thriving, and will continue to be so even after the release of Perl 6.0.

# The Continuing Mission

Much has changed since the early days of the project. New people join and others leave in a regular "changing of the guard" pattern. Plans change as the work progresses, and the demands of the work and the needs of the community become clearer. Today the Perl 6 project has two major parts: language design and internals. Each branch is relatively autonomous, though there is a healthy amount of coordination between them.

# Language Design

As with all things Perl, the central command of the language design process is Larry Wall, the creator of the Perl language. Larry is supported by the rest of the design team: Damian Conway, Allison Randal, Dan Sugalski, Hugo van der Sanden, and chromatic. We speak in weekly teleconferences and also meet face-to-face a few times a year to hash out ideas for the design documents, or to work through roadblocks standing in the way of design or implementation. The design team is a diverse group, including programmers-for-hire, Perl trainers, and linguists with a broad spectrum of interests and experiences. This diversity has proved quite valuable in the design process, as each member is able to see problems in the design or potential solutions that the other members missed.

## Requests For Comments (RFCs)

The first step in designing the new language was the RFC (Request For Comments) process. This spurred an initial burst of community involvement. Anyone was free to submit an RFC on any subject, whether it was as small as adding an operator, or as big as reworking OO syntax. Most of the proposals were really quite conservative. The RFCs followed a standard format so they would be easier to read and easier to compare.

Each RFC was subject to peer review, carried out in an intense few weeks around October 2000. One thing the RFC process demonstrated was that the Perl community still wasn't quite ready to move beyond the infighting that had characterized Perl 5 Porters earlier that year.[*] Even though few RFCs have been accepted without modification, the process identified a large number of irritants in the language. These have served as signposts for later design efforts.

## Apocalypses, Synopses, Exegeses

The Apocalypses,[†] Synopses, and Exegeses[‡] are an important part of the design process. Larry started the Apocalypse series as a systematic way of answering the RFCs. Each Apocalypse corresponds to a chapter in his book *Programming Perl*, and addresses the features in the chapter that are likely to change.

---

[*] Mark-Jason Dominus wrote an excellent critique of the RFC process (*http://www.perl.com/pub/a/2000/11/perl6rfc.html*). It may seem harsh to people accustomed to the more open and tolerant community of today, but it's an accurate representation of the time when it was written.

[†] An "apocalypse" in the sense of "revelation," not "end of the world."

[‡] An "exegesis" is an explanation or interpretation of a text.

---

However, the Apocalypses have become much more than a simple response to RFCs. Larry has a startling knack for looking at 12 solutions to a problem, pulling out the good bits from each one, and combining them into a solution that is 10 times better than any of the proposals alone. The Apocalypses are an excellent example of this "Larry Effect." He addresses each relevant RFC, and gives reasons why he accepted or rejected various pieces of it. But each Apocalypse also goes beyond a simple "yes" and "no" response to attack the roots of the problems identified in the RFCs.

The Synopses are summaries of each Apocalypse. These act as a quick reference for the current state of design, and are more approachable than the often lengthy Apocalypses. The Synopsis series didn't start until Apocalypse 5, but Luke Palmer is now working on the retroactive Synopses 2–4.

Damian Conway's Exegeses are extensions of each Apocalypse. The Exegeses are built around practical code examples that apply and explain the new ideas.

### The p6l mailing list

The next body of design work is the Perl 6 Language mailing list (*perl6-language@perl.org*), often fondly referred to as "p6l." Piers Cawley writes a weekly summary of all the Perl 6 mailing lists. Luke Palmer has been deputized as unofficial referee of the list. He answers questions that don't require the direct involvement of the design team or that have been answered before. The list has approximately 40 regular contributors in any given month, as well as a large number of occasional posters and lurkers. Some people have participated since the very beginning; others appear for a few months and move on.

Even though the individuals change, the general tone of p6l is the same. It's an open forum for any ideas on the user-visible parts of Perl 6. In the typical pattern, one person posts an idea and 5 to 10 people respond with criticisms or suggestions. The list periodically travels down a speculative thread like a runaway train, but these eventually run out of steam. Then Larry picks out the golden bits and gently tells the rest that no, he never intended Perl 6 to have neo-Vulcan mechanoid Scooby-Dooby-doos. Even when Larry doesn't post, he follows the list and the traffic serves as a valuable catalyst for his thoughts.

## Internals

The internals development for Perl 6 falls to the Parrot project. The heart of Parrot is a grandiose idea that turned out to be more realistic than anyone originally could have believed: why not have a single interpreter for several languages? Unlike the parent Perl 6 project, which was launched in a single day, the plan for Parrot formed in bits and pieces over the period of a year.

On April 1, 2001, Simon Cozens published an article titled "Programming Parrot" as an April Fools' joke (*http://www.perl.com/pub/a/2001/04/01/parrot.htm*). It was a contrived interview with Larry Wall and Guido van Rossum detailing their plans to merge Python and Perl into a new language called Parrot. A few months later, when Perl 6 internals began to take an independent path within the larger project, they dubbed the subproject "Parrot" in a fitting turn of life imitating art.

---

## Early Steps Toward Perl 6 Internals

The earliest progress toward implementing Perl 6 started before the current incarnation of Perl 6 was even conceived. The Topaz project, started in 1998, was spearheaded by Chip Salzenberg. It was a reimplementation of Perl 5 written in C++. The project was abandoned, but many of the goals and intended features for Topaz were adopted for Perl 6 internals, and the difficulties Topaz encountered were also valuable guides.

Sapphire was another early prototype that influenced the shape of Perl 6 internals. It was a one-week project in September 2000. The brainchild of Simon Cozens, Sapphire was another rewrite of Perl 5 internals. It was never intended for release, only as an experiment to see how far the idea could go in a week, and what lessons could be learned.

---

The plan for Parrot was to build a language-neutral run-time environment. It would support all the features of dynamic languages, such as Python, Ruby, Scheme, Befunge, and others. It would have threading and Unicode support (two of the most problematic features to add into Perl 5 code) designed in from the start. It would support exceptions and compilation to bytecode, and have clean extension and embedding mechanisms.

The language-neutral interpreter was originally just a side effect of good design. Keeping the implementation independent of the syntax would make the code cleaner and easier to maintain. One practical advantage of this design was that Parrot development could begin even though the Perl 6 language specification was still in flux.

The bigger win in the long term, though, was that since Parrot would support the features of the major dynamic languages and wasn't biased to a particular syntax, it could run all these languages with little additional effort.

---

It's generally acknowledged that different languages are suited to different tasks. Picking which language will be used in a large software project is a common planning problem. There's never a perfect fit. It usually boils down to picking the language with the most advantages and the least noticeable disadvantages. The ability to easily combine multiple languages within a project could be a huge benefit. Use well-tested libraries from one language for one task. Take advantage of a clean way of expressing a particular problem domain in a second, without being forced to use it in areas where it's weak.

The modular design also benefits future language designers. Instead of targeting *lex/yacc* and reimplementing low-level features such as garbage collection and dynamic types, designers can write a parser that targets the Parrot virtual machine.

Dan Sugalski leads the Parrot project as chief architect, and Leopold Tötsch is the current pumpking. The Parrot project is largely autonomous. Dan coordinates with the rest of the design team to ensure that Parrot will be able to support the semantics Perl 6 will require, but the language designers have very little input into the details of implementation. Parrot isn't developed solely for Perl, but Perl 6 is entirely dependent on Parrot—it is the only interpreter for Perl 6.

The core communication line for the Parrot project is the mailing list, *perl6-internals@perl.org*, otherwise known as "p6i." It's a much more business-like list than p6l. Workflow in Parrot takes the form of submitted patches. Anyone is free to submit a patch, and contributors who consistently submit valuable patches over a long period of time are granted check-in access to the CVS repository.

# Ponie

Ponie is an implementation of Perl 5 on Parrot, started in July 2003. Offically, Ponie stands for "Perl On New Internal Engine." The name was originally derived from a running gag in the London.pm Perl Mongers group where the phrase "I want a pony" appeared in lists of feature requests for Perl (and other unusual places).

The project, led by Artur Bergman, has taken the Perl 5 source code as a base and is gradually replacing the core elements with Parrot equivalents. Legacy code will be one of the biggest obstacles to projects considering the move from Perl 5 to Perl 6. Few companies have the resources to do a complete update to existing code every time a new version of the language is released. Ponie offers a smooth migration path that ensures Perl 5 code will function as long as it's needed. You'll even be able to use Perl 5 modules and Perl 6 modules side-by-side in the same program. The current plan is for Ponie to be the 5.14 or 5.16 release of Perl.

The mailing list for Ponie development is *ponie-dev@perl.org*.

## Supporting Structure

Last, but not least, is the glue that holds the project together. Ask Bjørn Hansen and Robert Spier manage the email, revision control, and bug-tracking systems, as well as the web pages for Perl 6, Parrot, and Ponie (*http://dev.perl.org*). Without these systems, the project would grind to a screeching halt.

Allison Randal is the project manager. As is typical of open source development projects, managing the Perl 6 project is quite different from managing a commercial project of the same size and complexity. There are no schedules, no deadlines, no hiring and firing, and no salaries, bonuses, or stock options. There are no employees or bosses; there is very little hierarchy whatsoever. Management in this context isn't about giving orders, it's about making sure everyone has what they need to keep moving forward.

In the end, it is the developers themselves who hold the project together. Individuals bear their own share of responsibility for finding tasks that suit their skills, coordinating with others to keep duplicated effort minimal, and making sure the job gets done.

# CHAPTER 2

# Project Development

The Perl community is rich and diverse. There are as many variations in skill sets and skill levels as there are people. Some are coders, some are testers, some are writers, some are teachers, some are theorists. For every skill, there is a task. It's the combination of all the skills that gets the job done. A team of workers all wielding hammers could never build a house. Someone has to cut the wood, sand it, apply plaster, paint it, and install windows, doors, electrical systems, and plumbing.

## Language Development

Theoretically, language design is the driving force behind all other parts of the project. In actual practice, Parrot development frequently affects the direction and focus of design efforts. A design that gave no consideration to what can be implemented efficiently wouldn't be much use. Equally, if the design work followed a strictly linear path, it would be a waste of developer resources. The Parrot project can't afford to go on hold every time they need information from a future area of design. For example, long before the design of OO syntax was completed, the design team took time to define enough of the required semantics so that development could move ahead.

### Development Cycles

Design work goes in cycles. Each cycle begins with a quiet period. During this time, the list traffic is fairly light, and Larry is rarely seen. It can seem as if the project is stalled, but in fact, this part of the cycle is where the bulk of original design work is done. Larry disappears when he's working on an Apocalypse. It's the most intense and creative phase.

The next phase is internal revision. Larry sends a draft of the Apocalypse to the design team for comments and makes changes based on their suggestions. Sometimes the changes are as simple as typo fixes, but sometimes they entirely alter the shape of the design. Larry repeats this several times before publishing the document. This is a very fast-paced and dynamic phase, but again, low on visible results.

Next is the community review. Usually the first day or two after an Apocalypse comes out are quiet, while the ideas soak in. Then the list begins to fly. Some people suggest changes, while others ask about the design. This phase reflects the most visible progress, but the changes are mostly refinements. The changes introduced at community review polish off the rough edges, add a few new tricks, or make simplifications for the average user. Here the community takes ownership of the design, as both the design and the people change until the two are a comfortable fit.

The Synopsis, a summary released by the design team soon after each Apocalypse, assists in the community review by breaking down the ideas from the Apocalypse into a simple list of points.

The Exegesis comes next, and its process is much like that of the Apocalypse. List traffic slows again while Damian writes and the design team revises. The Exegesis responds to the community review. The practical examples at the core of each Exegesis explain the parts of the Apocalypse that were hardest to understand and flesh out some of the holes found in the community review. The list bursts into another flurry of activity as the community reviews the Exegesis. Then the cycle starts all over again.

## Getting Involved

The primary cycle of Apocalypses, Synopses, and Exegeses is not the only movement in design. Constant activity on and off the list packs around the larger cycle. Old decisions are revisited; future decisions are previewed.

Getting involved in Perl 6 design work is as simple, and as difficult, as joining the p6l list. Subscribing to a list takes almost no effort, but the most valuable contributions don't come from people who respond to an idea here and there, though those are certainly welcome. The posts with the greatest impact come from people who take the time to learn the system—to figure out what Perl 6 is all about.

If you want to make a valuable contribution, get on the list and listen. Work to understand the issues behind each thread of discussion. Soon you'll find there are repetitions in the themes, guiding principles that shape the debates.

Form a mental map of the new syntax. It's not an easy task. There is is only a limited prototype interpreter available for Perl 6, so if you forget how a particular feature works you can't just experiment. Mainly, you'll have to search through the list archives—over, and over, and over again. And the syntax keeps changing. You'll have a perfect grasp on a feature just before it changes. It can be frustrating, but it is well worth it.

# Parrot Development

Parrot development is the productive core of Perl 6 development. If you want coding action, this is the place to be.

Organization of the Parrot project is lightweight but efficient. It's a meritocracy—people who make valuable contributions are offered more responsibility. Communication is relaxed and informal. As Dan is so fond of saying, "This is far too important to take seriously." It's a bit like a special forces unit—the work gets done not because of tight control from the top, but because the whole team knows the task at hand and does it.

## Development Cycles

The cycles in Parrot development center on "point releases." A point release is a version change, such as 0.0.8 to 0.0.9. The pumpking decides when point releases happen and what features are included. Usually one or two solid new features trigger a release.

Development proceeds at a steady pace of bug reports, patches submitted, and patches applied. The pace isn't so much a result of careful planning as it is the law of averages—on any given day, someone, somewhere, is working on Parrot. A release is a spike in that activity, but since Parrot tends to follow the "release early, release often" strategy, the spike is relatively small.

Typically, the pumpking declares a feature freeze a few days before each release and all development efforts center on bug squashing. This periodic cleanup is one of the most valuable aspects of a release.

## Getting Involved

Just like design work, the first step to participating in Parrot development is joining the list. The topics on p6i tend to stick to practical matters: bug reports, patches, notifications of changes committed to CVS, and questions on coding style. Occasionally, there are discussions about how to implement a particular feature. Generally, if you have a question about syntax or a speculation about whether Perl 6 should support a particular feature, that question belongs on the language list rather than the internals list.

## Use the source

The second step to participating in Parrot development is to get a copy of the source code. If you just want to try it out—experiment with a few features and see how it feels—you're probably best off downloading a tarball. For the most stable copy, grab the latest point release from CPAN. The sure way to get the most recent release is at *http://search.cpan.org/dist/parrot/* (or search for "parrot" in "Distributions"). If you want something a little more cutting edge than the packaged release, a new snapshot of the CVS repository is created every eight hours. The most recent snapshot is always available at *http://cvs.perl.org/snapshots/parrot/parrot-latest.tar.gz*.

If you plan to get involved in development, you'll want to check out the source from the CVS repository. Anyone can get anonymous access. Just log in as the "anonymous" user and check out the source. No password is necessary.

```
cvs -d :pserver:anonymous@cvs.perl.org:/cvs/public login
cvs -d :pserver:anonymous@cvs.perl.org:/cvs/public checkout parrot
```

There's also a web interface for viewing files in the repository at *http:// cvs.perl.org/cvsweb/parrot/*.

Now that you've got the source, take a moment to look around. The code changes constantly, so a detailed description of every file is impossible. But a few road signs are helpful starting out.

The most important top-level directory is *docs/*. The content isn't always up to date, but it is a good place to start. *parrot.pod* provides a quick overview of what is in each documentation file.

The *languages/* directory contains the code that implements various language compilers: Perl 6, as well as Forth, Scheme, Befunge, BASIC, etc. Most are in various stages of partial completion. *LANGUAGES.STATUS* provides meta information on the included languages, and on languages maintained outside the Parrot repository, such as Python (Pirate) and Ruby (Cardinal). If you have a language you're particularly interested to see implemented on Parrot, you might take a peek to see how far along it is.

The *lib/* directory contains Perl 5 classes currently used in developing Parrot. The *classes/* directory contains the C source code for Parrot classes (PMCs, which you'll read more about in Chapter 9). The *examples/* directory contains some example Parrot assembler code, as well as benchmarks.

For instructions on building Parrot, see "Getting Started" in Chapter 9.

## Patch submission

Parrot development is a continuous stream of patches. Patches are the currency of exchange in the project—the unit of work. They fix bugs, add features, modify features, remove features, and improve the documentation. Pretty much anything that changes, changes via a patch.

Although anyone is free to submit a patch, a small number of people have access to commit changes to the CVS repository. This system works well. It means the project can harness the efforts of a large group, but still keep the same high quality as a small group of experienced developers.

Every submitted patch is automatically forwarded to the p6i list where it's subject to peer review. Patches spark little debate. Parrot developers generally submit code that's clean and well thought-out, so there's rarely any need for debate. Also, patches are typically small modular changes, which makes them easy to evaluate. Occasionally an entire language implementation is submitted in a single patch, but these are the exceptions.

Submitting a patch is fairly straightforward. You create a file that lists all your changes and email it to the ticket tracking system at *bugs-parrot@bugs6.perl.org*. But a few common-sense guidelines will make your patches cleaner, better, and less likely to give the pumpking hives.

First off, create your patches from a checked-out CVS repository, not from a tarball, so your diff is running against the latest version of the files. Then, make sure the paths listed in the patch match those in the repository. There are two methods of creating patches that will do this for you. You can make changes directly in your checked-out copy of the CVS repository and then create diffs using `cvs diff -u`. Or you can make a copy of the repository and then create diffs between the two copies with the standard `diff -u` command. For example:

```
diff -u parrot/README parrot_changed/README
```

Either method is fine, and both are equally common on p6i. Your working style and the types of changes you make—small and modular versus large and sweeping—will influence which method you choose.

Next, when you're making changes, take some extra time to consider how your patch affects the rest of the system. If your patch adds a new file, patch the main *MANIFEST* file to include it. If you add a new feature, add a test for it. If you fix a bug, add a test for it. (See "Writing Tests" in Chapter 9.) Before you submit a patch, always recompile the system with your patch included and run all tests:

```
make clean
perl Configure.pl
```

```
make
make test
```

Then consider the people who will review and apply your patch, and try to make their jobs easier. Patch filenames should be as descriptive as possible: *fix_readme_typo.patch* is better than *README.patch*. An attached file is better than a diff pasted into an email, because it can be applied without manual editing. The conventional extension for patch files is *.patch*.

In the email message, always start the subject with "[PATCH]," and make the subject as clear as possible: "[PATCH] misspelled aardvark in main README file" is better than "[PATCH] typo." The body of the message should clearly explain what the patch is supposed to do and why you're submitting it. Make a note if you're adding or deleting files so they won't be missed.

Here is a good example of a patch submission using the CVS diff method (an actual patch from p6i). It's short, sticks to the point, and clearly expresses the problem and the solution. The patch filename and the subject of the message are both descriptive:

```
Subject: [PATCH] Pointers in List_chunk not initialized
From: Bruce Gray

On Win32, these tests are segfaulting due to invalid
pointers in List_chunk structs:
t/op/string.t          97-98
t/pmc/intlist.t        3-4
t/pmc/pmc.t            80

The problem is caused by list.c/allocate_chunk not
initializing the pointers. This patch corrects the problem.


--
Hope this helps,
Bruce Gray
```

The following includes the attached file *list_chunk_initialize.patch*:

```
Index: list.c
===============================================
RCS file: /cvs/public/parrot/list.c,v
retrieving revision 1.23
diff -u -r1.23 list.c
--- list.c        27 Dec 2002 09:33:11 -0000        1.23
+++ list.c        28 Dec 2002 03:37:35 -0000
@@ -187,6 +187,10 @@
     Parrot_block_GC(interpreter);
     chunk = (List_chunk *)new_bufferlike_header(interpreter,
sizeof(*chunk));
     chunk->items = items;
+    chunk->n_chunks = 0;
```

```
+    chunk->n_items  = 0;
+    chunk->next     = NULL;
+    chunk->prev     = NULL;
     Parrot_allocate_zeroed(interpreter, (Buffer *)chunk, size);
     Parrot_unblock_DOD(interpreter);
     Parrot_unblock_GC(interpreter);
```

## Bug tracking

Bug reports go to the same address as patch submissions (*bugs-parrot@bugs6.perl.org*). Similar conventions apply: make the subject and the message as clear and descriptive as possible. There's no set convention on subject lines, but you can't go wrong starting off with something like "[BUG]" or "[P6C BUG]" to make it immediately obvious what the message is about.

If you want to track a bug or patch you've submitted, the current queue of bugs and patches is publicly viewable at *http://bugs6.perl.org*. Bug tracking for Parrot is handled by the Request Tracker (RT) ticket tracking system from Best Practical Solutions.

# CHAPTER 3

# Design Philosophy

At the heart of every language is a core set of ideals that give the language its direction and purpose. If you really want to understand the choices that language designers make—why they choose one feature over another or one way of expressing a feature over another—the best place to start is with the reasoning behind the choices.

Perl 6 has a unique set of influences. It has deep roots in Unix and the children of Unix, which gives it a strong emphasis on utility and practicality. It's grounded in the academic pursuits of computer science and software engineering, which gives it a desire to solve problems the right way, not just the most expedient way. It's heavily steeped in the traditions of linguistics and anthropology, which gives it the goal of comfortable adaptation to human use. These influences and others like them define the shape of Perl and what it will become.

## Linguistic and Cognitive Considerations

Perl is a human language. Now, there are significant differences between Perl and languages like English, French, German, etc. For one, it is artificially constructed, not naturally occurring. Its primary use, providing a set of instructions for a machine to follow, covers a limited range of human existence. Even so, Perl is a language humans use for communicating. Many of the same mental processes that go into speaking or writing are duplicated in writing code. The process of learning to use Perl is much like learning to speak a second language. The mental processes involved in reading are also relevant. Even though the primary audience of Perl code is a machine, humans have to read the code while they're writing, reviewing, or maintaining it.

Many Perl design decisions have been heavily influenced by the principles of natural language. The following are some of the most important principles, the ones we come back to over and over again while working on the design and the ones that have had the greatest impact.

## The Waterbed Theory of Complexity

The natural tendency in human languages is to keep overall complexity about equivalent, both from one language to the next, and over time as a language changes. Like a waterbed, if you push down the complexity in one part of the language, it increases complexity elsewhere. A language with a rich system of sounds (phonology) might compensate with a simpler syntax. A language with a limited sound system might have a complex way of building words from smaller pieces (morphology). No language is complex in every way, as that would be unusable. Likewise, no language is completely simple, as too few distinctions would render it useless. This principle might just as well be called the "Conservation of Complexity."

The same is true of computer languages. They require a constant balance between complexity and simplicity. Restricting the possible operators to a small set leads to a proliferation of user-defined methods and subroutines. This is not a bad thing, in itself, but it encourages code that is verbose and difficult to read. On the other hand, a language with too many operators encourages code that is heavy in line noise and difficult to read. Somewhere in the middle lies the perfect balance.

## The Principle of Simplicity

Generally, a simple solution is preferable to a complex one. A simple syntax is easier to teach, remember, use, and read. But this principle is in constant tension with the waterbed theory. Simplification in the wrong area is one danger to avoid. Another is false simplicity or oversimplification. Some problems are complex and require a complex solution. Perl 6 grammars aren't simple, but they are complex at the language level in a way that allows simpler solutions at the user level.

## Huffman Coding

Huffman coding is a method of compressing data that replaces each character with a variable-length sequence of bits. To save space, frequent characters get shorter sequences and more rare characters get longer sequences.

When Larry talks about "Huffman coding" he means the idea that more commonly used features in the language deserve the best short-cuts. For example, the very limited set of easy-to-type, single-character, plain ASCII operators go to common operations: addition, subtraction, logical negation, etc. Less common operations get multiple character combinations or Unicode characters. Huffman coding is one of the moderating factors between simplicity and complexity.

## The Principle of Adaptability

Natural languages grow and change over time. They respond to changes in the environment and to internal pressure. New vocabulary springs up to handle new communication needs. Old idioms die off as people forget them, and newer, more relevant idioms take their place. Complex parts of the system tend to break down and simplify over time. Change is what keeps language active and relevant to the people who use it. Only dead languages stop changing.

The plan for Perl 6 explicitly includes plans for future language changes. No one believes that Perl 6.0.0 will be perfect, but at the same time, no one wants another change process quite as dramatic as Perl 6. So Perl 6 will be flexible and adaptable enough to allow gradual shifts over time. This has influenced a number of design decisions, including making it easy to modify how the language is parsed, lowering the distinctions between core operations and user-defined operations, and making it easy to define new operators.

## The Principle of Prominence

In natural languages, certain structures and stylistic devices draw attention to an important element. This could be emphasis, as in "The *dog* stole my wallet" (the dog, not something else), or extra verbiage, as in "It was the dog who stole my wallet," or a shift to an unusual word order, "My wallet was stolen by the dog" (my wallet, not my shoe, etc.), or any number of other verbal tricks.

Perl is designed with its own set of stylistic devices to mark prominence, some within the language itself, and some that give users flexibility to mark prominence within their code. The NAMED blocks use all capitals to draw attention to the fact that they're outside the normal flow of control. Perl 5 has an alternate syntax for control structures like if and for, which moves them to the end to serve as statement modifiers (the start of a line is a position of prominence). Perl 6 keeps this flexibility, and adds a few new control structures to the list.

The balance for design is to decide which features deserve to be marked as prominent, and where the syntax needs a little flexibility so the language can be more expressive.

## The Principle of End Weight

Natural languages place large, complex elements at the end of sentences. So, even though "I gave Mary the book" and "I gave the book to Mary" are equally comfortable, "I gave the book about the history of development of peanut-based products in Indonesia to Mary" is definitely less comfortable than the other way around. This is largely a mental parsing problem. It's easier to interpret the major blocks of the sentence all at once than to start with a few, work through a large chunk of minor information, and then go back to fill in the major sentence structure. Human memory is limited.

End weight is one of the reasons regular expression modifiers were moved to the front in Perl 6. It's easier to read a grammar rule when you know right at the start whether the rule is case insensitive or modified some other significant way. (It's also easier for the machine to parse, which is almost as important.)

## The Principle of Context

Natural languages use context when interpreting meaning. The meanings of "hot" in "a hot day," "a hot stereo," "a hot idea," and "a hot debate" are all quite different. The implied meaning of "it's wet" changes depending on whether it's a response to "Should I take a coat?" or "Why is the dog running around the kitchen?" The surrounding context allows us to distinguish these meanings. Context appears in other areas as well. A painting of an abstract orange sphere will be interpreted differently depending on whether the other objects in the painting are bananas, clowns, or basketball players. The human mind constantly tries to make sense of the universe, and it uses every available clue.

Perl has always been a context-sensitive language. It makes use of context in a number of different ways. The most obvious use is scalar and list contexts, where a variable or expression may return a different value depending on where and how it's used. These have been extended in Perl 6 to include string context, Boolean context, numeric context, and others. Another use of context is the $_ defaults, like print, chomp, matches, and the new when keyword.

Context-dependent features are harder to write an interpreter for, but they're easier on the people who use the language daily. They fit in with the way humans naturally think, which is one of Perl's top goals.

## The Principle of DWIM

In natural languages there is a notion called "native speaker's intuition." Someone who speaks a language fluently will be able to tell whether a sentence is correct, even if they can't consciously explain the rules. (This has little to do with the difficulty English teachers have getting their students to use "proper" grammar. The rules of formal written English are very different from the rules of spoken English.)

As much as possible, features should do what the user expects. This concept of DWIM, or "Do What I Mean," is largely a matter of intuition. The user's experiences, language exposure, and cultural background all influence their expectations. This means that intuition varies from person to person. An English speaker won't expect the same things as a Dutch speaker, and an Ada programmer won't expect the same things as a COBOL programmer.

The trick in design is to use the programmer's intuitions instead of fighting against them. A clearly defined set of rules will never match the power of a feature that "just seems right."

Perl 6 targets Perl programmers. What seems right to one Perl programmer may not seem right to another, so no feature will please everyone. But it is possible to catch the majority cases.

Perl generally targets English speakers. It uses words like "given," which gives English speakers a head start in understanding its behavior in code. Of course, not all Perl programmers are English speakers. In some cases idiomatic English is toned down for broader appeal. In grammar rules, ordinal modifiers have the form 1st, 2nd, 3rd, 4th, etc., because those are most natural for native English speakers. But they also have an alternate form 1th, 2th, etc., with the general rule Nth, because the English endings for ordinal numbers are chaotic and unfriendly to non-native speakers.

## The Principle of Reuse

Human languages tend to have a limited set of structures and reuse them repeatedly in different contexts. Programming languages also employ a set of ordinary syntactic conventions. A language that used braces ({ }) to delimit loops but paired keywords to delimit if statements (like if ... then ... end if) would be incredibly annoying. Too many rules make it hard to find the pattern.

In design, if you have a certain syntax to express one feature, it's often better to use the same syntax for a related feature than to invent something entirely new. It gives the language an overall sense of consistency, and makes the new features easier to remember. This is part of why Perl 6 grammars are structured as classes. (For more details on grammars, see Chapter 7.) Grammars could use any syntax, but classes already express many of the features grammars need, like inheritance and the concept of creating an instance.

## The Principle of Distinction

The human mind has an easier time identifying big differences than small ones. The words "cat" and "dog" are easier to tell apart than "snore" and "shore." Usually context provides the necessary clues, but if "cats" were "togs," we would be endlessly correcting people who heard us wrong ("No, I said the Johnsons got a new dog, not tog, *dog*.").

The design consideration is to build in visual clues to subtle contrasts. The language should avoid making too many different things similar. Excessive overloading reduces readability and increases the chance for confusion. This is part of the motivation for splitting the two meanings of eval into try and eval, the two meanings of for into for and loop, and the two uses of sub into sub and method.

Distinction and reuse are in constant tension. If too many features are reused and overloaded, the language will begin to blur together. Far too much time will be spent trying to figure out exactly which use is intended. But, if too many features are entirely distinct, the language will lose all sense of consistency and coherence. Again, it's a balance.

## Language Cannot Be Separated from Culture

A natural language without a community of speakers is a dead language. It may be studied for academic reasons, but unless someone takes the effort to preserve the language, it will eventually be lost entirely. A language adds to the community's sense of identity, while the community keeps the language relevant and passes it on to future generations. The community's culture shapes the language and gives it a purpose for existence.

Computer languages are equally dependent on the community behind them. You can measure it by corporate backing, lines of code in operation, or user interest, but it all boils down to this: a programming language is dead if it's not used. The final sign of language death is when there are no compilers or interpreters for the language that will run on existing hardware and operating systems.

For design work this means it's not enough to only consider how a feature fits with other features in the language. The community's traditions and expectations also weigh in, and some changes have a cultural price.

## The Principle of Freedom

In natural languages there is always more than one way to express an idea. The author or speaker has the freedom, and the responsibility, to pick the best phrasing—to put just the right spin on the idea so it makes sense to their audience.

Perl has always operated on the principle that programmers should have the freedom to choose how to express their code. It provides easy access to powerful features and leaves it to the individuals to use them wisely. It offers customs and conventions rather than enforcing laws. "There's more than one way to do it" (TMTOWTDI).

This principle influences design in several ways. If a feature is beneficial to the language as a whole, it won't be rejected just because someone could use it foolishly. On the other hand, we aren't above making some features difficult to use, if they should be used rarely.

Another part of the design challenge is to build tools that will have many uses. No one wants a cookbook that reads like a Stephen King novel, and no one wants a one-liner with the elaborate structure of a class definition. The language has to be flexible to accommodate freedom.

## The Principle of Borrowing

Borrowing is common in natural languages. When a new technology (food, clothing, etc.) is introduced from another culture, it's quite natural to adopt the original name for it. Most of the time borrowed words are adapted to the new language. In English, no one pronounces "tortilla," "lasagna," or "champagne" exactly as in the original languages. They've been altered to fit the English sound system.

Perl has always borrowed features, and Perl 6 will too. There's no shame in acknowledging that another language did an excellent job implementing a particular feature. It's far better to openly borrow a good feature than to pretend it's original. Perl doesn't have to be different just for the sake of being different. However, most features won't be adopted without any changes.

Every language has its own conventions and syntax, and many aren't compatible. So, Perl borrows features, but uses Perlish syntax to express them.

# Architectural Considerations

The second set of principles governs the overall architecture of Perl 6. These principles are connected to the past, present, and future of Perl, and define the fundamental purpose of Perl 6. No principle stands alone; each is balanced against the others.

## Perl Should Stay Perl

Everyone agrees that Perl 6 should still be Perl, but the question is, what exactly does that mean? It doesn't mean Perl 6 will have exactly the same syntax. It doesn't mean Perl 6 will have exactly the same features. If it did, Perl 6 would just be Perl 5. So, the core of the question is what makes Perl "Perl?"

### True to the original purpose

Perl will stay true to its designer's original intended purpose. Larry wanted a language that would get the job done without getting in his way. The language had to be powerful enough to accomplish complex tasks, but still lightweight and flexible. As Larry is fond of saying, "Perl makes the easy things easy and the hard things possible." The fundamental design philosophy of Perl hasn't changed. In Perl 6, the easy things are a little easier and the hard things are more possible.

### Familiarity

Perl 6 will be familiar to Perl 5 users. The fundamental syntax is still the same. It's just a little cleaner and a little more consistent. The basic feature set is still the same. It adds some powerful features that will probably change the way we code in Perl, but they aren't required.

Learning Perl 6 will be like American English speakers learning Australian English, not English speakers learning Japanese. Sure, there are some vocabulary changes, and the tone is a little different, but it is still—without any doubt—English.

### Translatable

Perl 6 will be mechanically translatable from Perl 5. In the long term, this isn't nearly as important as what it will be like to write code in Perl 6. But during the transition phase, automatic translation will be important. It will allow developers to start moving ahead before they understand every subtle nuance of every change. Perl has always been about learning what you need now and learning more as you go.

## Important New Features

Perl 6 will add a number of features such as exceptions, delegation, multi-method dispatch, continuations, coroutines, and currying, to name a few. These features have proven useful in other languages and provide a great deal of power for solving certain problems. They improve the stability and flexibility of the language.

Many of these features are traditionally difficult to understand. Perl takes the same approach as always: provide powerful tools, make them easy to use, and leave it up to the user to decide whether and how to use them. Most users probably won't even know they're using currying when they use the assuming method.

Features like these are an important part of preparing Perl for the future. Who knows what development paradigms might develop in a language that has this combination of advanced features in a form easily approachable by the average programmer? It may not be a revolution, but it's certainly evolution.

## Long-Term Usability

Perl 6 isn't a revision intended to last a couple of years and then be tossed out. It's intended to last 20 years or more. This long-range vision affects the shape of the language and the process of building it. We're not interested in the latest fad or in whipping up a few exciting tricks. We want strong, dependable tools with plenty of room to grow. And we're not afraid to take a little extra time now to get it right. This doesn't mean Perl 6.0 will be perfect, any more than any other release has been perfect. It's just another step of progress.

# CHAPTER 4

# Basic Syntax

Perl 6 is a work in progress, so the syntax is rapidly changing. The next four chapters are likely to be outdated by the time you read them. Even so, they provide a good baseline. If you start here, you'll only have to catch up on a few months of changes (starting with the design documents after Apocalypse 12), instead of several years worth.

Pretend for a moment that you don't know anything about Perl. You heard the language has some neat features, so you thought you might check it out. You go to the store and pick up a copy of *Programming Perl* because you think this Larry Wall guy might know something about it. It's the latest version, put out for the 6.0.1 release of Perl. It's not a delta document describing the changes, it's an introduction, and you dive in with the curiosity of a kid who got a telescope for his birthday. These chapters are a glimpse down that telescope.

There's plenty of time later to analyze each feature and decide which you like and which you don't. For now, take a step back and get a feel for the system as a whole, for what it'll be like to work in it.

## Variables

The most basic building blocks of a programming language are its nouns, the chunks of data that get sucked in, pushed around, altered in various ways, and spat out to some new location. The chunks of data are values: strings, numbers, etc., or composites of the simpler values. Variables are just named containers for those values. The three kinds of variables in Perl 6 are scalars, arrays, and hashes. Each has an identifying symbol (or sigil) as part of the name of the variable: $ for scalars, @ for arrays, and % for hashes. The sigils provide a valuable visual distinction by making it immediately obvious what kinds of behavior a particular variable is likely to have. But, fundamentally, there's little difference between the three. Each variable is essentially a container for a value, whether that value is single or collective. (This statement is an oversimplification, as you'll soon see.)

## Scalars

Scalars are all-purpose containers. They can hold strings, integers, floating-point numbers, and references to all kinds of objects and built-in types. For example:

```
$string = "Zaphod's just this guy, you know?";
$int = 42;
$float = 3.14159;
$arrayref = [ "Zaphod", "Ford", "Trillian" ];
$hashref = { "Zaphod" => 362, "Ford" => 1574, "Trillian" => 28 };
$subref = sub { print $string };
$object = Android.new;
```

A filehandle is just an ordinary object in an ordinary scalar variable. For example:

```
$filehandle = open $filename;
```

## Arrays

Array variables hold simple ordered collections of scalar values. Individual values are retrieved from the array by numeric index. The 0 index holds the first value. The @ sigil is part of the name of the variable and stays the same no matter how the variable is used:

```
@crew = ( "Zaphod", "Ford", "Trillian" );

$second_member = @crew[1]; # Ford
```

To get the the number of elements in an array use the .elems method. The .last method returns the index of the last element in an array—that is, the highest index in an array.

```
$count_elements = @crew.elems;
$last_index = @crew.last;
```

## Pairs

Pairs hold a single key and a single value. They don't have a unique sigil because they rarely appear alone, so they're stored in scalars, arrays, or hashes. The pair constructor => forms a pair, with the key on the left and value on the right.

```
$pair = 'key' => 'value';
```

The alternate *option* syntax also constructs a pair, with a colon before the key and parentheses around the value:

```
$pair = :key('value');
```

The option syntax is useful for subroutine calls, as you'll see in "Named Argument Passing" in Chapter 5.

# Hashes

Hashes are unordered collections of scalar values, stored and retrieved by a key index. The simplest way to build a hash is by passing it a list of anonymous pair objects. For example:

```
%hash = ( "Zaphod" => 362, "Ford" => 1574, "Trillian" => 28 );
```

The key for each value may be a string or an object, though there are some restrictions on object keys. Hashes that use object keys must be declared as such, for the sake of efficiency. Any object used as a hash key must have a .id method that returns a unique value for each unique object to avoid hashing collisions. This method is provided by default in the universal base class, so you only have to worry about uniqueness when you define your own .id methods:

```
$age = %hash{"Zaphod"}; # string
$age = %hash{$name};    # string variable
$age = %hash{$person};  # object
```

Quotes are required around literal string keys, so you can call a subroutine to retrieve a key and the subroutine name won't act as a string key:

```
$age = %hash{get_key};  # subroutine call
```

If you really don't want to type the quotes, substitute auto-quoting brackets for the ordinary curly braces around the key:

```
$age = %hash«Zaphod»;               # string
$age = %hash<<Zaphod>>;             # ASCII equivalent
```

In list context, a hash returns a list of key/value pair objects. The .kv method returns a flattened list of keys and values from a hash. So the assignment of a hash directly to an array:

```
@pairs = %hash;
```

creates an array of pairs that looks like:

```
(pair1, pair2, pair3, etc...)
```

However, the assignment of the flattened key/value list:

```
@flat = %hash.kv;
```

creates an array of alternating keys and values that looks like:

```
(key1, value1, key2, value2, etc...)
```

The .keys method returns a flattened list of all the keys in a hash. The .values method returns a flattened list of all the values:

```
@keys = %hash.keys;
@values = %hash.values;
```

# References

References are largely transparent in Perl 6. There is a distinction between references and ordinary variables, but it's minimized as much as possible in actual use, with automatic referencing and dereferencing where appropriate. Creating a reference to an array or hash requires no special syntax. You simply assign it to a scalar variable:

```
$arrayref = @array;
$hashref = %hash;
```

References are implicitly dereferenced in many contexts, so array indexes and hash keys access individual elements directly from hashrefs and arrayrefs, just like they do with hashes and arrays:

```
$arrayref[1]
$hashref{"Zaphod"}
```

Methods are called on arrayrefs and hashrefs just like they are on arrays and hashes. The referent—the underlying data type or object—determines which methods can be used with a particular reference, what those methods do, and whether the reference can support indexed access:

```
$arrayref.elems
$hashref.keys
```

References to subroutines can be executed simply by passing the reference an argument list. The list can be empty, but the parentheses are required.

```
$subref($arg);
```

Arrayrefs and hashrefs have special syntax (@{ ... } and %{ ... }) for dereferencing them in contexts that normally wouldn't:

```
@array = @{$arrayref};
# or
@array = @$arrayref;
```

Ordinarily, an array reference assigned to an array would produce an array with a single arrayref element. To copy the individual elements of $arrayref to @array you need to dereference it first.

# Variables and Context

One of the main differences between variables with the $, @, or % sigils is that they each impose a different context. The $ sigil imposes a scalar context, @ imposes list context, and % imposes hashlist context.*

## Scalar context

Scalar context expects a single value. Any array or list evaluated in scalar context returns an arrayref. This means that assigning an array:

```
@array = ( "Zaphod", "Ford", "Trillian" );
$arrayref = @array;
```

a list:

```
$arrayref = ( "Zaphod", "Ford", "Trillian" );
```

or an explicit anonymous arrayref:

```
$arrayref = [ "Zaphod", "Ford", "Trillian" ];
```

to a scalar variable all produce exactly the same structure: a reference to an array with three elements.

The comma is the list constructor, even in scalar context. Parentheses only group. When a single element in parentheses is assigned in scalar context, it stays a simple scalar value:

```
$value = (20);
```

If you want to create an arrayref of one element in scalar context, use square brackets ([ . . . ]) to explicitly construct an anonymous array reference:

```
$arrayref = [20];
```

A hash-like list assigned to a scalar variable creates a reference to an ordered array of pairs, following the rule that a list in scalar context is an arrayref:

```
$pair_list = ( "Zaphod" => 362, "Ford" => 1574, "Trillian" => 28 );
```

You have to use curly braces ({ . . . }) to explicitly construct a hash reference in scalar context:

```
$hashref = { "Zaphod" => 362, "Ford" => 1574, "Trillian" => 28 };
```

## List context

Variables with the @ sigil impose flattening-list context. This means that if you assign one array to another array, the original array is flattened—treated

---

* These three are not the only contexts in Perl 6. A complete discussion of Perl 6 contexts appears in "Context Forcing Operators" later in this chapter.

as if it were a simple list of values—and every element from the original array is copied to the new array. The result is that the two array variables contain different data structures, each with identical values:

```
@copy = @original;
```

Lists also impose flattening-list context. Assigning an array to a list flattens the array and assigns each array element to the corresponding element in the list. If the array has more elements than the list, the remaining elements are simply discarded:

```
($first, $second, $third) = @array;
```

A single value in list context is a one-element list, so it produces a one-element array on assignment:

```
@array = (20);
@array = 20;    # same
```

The anonymous arrayref constructor [ . . . ] imposes flattening-list context internally. It doesn't flatten when used in list context, though, because flattening-list context doesn't flatten references. In scalar context, a simple list and an arrayref construct produce the same result. But in list context, a simple list is treated as a flattened list, while an arrayref construct is treated as a list of one element, an arrayref:

```
@array = ( "Zaphod", "Ford", "Trillian" );
@array = [ "Zaphod", "Ford", "Trillian" ];
```

The first example above produces an array with three elements. The second produces an array with one element and that element is a reference to an array with three elements. This is useful for building up complex data structures.

```
@array = ( "Marvin", [ "Zaphod", "Ford", "Trillian" ], "Zarniwoop" );
```

Similarly, in flattening-list context a list of array variables are flattened into a single list, while a list of scalar variables are treated as a simple list, even if the scalar variables are arrayrefs:

```
@array = ( @array1, @array2, @array3 ); # single flattened list
@array = ( $arrayref1, $arrayref1, $arrayref3 ); # 3-element list
```

So, the first example above produces an array containing all the elements of the three arrays, while the second produces an array of three arrayrefs.

A lone pair of parentheses is a special token representing an empty list. It produces an array structure with no elements in both scalar and list context:

```
$arrayref = ( ); # 0-element arrayref
@array = ( );    # 0-element array
```

### Hashlist context

Variables with % sigils impose hashlist context, which expects a list of pair objects. This is typically simply a list of anonymous pairs built with the pair constructor (=>):

```
%hash = ( "Zaphod" => 362, "Ford" => 1574, "Trillian" => 28 );
```

A list of simple values in hashlist context is treated as a list of pairs. You can substitute two values for a pair object only in hashlist context:

```
%hash = ( "Zaphod", 362, "Ford", 1574, "Trillian", 28 );
```

Curly braces { . . . } are the anonymous hash reference constructor, but they don't impose hashlist context. This is because an ordinary structure wrapped in curly braces and assigned to a scalar variable defines an anonymous subroutine:

```
# a sub reference that returns a list
$subref = { "Zaphod", 362, "Ford", 1574, "Trillian", 28 };
```

The hash reference constructor isn't really { . . . }, but { . . . => . . . }, so you can't use commas in place of pair constructors when assigning a hash reference to a scalar variable. It's the => that marks the structure as a hash. When there is ambiguity, you can force the right context by specifying hash or sub before the block:

```
$subref = sub { print "Lost luggage.\n"; }
$hashref = hash { "Zaphod", 362, "Ford", 1574, "Trillian", 28 };
```

## Properties and Traits

Properties allow additional information to be attached to variables and values. As Damian likes to explain it, they're much like sticky notes. You can take a note, scribble some important information on it, and slap it onto the refrigerator, your monitor, or the dashboard of your car. When you're done, you peel it off and throw it away.

Some properties are attached at compile time. These are known as *traits*. Traits are still properties, just a particular kind of property. Traits are fixed to the variable when it is declared and cannot be changed later. Compile-time traits are set with the is keyword:

```
my $pi is constant = 3.14159;
```

The constant trait specifies that the value of the variable can't be changed.

Other properties are attached at run-time. They only modify values, not variables. They can be added and removed at any time during the execution of the code. Run-time properties are set with the but keyword:

```
$true_value = 0 but true;
```

The true property specifies that the value will evaluate as true in a Boolean context, no matter what the actual value is. This particular property means the Perl 6 system call can be checked with a simple conditional. It still returns the same numeric values it always has (0 on success and a numeric error code on failure), but it flags the value with a property as true when the call succeeds and false when it fails.

Properties and traits can also store a value. Both constant and true define their own values when they're set. Some properties take arguments for their value:

```
my @array is dim(2,5,42); # specify dimensions
```

Properties have proven to be an incredibly useful and extensible syntax. You'll see them again and again throughout the next few chapters. They aren't restricted to variables and values, but appear on subroutines, methods, classes, grammars, rules, and in parameter lists.

# Types

Perl 6 allows you to specify the types of variables and values much more precisely than Perl 5, but keep in mind that explicit types are completely optional. If you choose to use them, you'll gain some benefits in optimization and interfacing between languages. The design of the type system isn't complete, but the basic groundwork is in place.

Perl 6 makes a distinction between the type of a value and the type of a variable. The *value* type specifies what kind of values a variable can hold. Putting an Int value type on a scalar says that the scalar can only hold an integer value:

```
my Int $scalar;
```

Putting an Int value type on an array says that the array holds integer values:

```
my Int @array;
```

And putting an Int value type on a hash says that the hash holds integer values (but says nothing about the type of the keys):

```
my Int %hash;
```

The *variable* type specifies what kind of container the variable is. This is basically like a tie in Perl 5. Variable types are defined as traits of the variable, with the is keyword. The sigils provide an implicit variable type, so a variable with no type is just:

```
my $scalar is Scalar;
my @array is Array;
my %hash is Hash;
```

But you can also define your own classes to implement a variable type:

```
my $scalar is FileHandle;
my @array is Matrix;
my %hash is BerkeleyDB;
```

Hierarchical data structures can have a complex value type. A hash that holds integer arrays has the value type `Array of Int`:

```
my Array of Int %hash;
```

The type syntax is flexible, so you could also write that as:

```
my %hash is Hash of Array of Int;
# or
my %hash of Array of Int;
```

and get the same data structure. This improves readability, especially in multilevel data structures:

```
my Array of Hash of Array of Int %hash;
my %hash is Hash of Array of Hash of Array of Int;
```

# Operators

Operators provide a simple syntax for manipulating values. A few characters take the place of a function call, or even several function calls. On the positive side this makes them incredibly convenient. On the negative side they're also sometimes difficult to learn because they pack so much meaning into a small space. Many of the Perl 6 operators will be familiar, especially to Perl 5 programmers. The new operators either add new features to the language, or move Perl's operator set toward a more consistent system.

## Assignment and Binding

The = operator is for ordinary assignment. It creates a copy of the values on the righthand side and assigns them to the variables or data structures on the lefthand side:

```
$copy = $original;
@copies = @originals;
```

$copy and $original both have the same value, and @copies has a copy of every element in @originals.

The := operator is for binding assignment. Instead of copying the value from one variable or structure to the other, it creates an alias. An alias is an additional entry in the symbol table with a different name for the one container:

```
$a := $b;  # $a and $b are aliases
@c := @d;  # @c and @d are aliases
```

In this example, any change to $a also changes $b and vice versa, because they're just two separate names for the same container. Binding assignment requires the same number of elements on both sides, so both of these would be an error:

```
# ($a, $b) := ($c);          # error
# ($a, $b) := ($c, $d, $e);  # error
```

The ::= operator is a variant of the binding operator that binds at compile time.

## Arithmetic Operators

The arithmetic operators are addition (+), subtraction (-), multiplication (*), division (/), modulus (%), and exponentiation (**). Each has a corresponding assignment operator (+=, -=, *=, /=, %=, **=) that combines the arithmetic operation with assignment:

```
$a = 3 + 5;
$a += 5;      # $a = $a + 5
```

The unary arithmetic operators are the prefix and postfix autoincrement (++) and autodecrement (--) operators. The prefix operators modify their argument before it's evaluated, and the postfix operators modify it afterward:

```
$a++;
$a--;
++$a;
--$a;
```

## String Operators

The ~ operator concatenates strings. The corresponding ~= operator concatenates the righthand side of the assignment to the end of the string:

```
$line = "The quick brown " ~ $fox ~ jumps_over() ~ " the lazy " ~ $dog;
$line ~= "Belgium"; # appends to the string
```

The x operator replicates strings. It always returns a string no matter whether the left side of the operation is a single element or a list. The following example assigns the string "LintillaLintillaLintilla":

```
$triplet = "Lintilla" x 3;
```

The corresponding x= operator replicates the original string and assigns it back to the original variable:

```
$twin = "Lintilla";
$twin x= 2;          # "LintillaLintilla"
```

# List Operators

The xx operator replicates lists. It returns a list no matter whether it operates on a list of elements or a single element. The following example assigns a list of three elements to @array, each with a copy of the value "Lintilla":

```
@array = "Lintilla" xx 3; # ("Lintilla", "Lintilla", "Lintilla")
```

The corresponding xx= operator creates a list that contains the specified number of copies of every element in the original array and assigns it back to the array variable:

```
@array = (4, 2);
@array xx= 2;              # now (4, 2, 4, 2)
@array = (@array, @array); # equivalent
```

The range operator .. returns a list of values from a starting point to an ending point:

```
@range = 3..7;   # 3,4,5,6,7
```

Ranges evaluate lazily, so a range containing an infinite value won't try to calculate all the values before assigning the list. Instead, it returns a list generator that only generates elements as they're requested.

```
@range = 3..Inf; # lazy
```

The ... operator is equivalent to ..Inf:

```
@range = 3...;
```

# Comparison

Each comparison operator has two forms, one for numeric comparisons and one for string comparisons. The comparison operators are greater-than (>, gt), less-than (<, lt), greater-than-or-equal (>=, ge), less-than-or-equal (<=, le), equal (==, eq), and not-equal (!=, ne). The identity operator (=:=) tests whether the two arguments are aliases to the same object. Each returns a true value if the relation is true and a false value otherwise. The generic comparison operators (<=>, cmp) return 0 if the two arguments are equal, 1 if the first is greater, and -1 if the second is greater:

```
if ($age > 12) {...}
```

Comparison operators can also be chained. Chained comparisons evaluate each value in the chain only once:

```
if (24 < $age < 42) {...} # 24 < $age and $age < 42
```

# Logical Operators

The binary logical operators test two values and return one value or the other depending on certain truth conditions. They're also known as the short-circuit operators because the righthand side will never be evaluated if the overall truth value can be determined from the lefthand side. This makes them useful for conditionally assigning values or executing code.

The AND relation has the && operator and the low-precedence and operator. If the lefthand side evaluates as false, its value is returned. If the lefthand value is true, the righthand side is evaluated and its value is returned:

```
$splat = $whale && $petunia;
$splat = ($whale and $petunia);
```

The OR relation has the || operator and the low-precedence or operator. The lefthand value is returned if it is true; otherwise, the righthand value is evaluated and returned:

```
$splat = $whale || $petunia;
$splat = ($whale or $petunia);
```

A variant of the OR relation tests for definedness instead of truth. It uses the // operator and the low-precedence err operator. The lefthand value is returned if it is defined; otherwise, the righthand side is evaluated and its value returned:

```
$splat = $whale // $petunia;
$splat = ($whale err $petunia);
```

The XOR relation has the ^^ operator and the low-precedence xor operator. It returns the value of the true operand if any one operand is true, and a false value if both are true or neither is true. xor isn't short-circuiting like the others, because it always has to evaluate both arguments to know if the relation is true:

```
$splat = $whale ^^ $petunia;
$splat = ($whale xor $petunia);
```

Perl 6 also has Boolean variants of the logical operators: ?& (AND), ?| (OR), and ?^ (XOR). These always return a true or false value.

```
$whale = 42;
$petunia = 24;
$value = $whale || $petunia   # $value is 42
$truth = $whale ?| $petunia   # $truth is 1
```

# Context Forcing Operators

The context of an expression specifies the type of value it is expected to produce. An array expects to be assigned multiple values at the same time, so

---

assignment to an array happens in *list* context. A scalar variable expects to be assigned a single value, so assignment to a scalar happens in *scalar* context. Perl expressions often adapt to their context, producing values that fit with what's expected.

Contexts have proven to be valuable tools in Perl 5, so Perl 6 has a few more added. Void context still exists. Scalar context is subdivided into Boolean, integer, numeric, string, and object contexts. List context is subdivided into flattening-list context, nonflattening-list context, lazy list context, and hashlist context.

*Void context*
    Expects no value.

*Scalar context*
    Expects a single value. A composite value returns a reference to itself in scalar context.

*Boolean context*
    Expects a true or false value. This includes the traditional definitions of truth—where 0, undef, and the empty string are false and all other values are true—and values flagged with the properties true or false.

*Integer context*
    Expects an integer value. Strings are treated as numeric and floating-point numbers are truncated.

*Numeric context*
    Expects a number, whether it's an integer or floating-point, and whether it's decimal, binary, octal, hex, or some other base.

*String context*
    Expects a string value. It interprets any information passed to it as a string of characters.

*Object context*
    Expects an object, or more specifically, a reference to an object. It may also expect an object of a particular type.

*List context*
    Expects a collection of values. Any single value in list context is treated as a one-element list.

*Flattening-list context*
    Expects a list. Flattens out arrays and hashes into their component parts.

*Nonflattening-list context*
    Expects a list. Treats arrays, hashes, and other composite values as discrete entities.

*Lazy list context*

Expects a list, just like nonflattening-list context, but doesn't require all the elements at once.

*Hashlist context*

Expects a list of pairs. A simple list in hashlist context pairs up alternating elements.

The unary context operators force a particular context when it wouldn't otherwise be imposed. Generally, the default context is the right one, but at times you might want a little more control.

The unary ? operator and its low-precedence equivalent true force Boolean context. Assignment of a scalar to a scalar only imposes generic scalar context, so the value of $number is simply copied. With the ? operator, you can force Boolean context and assign the truth value of the variable instead of the numeric value:

```
$value = $number;
$truth = ?$number;
```

The unary ! operator and the low-precedence not also force Boolean context, but they negate the value at the same time. They're often used in a Boolean context, where only the negating effect is visible.

```
$untruth = !$number;
```

The unary + operator forces numeric context, and - forces numeric context and negates the number at the same time:

```
$number = +$string;
$negnum = -$string;
```

The unary ~ operator forces string context:

```
$string = ~$number;
```

You can also create a scalar, list, or hashlist context with $( ... ), @( ... ), and %( ... ).

## Bitwise Operators

Perl 6 has two sets of bitwise operators, one for integers and one for strings. The integer bitwise operators combine the AND, OR, and XOR relation symbols with the general numeric symbol + (the unary numeric context operator). These are the binary +&, +|, and +^ and the unary +^ for bitwise negation (ones complement). The default integer type in Perl 6 is a signed int, so the results are equivalent to working with the use integer pragma turned on in Perl 5:

```
$number = 42 +& 18; # $number is 2
$number = 42 +| 18; # $number is 58
```

```
$number = 42 +^ 18; # $number is 56
$number = +^ 42;    # $number is -43
```

The numeric bitwise shift operators shift the value of the left operand by the number of bits in the right operand, either to the left (<<) or to the right (>>):

```
$number = 4 << 1; # $number is 8
$number = 4 >> 1; # $number is 2
```

The string bitwise operators combine the AND, OR, and XOR relation symbols with the general string symbol ~ (the same symbol as string concatenation and the unary string context operator). These are ~&, ~|, and ~^.

```
$string = 'jj' ~& 'gg'; # $string is 'bb'
$string = 'aa' ~| 'bb'; # $string is 'cc'
$string = "GG" ~^ "**"; # $string is 'mm'
```

Each of the binary bitwise operators has an assignment counterpart: +&=, +|=, +^=, <<=, >>=, ~&=, ~|=, and ~^=.

# Conditional

The ternary ??:: operator evaluates either its second or third operand, depending on whether the first operand evaluates as true or false. It's basically an if-then-else statement acting as an expression:

```
$form = ($heads == 2) ?? "Zaphod" :: "ape-descended lifeform";
```

# Hyper Operators

The hyper operators are designed to work with lists. They're simply modified versions of the standard scalar operators. Every operator has a hyper version, even user-defined operators. They have the same basic forms as their scalar counterparts, but are marked with the bracketing characters » and «,* or their plain-text equivalents >> and <<. For example, the hyper addition operator is >>+<<.

Hyper operators impose list context on their operands and distribute their operations across all the operands' elements. Hyper addition takes each element from the first list and adds it to the corresponding element in the second list:

```
@sums = @first >>+<< @second;
```

The resulting array contains the sums of each pair of elements, as if each pair were added with the scalar operator:

```
@sums = ( (@first[0] + @second[0]), (@first[1] + @second[1]), etc...);
```

---

* These are the Unicode RIGHT POINTING GUILLEMET (U+00BB) and LEFT POINTING GUILLEMET (U+00AB) characters.

If one side of a hyper operation is a simple scalar, it is distributed across the list as if it were a list of identical elements:

```
@sums = @numbers >>+<< 5;

@sums ( (@numbers[0] + 5), (@numbers[1] + 5), etc... );
```

Unary operators may also take a one-sided hyper on the side of their single operand:

```
@less = @numbers >>--;
@nums = +<< @strings;
```

## Junctions

At the simplest level, junction operators are no more than AND, OR, XOR, and NOT for values instead of expressions. The binary junction operators are & (AND), | (OR), and ^ (XOR). There isn't an operator for junctive NOT, but there is a function, as you'll see shortly. So, while || is a logical operation on two expressions:

```
if ($value == 1) || ($value == 2) { ... }
```

| is the same logical relation between two values:

```
if $value == 1 | 2 { ... }
```

In fact, those two examples have exactly the same result: they return true when $value is 1 or 2 and false otherwise. In the common case, that's all you'll ever need to know.

But junctions are a good deal more powerful than that, once you learn their secrets. A junctive operation doesn't return an ordinary single value, it returns a composite value containing all of its operands. This return value is a junction, and it can be used anywhere a junction operation is used:

```
$junc = 1 | 2;
if ($value == $junc) { ... }
```

Here, the variable $junc is used in place of 1 | 2, and has exactly the same effect as the earlier example.

A junction is basically just an unordered set with a logical relation defined between its elements. Any operation on the junction is an operation on the entire set. Table 4-1 shows the way the four different types of junctions interact with other operators.

*Table 4-1. Picture junctions*

| Function | Operator | Relation | Meaning |
|----------|----------|----------|---------|
| all | & | AND | Operation must be true for all values |
| any | | | OR | Operation must be true for at least one value |
| one | ^ | XOR | Operation must be true for exactly one value |
| none | | NOT | Operation must be false for all values |

The simplest possible example is the result of evaluating a junction in Boolean context. The operation on the set is just "is it true?" This operation on an all junction is true if *all* the values are true:

```
true( $a & $b )
true( all($a,$b) )
```

So, if both $a and $b are true, the result is true.

On an any junction, it's true if *any* one value is true:

```
true( $a | $b )
true( any($a,$b) )
```

So, if $a or $b is true or if both are true, the result is true.

On a one junction, it's true only if exactly *one* value is true:

```
true( $a ^ $b )
true( one($a,$b) )
```

So, if either $a or $b is true, the result is true. But, if $a and $b are both true or neither is true, the result is false.

On a none junction, it's true only when *none* of the values are true—that is, when all the values are false:

```
true( none($a,$b) )
```

So, if $a and $b are both false, the result is true.

Ordinary arithmetic operators interact with junctions much like hyper operators on arrays. A junction distributes the operation across all of its elements:

```
$junc = any(1, 2);
$junc += 5; # $junc is now any(6, 7)
```

Junctions can be combined to produce compact and powerful logical comparisons. If you want to test that two sets have no intersection, you might do something like:

```
if all($a, $b) == none($c, $d) { ... }
```

which tests that all of the elements of the first set are equal to none of the elements of the second set. Translated to ordinary logical operators that's:

```
if ($a != $c) && ($a != $d) && ($b != $c) && ($b != $d) { ... }
```

If you want to get back a flat list of values from a junction, use the `.values` method:

```
$junc = all(1, 2, 3);      # create a junction
$sums = $junc + 3;         # add 3
@set  = $sums.values();  # (4, 5, 6)
```

The `.dump` method returns a string that shows the structure of a junction:

```
$string = $sums.dump(); # "all(4,5,6)"
```

The `.pick` method selects one value from an any junction or a one junction that has exactly one value, and returns it as an ordinary scalar:

```
$junc = any(1, 2, 3);
$single = $junc.pick();  # may be 1, 2, or 3
```

On an all junction, a none junction, or a one junction with more than one value, `.pick` returns undef. (With some levels of error strictness, it may raise an exception.)

# Smart Match

The binary `~~` operator makes a smart match between its two terms. It returns a true value if the match is successful and a false value if the match fails.[*] The negated smart match operator `!~` does the exact opposite: it returns true if the match fails and false if it is successful. The kind of match a smart match does is determined by the kind of arguments it matches. If the types of the two arguments can't be determined at compile time, the kind of match is determined at run time. Smart match is usually a symmetric operator, so you can reverse A `~~` B to B `~~` A and it will have the same truth value.

## Matching scalars

Any scalar value (or any code that results in a scalar value) matched against a string tests for string equality. The following match is true if `$string` has the value "Ford":

```
$string ~~ "Ford"
```

---

[*] This is an oversimplification. Some matches return a more complex value, but in Boolean context it will always evaluate as true for a successful match, and false for a failed match.

Any scalar value matched against a numeric value tests for numeric equality. The following is true if $number has the numeric value 42, or the string value "42":

```
$number ~~ 42
```

An expression that results in the value 42 is also true:

```
( (5 * 8) + 2 ) ~~ 42
```

Any scalar value matched against an undefined value checks for definedness. The following matches are true if $value is an undefined value and false if $value is any defined value:

```
$value ~~ undef
$value ~~ $undefined_value
```

Any scalar value matched against a rule (regex) does a pattern match. The following match is true if the sequence "towel" can be found anywhere within $string:

```
$string ~~ /towel/
```

Any scalar value matched against a substitution attempts that substitution on the value. This means the value has to be modifiable. The following match is true if the substitution succeeds on $string and false if it fails:

```
$string ~~ s/weapon/towel/
```

Any scalar value matched against a Boolean value simply takes the truth value of the Boolean. The following match will always be true, because the Boolean on the right is always true:*

```
$value ~~ (1 == 1)
```

The Boolean value on the right must be an actual Boolean: the result of a Boolean comparison or operation, the return value of a not or true function, or a value forced into Boolean context by ! or ?. The Boolean value also must be on the right; a Boolean on the left is treated as an ordinary scalar value.

## Matching lists

Any scalar value matched against a list compares each element in sequence. The match is true if at least one element of the list would match in a simple expression-to-expression match. The following match is true if $value is the same as any of the three strings on the right:

```
$value ~~ ( "Zaphod", "Ford", "Trillian" )
```

---

* At the moment this relation won't seem particularly useful. It makes much more sense when you realize that the switch statement duplicates all the smart match relations. More on that in "The switch statement" later in this chapter.

This match is short-circuiting: it stops after the first successful match. It has the same truth value as a series of or-ed matches:

```
($value ~~ "Zaphod") or ($value ~~ "Ford") or ($value ~~ "Trillian")
```

A smart-matched list can contain any combination of elements: scalar values, rules, Boolean expressions, arrays, hashes, etc.:

```
$value ~~ ( "Zaphod", 5, /petunias/ )
```

A match of a list against another list sequentially compares each element in the first list to the corresponding element in the second list. The match is true if every element of the first list matches the corresponding element in the second list. The following match is true, because the two lists are identical:

```
( "Zaphod", "Ford", "Trillian" ) ~~ ( "Zaphod", "Ford", "Trillian" )
```

The two lists don't have to be identical, as long as they're the same length and their corresponding elements match:

```
( $zaphod, $ford, $trillian ) ~~ ( "Zaphod", /Ford/, /^T/ )
```

The list-to-list match is also short-circuiting. It stops after the first failed match. This has the same truth value as a series of single-element smart matches linked by and:

```
($zaphod ~~ "Zaphod") and ($ford ~~ /Ford/) and ($trillian ~~ /^T/)
```

## Matching arrays

A nonnumeric expression matched against an array sequentially searches for that value in the array. The match is true if the value is found. If @array contains the values "Zaphod", "Ford", and "Trillian", the following match is true when $value matches any of those three strings:

```
$value ~~ @array
```

An integer value matched against an array tests the truth of the value at that numeric index. The following match is true if the element @array[2] exists and has a true value:

```
2 ~~ @array
```

An integer value matched against an array reference also does an index lookup:

```
2 ~~ [ "Zaphod", "Ford", "Trillian" ]
```

This match is true, because the third element of the array reference is a true value.

An array matches just like a list of scalar values if it's flattened with the * operator (See "Referencing (or Not)" later in this chapter). So, the following

---

example searches the array for an element with the value 2, instead of doing an index lookup:

```
2 ~~ *@array
```

An array matched against a rule does a pattern match against every element of the array. The match is true if any element matches the rule. If "Trillian", "Milliways", or "million" is an element of @array, the following match is true, no matter what the other elements are:

```
@array ~~ /illi/
```

A match of an array against an array sequentially compares each element in the first array to the corresponding element in the second array:

```
@humans ~~ @vogons
```

This match is true if the two arrays are the same length and @humans[0] matches @vogons[0], @humans[1] matches @vogons[1], etc.

## Matching hashes

A hash matched against any scalar value tests the truth value of the hash entry with that key:

```
$key ~~ %hash
```

This match is true if the element %hash{$key} exists and has a true value.

A hash matched against a rule does a pattern match on the hash keys:

```
%hash ~~ /blue/
```

This match is true if at least one key in %hash matches the string "blue".

A hash matched against a hash checks for intersection between the keys of the two hashes:

```
%vogons ~~ %humans
```

So, this match is true if at least one key from %vogons is also a key of %humans. If you want to see that two hashes have exactly the same keys, match their lists of keys:

```
%vogons.keys.sort ~~ %humans.keys.sort
```

A hash matched against an array checks a slice of a hash to see if its values are true. The match is true if any element of the array is a key in the hash and the hash value for that key is true:

```
%hash ~~ @array
```

If @array has one element "blue" and %hash has a corresponding key "blue", the match is true if %hash{'blue'} has a true value, but false if %hash{'blue'} has a false value.

## Matching junctions

An expression matched against an any junction is a recursive disjunction. The match is true if at least one of the elements of the list would match in a simple expression-to-expression match:

```
$value ~~ any("Zaphod", "Ford", "Trillian")
```

This example matches if $value is the same as any of the three strings on the right. The effect of this comparison is the same as a simple comparison to a list, except that it isn't guaranteed to compare in any particular order.

A smart match of an all junction is only true when the expression matches every value in the junction:

```
/illi/ ~~ all("Gillian", "million", "Trillian")  # match succeeds
/illi/ ~~ all("Zaphod", "Ford", "Trillian")      # match fails
```

A smart match of a one junction is only true when the expression matches exactly one value in the junction:

```
/illi/ ~~ one("Zaphod", "Ford", "Trillian")      # match succeeds
/illi/ ~~ one("Gillian", "million", "Trillian")  # match fails
```

A smart match of a none junction is true when it doesn't match any values in the junction:

```
/illi/ ~~ none("Zaphod", "Ford", "Marvin")    # match succeeds
/illi/ ~~ none("Zaphod", "Ford", "Trillian")  # match fails
```

An any junction matched against another any junction is a recursive disjunction of every value in the first junction to every value in the second junction. The match is true if at least one value of the first junction matches at least one value in the second junction:

```
any("Ford", "Trillian") ~~ any("Trillian", "Arthur")
```

This match is true, because "Trillian" is in both junctions.

## Matching objects

An object matched against a class name is true if the object belongs to that class or inherits from that class. It's essentially the same as calling the .isa method on the object:

```
$ship ~~ Vogon::Constructor   # $ship.isa(Vogon::Constructor)
```

## Matching subroutines

Any expression matched against a subroutine tests the return value of the subroutine. If the subroutine takes no arguments, it is treated as a simple Boolean:

```
$value ~~ my_true
```

If the subroutine has a one argument signature and it is compatible with the variable type of the expression, the subroutine is called with the expression as its argument:

```
$value  ~~ &value_test    # value_test($value)
@array  ~~ &array_test     # array_test(@array)
%hash   ~~ &hash_test      # hash_test(%hash)
```

The return value of the subroutine determines the truth of the match.

A block matches as an anonymous subroutine. The return value of the block determines the truth of the match. It's treated as a simple Boolean if it takes no arguments, or passed the value on the left side if it uses $_ or placeholder variables inside the block (see "Placeholder Variables" in Chapter 5).

```
$value  ~~ { $_ + 5; }     # $_ is $value
%hash   ~~ { $_.keys; }    # $_ is \%hash
@array  ~~ { @^a.elems; }  # @^a is @array
```

# Referencing (or Not)

The unary \ operator returns a reference to its operand. The referencing operator isn't needed very often, since scalar context automatically generates references to arrays, hashes, and functions, but it is still needed in flattening contexts and other contexts that don't auto-reference:

```
@array_of_refs = ( \@a, \@b, \@c );
```

Ordinarily, an array assigned a list of arrays would flatten the elements of all the arrays into a single array. With the referencing operator, @array_of_refs is assigned a list of three arrayrefs.

The unary * operator (known as the splat operator) flattens a list in a context where it would usually be taken as a reference. On an rvalue, * causes the array to be treated as a simple list:

```
@combo = (\@array, \%hash);
@a := @combo; # @a is @combo
(@b, %c) := *@combo; # @b is @array, %c is %hash
```

Since the @combo array contains an arrayref and a hashref, an ordinary binding assignment of @combo to @a treats @combo as a single element and binds it to @a. With the flattening operator, the @combo array is treated as a simple list, so each of its elements are bound to a separate element on the lefthand side. @b is bound to the original @array and %c is bound to the original %hash.

On an lvalue, * tells the array to slurp all available arguments. An ordinary binding of two arrays to two arrays simply binds the first element on the righthand side to the first element on the lefthand side, and the second to the second. So, @a is bound to @c, and @b is bound to @d:

```
(@a, @b) := (@c, @d); # @a is @c, @b is @d
```

With the * operator, the first element on the lefthand side flattens all the elements on the righthand side into a list before the binding assignment. So, @a contains all the elements from @c and @d:

```
*@a := (@c, @d); # @a contains @c and @d
```

One common use for * is in defining subroutine and method signatures, as you will see in "Variadic Parameters" in Chapter 5.

## Zip Operator

The ¦ operator takes two or more lists (arrays, hash keys, etc.) and returns a single list with alternating elements from each of the original lists. This allows loops and other iterative structures to iterate through the elements of several lists at the same time:

```
@a = (1, 2, 3);
@b = (4, 5, 6);

@c = @a ¬¦ @b; # @c is (1, 4, 2, 5, 3, 6)
```

There is no equivalent ASCII operator for the zip operator, but the zip function is much more fully featured than the operator. It is described in "The for loop" later in this chapter.

# Control Structures

The simplest flow of control is linear—one statement follows the next in a straight line to the end of the program. Since this is far too limiting for most development tasks, languages provide ways to alter the control flow.

## Selection

Selection executes one set of actions out of many possible sets. The selection control structures are if, unless, and given/when.

### The if statement

The if statement checks a condition and executes its associated block only if that condition is true. The condition can be any expression that evaluates to a truth value. Parentheses around the condition are optional:

```
if $blue {
    print "True Blue.";
}
```

The if statement can also have an unlimited number of elsif statements that check additional conditions when the preceding conditions are false.

The final else statement executes if all preceding if and elsif conditions are false:

```
if $blue {
    print "True Blue.";
} elsif $green {
    print "Green, green, green they say...";
} else {
    print "Colorless green ideas sleep furiously.";
}
```

### The unless statement

The unless statement is the logical opposite of if. Its block executes only when the tested condition is false:

```
unless $fire {
    print "All's well.";
}
```

There is no elsunless statement, though else works with unless.

### The switch statement

The switch statement selects an action by comparing a given expression (the *switch*) to a series of when statements (the *cases*). When a case matches the switch, its block is executed:

```
given $bugblatter {
    when Beast::Trall { close_eyes(); }
    when 'ravenous'   { toss('steak'); }
    when .feeding     { sneak_past(); }
    when /grrr+/      { cover_ears(); }
    when 2            { run_between(); }
    when (3..10)      { run_away();   }

}
```

If these comparisons are starting to look familiar, they should. The set of possible relationships between a given and a when are exactly the same as the left and right side of a smart match operator (~~). The given aliases its argument to $_. $_ is always the current topic (think "topic of conversation"), so the process of aliasing a variable to $_ is known as *topicalization*. The when is a defaulting construct that does an implicit smart match on $_. The result is the same as if you typed:

```
given $bugblatter {
    when $_ ~~ Beast::Trall { close_eyes(); }
    when $_ ~~ 'ravenous'   { toss('steak'); }
    when $_ ~~ .feeding     { sneak_past(); }
    when $_ ~~ /grrr+/      { cover_ears(); }
```

```
    when $_ ~~ 2          { run_between( ); }
    when $_ ~~ (3..10)    { run_away( );   }
}
```

but more convenient. Generally, only one case is ever executed. Each when statement has an implicit break at the end. It is possible to fall through a case and continue comparing, but since falling through is less common, it has to be explicitly specified with a continue:

```
given $bugblatter {
    when Beast::Trall { close_eyes( ); continue; }
    when 'ravenous'   { toss('steak'); continue; }
    when 'attacking'  { hurl($spear, $bugblatter); continue; }
    when 'retreating' { toss('towel'); }
}
```

The default case executes its block when all other cases fail:

```
given $bugblatter {
    when Beast::Trall { close_eyes( ); }
    when 'ravenous'   { toss('steak'); }
    default           { run('away'); }
}
```

Any code within a given will execute, but a successful when skips all remaining code within the given, not just the when statements:

```
given $bugblatter {
    print "Slowly I turn...";
    when Beast::Trall { close_eyes( ); }
    print "Step by step...";
    when 'ravenous'   { toss('steak'); }
    print "Inch by inch...";
}
```

This means the default case isn't really necessary, because any code after the final when just acts like a default. But an explicit default case makes the intention of the code clearer in the pure switch. The difference is also significant when trapping exceptions. More on that in "Exceptions" later in this chapter.

A when statement can also appear outside a given. When it does, it simply smart match against $_. when statements also have a statement modifier form that doesn't have an implicit break:

```
print "Zaphod" when 'two heads';    # if $_ ~~ 'two heads'
```

# Iteration

Iteration constructs allow you to execute a set of statements multiple times. Perl 6's loop constructs are while, until, loop, and for.

## The while loop

A while loop iterates as long as a condition is true. The condition may be complex, but the result is always a single Boolean value because while imposes Boolean context on its condition:

```
while $improbability > 1 {
    print "$improbability to 1 against and falling.";
    $improbability = drive_status('power_down');
}
```

until is like while but continues looping as long as the condition is false:

```
until $improbability <= 1 {
    print "$improbability to 1 against and falling.";
    $improbability = drive_status('power_down');
}
```

## The simple loop

In its simplest form, the loop construct is infinite. It will iterate until a statement within the loop explicitly terminates it:

```
loop {
    print "One more of that Ol' Janx.";
    last if enough();
}
```

loop is also the counter iterator. Like while, it tests a condition before executing its block each time, but it has added expression slots for initialization and execution between iterations that make it ideal for counter loops:

```
loop ($counter = 1; $counter < 20; $counter++) {
    print "Try to count electric sheep...";
}
```

The parentheses around the loop condition are optional.

## The for loop

The for loop is the list iterator, so it imposes lazy list context. It takes a list or array, or any expression that produces a list, and loops through the list's elements one at a time. On each iteration, for aliases $_ to the current loop element. This means all the constructs that default to $_, like print and when, can default to the loop variable:

```
for @useful_things {
    print; # prints $_, the current loop variable
    print " You're one hoopy frood." when 'towel';
}
```

The arrow operator, ->, makes a named alias to the current element, in addition to the $_ alias.* All aliases are lexically scoped to the block.

```
for %people.keys -> $name {
    print; # prints $_ (same as $name)
    print ":", %people{$name}{'age'};
}
```

The arrow operator also makes it possible to iterate over multiple loop elements at the same time:

```
for %ages.kv -> $name, $age {
    print "$name is now $age";
}
```

You can combine the arrow operator with the zip function or zip operator to loop over several lists, taking some specified number of elements from each list on every iteration, as in the following code.

```
# one from each array
for zip(@people,@places,@things) -> $person, $place, $thing {
    print "Are you a $person, $place, or $thing?";
}
```

This example iterates over three arrays, taking one element from each array on each iteration and creating named aliases for the three elements.

```
# two from each array
for zip( @animals, @things, :by(2) )
        -> $animal1, $animal2, $thing1, $thing2 {

    print "The animals, they came, they came in by twosies, twosies: ";
    print "$animal1 and $animal2";

    print "Two things. And I call them, $thing1 and $thing2.";

}
```

This example iterates over two arrays, taking two elements from each array on each iteration and creating named aliases for them.

```
# two from the first array and one from the second
for zip(@colors=>2, @textures=>1) -> $color1, $color2, $texture {
    $mix = blend($color1, $color2);
    draw_circle($mix, $texture);
}
```

This example iterates over two arrays, taking two elements from the first array and one element from the second array on each iteration and creating named aliases for them.

---

* The arrow isn't restricted to for; it also works on given and other control flow structures.

---

If zip is called with arrays or lists of different lengths, it will fill in undef values for the named aliases pulled from the shorter lists.

## Breaking out of loops

The next, redo, and last keywords allow you to interrupt the control flow of a loop. next skips the remaining code in the loop and starts the next iteration. redo skips the remaining code in the loop and restarts the same iteration over again without incrementing counters or reevaluating loop conditions. last skips the remaining code in the loop and terminates the loop.

```
for @useful_things -> $item {
    next when 'towel';
    redo when .try_again;
    last when 'bomb';
    print "Are you sure you need your $item?";
}
```

# Blocks

In Perl 6, every block is a closure, so you get consistent behavior throughout the language, whether the block is a control structure, an argument passed to a subroutine, an anonymous subroutine reference, or the definition of a named element such as a subroutine, method, or class. What is a closure? Closures are chunks of code that are tied to the lexical scope in which they're defined. When they're stored and later executed at some point far removed from their definition, they execute using the variables in their original scope, even if those variables are no longer accessible any other way. It's almost as if they package up their lexical scope to make it portable. This example creates a closure that prints a lexical variable. When the closure is executed (from some other lexical scope), it prints the variable from the scope where it was defined, not the scope where it's executed:

```
my $person = "Zaphod";
$closure = { print $person; }
...
my $person = "Trillian";
$closure(); # prints "Zaphod"
```

The fact that all blocks are closures has some implications. Every block can take arguments. This is how for creates a $_ alias for the iterator variable. Every block defines a lexical scope. Every block has the potential to be stored and executed later. Whether a block is stored or executed immediately depends on the structure that uses it. The control structures we've discussed so far all execute their blocks where they're defined. A bare block executes immediately when it's alone, but is stored when it's in an assignment context or passed as a parameter:

```
# executed immediately
{
    print "Zaphod";
}

# stored
$closure = {
    print "Trillian";
}
```

### my, our, temp, and let

my and our are different ways of declaring variables. my declares a variable in the current lexical scratchpad, while our declares a lexical alias to a variable in the package symbol table:

```
my $lexical_var;
our $package_var;
```

state declares a lexical variable similar to my, but instead of reinitializing the value every time the block is executed it preserves the previous value:

```
state $static_var;
```

temp and let are not declarations; they are run-time commands to store the current value of a variable so it can be restored later. temp variables always restore their previous value on exiting the lexical scope of the temp, while let variables keep the temporary value, unless the lexical scope of the let is exited under an error condition (an undef or empty-list return value, or an exception):

```
temp $throwaway;
let $hypothetical;
```

temp and let don't change the value of the variable, they only store it.

### Property blocks

Every block may have a series of control flow handlers attached to it. These are called *property blocks* because they are themselves blocks (i.e., closures), attached as properties on the block that contains them. Property blocks are defined within the block they modify, by an uppercase keyword followed by a block (they're also sometimes called NAMED blocks):

```
NEXT {
    print "Coming around again."
}
```

Property blocks aren't executed in sequential order with the other code in the enclosing block—they are stored at compile time and executed at the appropriate point in the control flow. NEXT executes between each iteration of a loop, LAST executes at the end of the final iteration (or simply at the end of an ordinary block). PRE executes before everything else—before all other properties and code in an ordinary block and before the first iteration of a loop. POST executes after everything else—after all code and properties in an ordinary block and after the last iteration of a loop. PRE and POST are intended for assertion checking and cannot have any side effects. CATCH, KEEP, and UNDO are related to exception handling. KEEP and UNDO are variants of LAST and execute after CATCH. KEEP executes when the block exits with no exceptions, or when all exceptions have been trapped and handled; UNDO executes when the block exits with untrapped exceptions. There can be only one CATCH in a block, but there's no limit on the other types of property blocks.

This example prints out its loop variable in the body of the block:

```
for 1..4 {
    NEXT { print " potato, "; }
    LAST { print "." }
    print;

}
```

Between each iteration, the NEXT block executes, printing "potato". At the end of the final iteration, the LAST block prints a period. So the final result is:

```
1 potato, 2 potato, 3 potato, 4.
```

Property blocks are lexically scoped within their enclosing block, so they have access to lexical variables defined there:

```
for 5..7 -> $count {
    my $potato = "$count potato, ";
    NEXT {
        print $potato;
    }
    LAST {
        print $potato, "more.";
    }
}
```

In this example, the lexical variable $potato is redefined on every iteration and then printed from within the NEXT or LAST block. So the final result is:

```
5 potato, 6 potato, 7 potato, more.
```

## Exceptions

There are two types of exceptions: error exceptions and control flow exceptions. All exceptions are stored in the error object $!. All exception classes inherit from the Exception class.

Error exceptions are thrown by die or (under use fatal) fail. Any block can be an error exception handler—all it needs is a CATCH block. CATCH blocks always topicalize $!, so the simplest way to test for a particular exception is to compare it to a class name using a when statement (see the section "Smart Match" earlier in this chapter):

```
CATCH {
    when Err::Danger { warn "fly away home"; }
}
```

The $! object will also stringify to its text message if you match it against a pattern:

```
CATCH {
    when /:w I'm sorry Dave/ { warn "HAL is in the house."; }
}
```

If the CATCH block is exited by an explicit break statement, or by an implicit break in a when or default case, it marks the exception as clean. A when case with a continue statement leaves the exception unhandled, since continue skips the implicit break. If the exception isn't marked clean by the end of the CATCH block, CATCH rethrows the exception so an outer block can catch it.

Once an exception is thrown, execution skips straight to the CATCH block and the remaining code in the block is skipped. If the block has POST, KEEP, or UNDO property blocks, they will execute after the CATCH block.

If you want to limit the effects of an error exception, you can wrap the error throwing code in a try block. A try block without a CATCH block provides a default CATCH that catches all exceptions and, marks them as clean, and causes the try to return undef when any exception was caught. A try block is also a handy bit of self-documentation.

```
try {
    may_throw_exception();

    CATCH {
        when Error::Moof { warn "Caught a Moof error."; }
    }
}
```

Control flow exceptions handle alterations in the flow of control that aren't errors. When you call next to skip the remaining code in the loop and go on to the next iteration, you're actually throwing a control exception. These exceptions are caught by the relevant control structure: next and last exceptions are caught by loops, a return exception is caught by a subroutine or method, etc.

# CHAPTER 5
# Subroutines

Subroutines are reusable units of code. They can be called from just about anywhere, and return control to the point of the call when they finish executing. They can be passed zero or more arguments[*] and return zero or more results. Subroutines can be named or anonymous. They can be lexically scoped, package scoped, or globally scoped. "Multi" subs allow multiple subroutines to have the same name as long as they have different parameter lists.

Methods are significantly different from subroutines. In Perl 6, they're even distinguished by a separate keyword, method. These differences will be discussed in Chapter 6.

## Using Subroutines

The most basic subroutine declaration is simply the sub keyword, followed by the name of the sub, followed by the block that defines the sub:

```
sub alert {
    print "We have normality.";
}
```

The simplest subroutine call is just the subroutine name followed by a comma-separated list of variables or values:

```
$result = sum($a, $b, 42, 57);
```

Arguments are also sometimes passed as anonymous pairs:

```
$result = sum(first => 12, second => 21);
```

---

[*] Following the example set in Apocalypse 6, throughout this chapter we'll use the term "argument" for the values passed into a subroutine call and "parameter" for the lexical variables declared in the subroutine's signature.

Parentheses are optional on calls to subroutines that have been predeclared, but required for all other calls. Including the & sigil before the subroutine name in a call will not turn off signature checking. In fact, in most contexts prefixing the subroutine name with & will return a reference to the subroutine instead of calling the subroutine.

# Parameters

One of the most significant additions to subroutines in Perl 6 is named formal parameters. The parameter list, often called the *signature* of the subroutine, is part of the subroutine declaration:

```
sub standardize ($text, $method) {
    my $clean;
    given $method {
        when 'length' { $clean = wrap($text, 72); }
        when 'lower'  { $clean = lowercase($text); }
        ...
    }
    return $clean;
}
```

The subroutine standardize has two scalar parameters, $text and $method, so it is called with two arguments, each a scalar value. The parameters are lexical variables within the body of the sub. They never need to be explicitly declared as my, even under use strict because they're declared by the subroutine declaration.

In a sub with no parameter list, all arguments are passed in the @_ array:

```
sub sum {
    my $sum;
    for @_ -> $number {
        $sum += $number;
    }
    return $sum;
}
```

Subroutines with defined parameter lists don't get an @_ array.* If you want a subroutine that takes no arguments (and complains when arguments are passed), define it with an empty parameter list ( ).

Subroutine calls normally provide a nonflattening list context, which means that any array or hash passed into a subroutine is treated as a single argument. An array parameter in the signature expects to be passed an actual

---

* In fact, a simple subroutine without a signature actually has an implicit signature of *@_. See "Variadic Parameters" later in this chapter.

array or arrayref argument, and a hash parameter expects a hash or hashref argument:

```
sub whole (@names, %flags) {
    ...
}

whole(@array, %hash);
```

## Optional Parameters

Every subroutine call checks its signature to make sure the arguments it gets match the declared parameter list. A mismatch in the number or kind of arguments is an error. But since requiring every declared parameter to be passed in on every call isn't nearly flexible enough for the average programmer, Perl 6 also allows optional parameters. Each optional parameter is marked with a ? before the parameter name:

```
sub someopt ($required1, $required2, ?$optional1, ?$optional2) {
    ...
}
```

So, someopt will accept anywhere from two to four arguments. You can have any number of required and optional parameters, but all the required parameters must come before the first optional parameter. This is largely a common sense restriction. If you want to leave some elements off a list of arguments, it has to be the ones at the end, because positional arguments are bound to the parameters in strict linear order. All these calls to someopt are fine:

```
someopt('req1', 'req2', 'opt1', 'opt2');
someopt('req1', 'req2', 'opt1');
someopt('req1', 'req2');
```

## Named Parameters

Any argument can be passed either by position with an ordered list of arguments, or by name with an unordered list of pairs. (See "Named Argument Passing" later in this chapter for more details.) Sometimes you'll want to specify that certain parameters will be passed only by name, never by position. Named parameters are marked with a + before the parameter name:

```
sub namedparams ($first, +$second, +$third) {
    ...
}

namedparams(1, second => 2, third => 3);
```

Named parameters are always optional. They must come after all positional parameters—that is, after the unmarked required parameters and the optional parameters marked with a ?. Again, this is largely a matter of common sense. Though named parameters are completely ignored when binding a list of positional arguments, the parser and the person maintaining your code will both be profoundly grateful they don't have to sort through a mixed bag of positional and named parameters to find the positional parameter list.

## Variadic Parameters

Another element of flexibility Perl developers will expect is the ability to pull a list of arguments into an array or hash parameter. These are known as *variadic* parameters because they can take a variable number of arguments. In Perl 6, an array parameter with a * before the parameter name will slurp up all the *positional* arguments that haven't already been bound to another positional parameter.* So, the following call to transport binds $arthur to @names[0], and $ford to @names[1]:

```
sub transport ($planet, *@names) {
    ...
}

transport('Magrathea', $arthur, $ford);
```

If the variadic array parameter is the only positional parameter in the signature, it will take all the positional arguments:

```
sub simple (*@_) {...}
# is the same as
sub simple {...}
```

A hash parameter with a * before the name will slurp up all the *named* arguments that haven't already been bound to another parameter. So, the following call to transport binds the value of the pair argument with the key 'planet' to the parameter $planet, but all the other pairs become part of the %flags hash (more on this in "Named Argument Passing" later in this chapter):

```
sub transport ($planet, *%flags) {...}

transport('name'    => 'Arthur',
          'luggage' => 'lost',
          'planet'  => 'Magrathea',
          'towel'   => 'required');
```

---

* You may notice that this is the same symbol as the flattening/slurping operator from "Smart Match" in Chapter 4.

When they're combined with other kinds of parameters, variadic parameters must come after all positional parameters in the signature. They can either precede or follow the named parameters.

## Typed Parameters

Signature checking is sensitive not only to the number of arguments and the variable type (defined by the $, @, %, or & symbol), but also to the value type. (See "Types" in Chapter 4 for more details on value and variable types.) The parameter type is defined before the parameter name and before any symbols for optional, named, or variadic parameters:

```
sub typedparams (Int $first, Str ?$second) {...}
```

The parameter type declares the type of argument that can be bound to it. The parameter and argument types have to be compatible, but not identical.

Type checking happens at compile time whenever possible, because it's faster and allows for optimizations. Otherwise, type checking happens at run time. So, if all the arguments passed to the subroutine are explicitly typed, the types will be checked at compile time. If the arguments aren't explicitly typed, the run-time checks will make sure the scalars contain an integer value and a string value.

## Properties on Parameters

By default, parameters are aliases to the original arguments (pass-by-reference), but they're marked as constant so they cannot be modified within the body of the subroutine. The is rw property marks a parameter as modifiable, so changes to the parameter within the body of the sub modify the original variable passed in:

```
sub modifyparams ($first is rw, $second is rw) {...}
```

The is copy property marks a parameter as pass-by-value, so the parameter is a lexically scoped copy of the original value passed in:

```
sub passbyvalue ($first is copy, $second is copy) {...}
```

## Default Values for Parameters

Sometimes it is useful to be able to define a default value for an optional or named parameter. The = operator marks the default value.* The parameter

---

* This isn't an assignment; it's only a reuse of the = symbol in a different context.

takes the default value only if the call doesn't pass an argument for that parameter.

```
sub default_vals ($required, ?$optional = 5) {...}
```

# Placeholder Variables

Placeholder variables are a simple alternative to formal parameter lists. They have many of the advantages of ordinary parameters, without the inconvenience of declaring a signature. You just use variables with a caret after the sigil—$^name, @^name, %^name, or &^name—within the subroutine's block, and the arguments passed into the subroutine are bound to them.

```
@sorted = sort { $^a <=> $^b } @array;
```

The order of the parameters is determined by the Unicode sorting order of the placeholders' names, so the following example acts as if it has a formal parameter list of ($^milk, $^sugar, $^tealeaves):

```
$make_tea = {
    my $tea = boil $^tealeaves;
    combine $tea, $^sugar, $^milk;
    return $tea;
}
```

Placeholders are handy in short subroutines and bare blocks, but soon become unwieldy in anything more complicated.

# Return Values

In addition to a signature for the incoming parameters to a subroutine, you can also declare a partial signature, or *siglet*, for the values returned from a subroutine. Return siglets declare the type of each return value, but they don't bind a named variable to the returned value and can't define a default value for the return. In the declaration, the return signature goes before the sub keyword or after the parameter list attached with the returns keyword.

```
sub get_value (Int $incoming) returns Int {...}
# same as
Int sub get_value (Int $incoming) {...}
```

Both syntaxes have exactly the same effect, but using the returns keyword is usually clearer when the sub has multiple return values:

```
sub get_values (Str $incoming) returns (Int, Str) {...}
```

# Arguments

The standard way of passing arguments is by position. The first argument passed in goes to the first parameter, the second to the second, and so on:

```
sub matchparams ($first, $second) {...}

matchparams($one, $two);  # $one is bound to $first
                          # $two is bound to $second
```

## Named Argument Passing

You can also pass arguments in by name, using a list of anonymous pairs. The key of each pair gives the parameter's name and the value of the pair gives the value to be bound to the parameter. When passed by name, the arguments can come in any order. Optional parameters can be left out, even if they come in the middle of the parameter list. This is particularly useful for subroutines with a large number of optional parameters:

```
sub namedparams ($first, ?$second, ?$third is rw) {...}

namedparams(third => 'Trillian', first => $name);
```

Sometimes the *option* syntax for pairs is clearer than the pair constructor syntax:

```
namedparams :third('Trillian'), :first($name);
```

## Flattening Arguments

To get the Perl 5–style behavior where the elements of an array (or the pairs of a hash) flatten out into the parameter list, use the flattening operator in the call to the subroutine. Here, $first binds to @array[0] and $second binds to @array[1]:

```
sub flat ($first, $second) {...}

flat(*@array);
```

A flattened hash argument acts as a list of pairs, which are bound to the parameters just like ordinary named arguments. So, $first is bound to %hash{'first'}, and $second is bound to %hash{'second'}:

```
sub flat_hash ($first, $second) {...}

%hash = (first => 1, second => 2);
flat_hash(*%hash);
```

Flattened hash arguments are useful for building up hashes of named arguments to pass in all at once.

## Argument Order Constraints

Arguments to subroutine calls have a standard general order. Positional arguments, if there are any, always go first. Named arguments go after any positional arguments. Variadic arguments always go at the end of the list.

```
order($positional, named => 1, 'va', 'ri', 'ad', 'ic');
```

Positional arguments are first so the parser and the person maintaining the code have an easier time associating them with positional parameters. Variadic arguments are at the end because they're open-ended lists.

If a subroutine has only required and variadic parameters, you can always call it with a simple list of positional arguments. In this example, 'a' is bound to $req and the rest of the arguments go to the slurpy array:

```
sub straight_line ($req, *@slurpy) {...}

straight_line('a', 'b', 'c', 'd', 'e');
```

If a subroutine has some optional parameters and a variadic array you can call it with a simple list of positional arguments, but only if you have arguments for all the optional parameters. In this example, 'a' is bound to $req, 'b' is bound to $opt, and the rest of the arguments go to the slurpy array:

```
sub mixed ($req, ?$opt, *@slurpy) {...}

mixed('a', 'b', 'c', 'd', 'e');
```

If you want to skip some of the optional parameters, you have two choices. When the argument list has at least one named argument, the parser knows to start the variadic list right after the named arguments end. This example binds 'a' to $req, binds 'opt' to $opt, skips $another, and puts the rest of the arguments in the variadic array:

```
sub mixed ($req, ?$opt, ?$another, *@slurpy) {...}

mixed('a', 'opt' => 1, 'b', 'c', 'd', 'e');
```

If you want to skip all the optional parameters you need to use the <= = operator in place of the comma to mark where the variadic list starts. This example binds 'a' to $req, skips $opt and $another, and puts all the rest of the arguments in the variadic array:

```
mixed('a' <= =  'b', 'c', 'd', 'e');
```

You have to watch out for optional and variadic parameters when you modify subroutines already in use. Adding an extra optional parameter to a signature with a variadic array will break any calls that passed all positional arguments. You could suggest that all users call your subroutines with <== in case you decide to change them later, or you could just add the new parameters as named parameters instead of optional parameters. Named parameters ignore positional arguments, so this version of the subroutine puts 'b' through 'e' in the variadic array with or without any named arguments in the call:

```
sub mixed ($req, +$opt, +$another, *@slurpy) {...}

mixed('a', 'opt' => 1, 'b', 'c', 'd', 'e');
mixed('a', 'b', 'c', 'd', 'e');
```

As usual, there's more than one way to do it.

# Subroutine Stubs

To declare a subroutine without defining it you give it a body consisting of nothing but the ... (or "yada, yada, yada") operator. So, all the preceding examples that look like pseudocode with {...} for their body are actually valid subroutine declarations.

```
sub stubbly (Str $name, Int ?$days) {...}
```

When you later define the subroutine, the signature and defined traits must exactly match the declaration.

```
sub stubbly (Str $name, Int ?$days) {
    print "$name hasn't shaved in $days day";
    print "s" if $days > 1;
}
```

# Subroutine Scope

Just like variables, subroutine names are simply entries in a symbol table or lexical scratchpad. So, all subroutines live in a particular scope, whether it's lexical, package, or global scope.

## Package-Scoped Subroutines

Package scope is the default scope for subs. A sub that is declared without any scope marking is accessible within the module or class where it's defined with an unqualified call, like subname(), and accessible elsewhere with a fully qualified call using the Package::Name::subname() syntax.*

---

* Certain levels of strictness may require the fully qualified name everwhere.

```
module My::Module {
  sub firstsub ($param) {...}

  sub secondsub {
    mysub('arg'); # call the subroutine
  }
}

module Other::Module {
  use My::Module;

  sub thirdsub {
    My::Module::firstsub('arg');
  }
}
```

This example declares two modules, My::Module and Other::Module. My::Module declares a subroutine firstsub and calls it from within secondsub. Other::Module declares a subroutine thirdsub that calls firstsub using its fully qualified name.

## Lexically Scoped Subroutines

Subroutines can also be lexically scoped, just like variables. A myed subroutine makes an entry in the current lexical scratchpad with a & sigil. Lexically scoped subs are called just like a normal subroutine:

```
if $dining {
    my sub dine ($who, $where) {
        ...
    }

    dine($zaphod, "Milliways");
}

# dine($arthur, "Nutri-Matic");  # error
```

The first call to the lexically scoped dine is fine, but the second would be a compile-time error because dine doesn't exist in the outer scope.

The our keyword declares a lexically scoped alias to a package scoped subroutine (it has an entry both in the symbol table of the current package and in the current lexical scratchpad). This is useful under certain levels of strictness.

```
if $dining {
    our sub pay ($when, $what) {
        ...
    }

    pay($tuesday, "hamburger");
}
```

## Globally Scoped Subroutines

Globally scoped subroutines are visible everywhere, unless they're overridden by a lexical or package scoped subroutine of the same name. They are declared with the * symbol before the name of the subroutine:

```
sub *seen_by_all ($why, $how) {...}
```

Most built-ins will be globally scoped.

# Anonymous Subroutines

Anonymous subroutines do everything that ordinary subroutines do. They can declare a formal parameter list with optional and required parameters, take positional and named arguments, and do variadic slurping. The only difference is that they don't define a name. But since you can't call a subroutine if you have no way to refer to it, they have to get the equivalent of a name somewhere, whether they're assigned to a variable, passed as a parameter, or aliased to another subroutine.

```
$make_tea = sub ($tealeaves, ?$sugar, ?$milk) {...}
```

The arrow operator used with for and given is just another way of defining anonymous subroutines. The arrow doesn't require parentheses around its parameter list. It can't declare named subs, and can't declare a return type.

```
$make_tea = -> $tealeaves, ?$sugar, ?$milk {...}
```

A bare block can also define an anonymous subroutine, but it can't define a formal parameter list on the sub and can't define a named sub:

```
$make_tea = {
    my $tea = boil 'tealeaves';
    combine $tea, 'sugar', 'milk';
}
```

You can't use the return statement within an arrow sub or bare block sub to return from an anonymous sub. Blocks and arrow subs are commonly used for ordinary control flow, so return ignores them and only returns from subroutines defined with sub keyword or methods.

# Multi Subroutines

You can define multiple routines with the same name but different signatures. These are known as "multisubs" and are defined with the multi keyword before sub. They're useful if you want a routine that can handle different types of arguments in different ways, but still appear as a single subroutine to the user. For example, you might define an add multisub with different behavior for integers, floats, and certain types of numeric objects:

```
multi sub add (Int $first, Int $second) {...}
multi sub add (Num $first, Num $second) {...}
multi sub add (Imaginary $first, Imaginary $second) {...}
multi sub add (MyNum $first, MyNum $second) {...}
```

When you later call the routine:

```
add($apples, $oranges);
```

it will dispatch to the right version of add based on the types of the arguments passed to it. The parameters used for dispatch selection are called *invocants*. If you want to use a limited set of parameters as invocants, mark the boundary between invocant parameters and the rest of the signature with a semicolon:

```
multi sub add (Int $first, Int $second: Int $third) {...}
```

This version of add will dispatch based on the types of the first two arguments passed in, and ignore the type of the third.

# Curried Subroutines

Currying* allows you to create a shortcut for calling a subroutine with some preset parameter values. The assuming method takes a list of named arguments and returns a subroutine reference, with each of the named arguments bound to the original subroutine's parameter list. If you have a subroutine multiply that multiplies two numbers, you might create a subref $six_times that sets the value for the $multiplier parameter, so you can reuse it several times:

```
sub multiply ($multiplicand, $multiplier) {
    return $multiplicand * $multiplier;
}

$six_times = &multiply.assuming(multiplier => 6);

$six_times(9); # 54
$six_times(7); # 42
...
```

---

* The term "currying" is drawn from functional languages and is named in honor of logician Haskell Curry.

You can also use binding assignment to alias a curried subroutine to an ordinary subroutine name instead of a scalar variable:

```
&six_times := &multiply.assuming(multiplier => 6);

six_times(7); # 42
```

# Wrapped Subroutines

Sometimes you might want to wrap extra functionality around a subroutine that was already defined (perhaps in a standard module), but still call it with the same name. The .wrap method is similar to the .assuming method, but more powerful. It takes a subroutine reference as an argument and returns an ID object. Inside the subref wrapper, the call statement marks the point where the original subroutine will be executed.

```
$id = &subname.wrap ({
    # preprocess arguments
    # or execute additional code
    call;
    # postprocess return value
    # or execute additional code
})

subname(...); # call the wrapped subroutine
```

By default, the inner subroutine is passed the same arguments as the wrapping subroutine, and the wrapping subroutine returns the same result as the inner subroutine. You can alter the arguments passed to the inner subroutine by adding an explicit argument list to call, and alter the outer return value by capturing the result from call and explicitly returning a value in the wrapper.

```
$id = &subname.wrap (sub (*@args) {
    # preprocess arguments
    $result = call('modified', 'arguments');
    # postprocess return value
    return $result;
})
```

A subroutine can have multiple wrappers at the same time. Each new wrapper wraps around the previous one, and the outermost wrapper executes first. The ID object returned by .wrap allows the .unwrap method to remove a specific wrapper:

```
&subname.unwrap($id);
```

If you'd rather not manually unwrap your sub, wrap a temped version instead. The temp automatically removes the wrapper at the end of its scope.

```
{
    temp &subname.wrap ({...})

    subname(...);
}
```

# Lvalue Subroutines

Lvalue subroutines pretend to be assignable values, just like any ordinary variable. They do this by returning a proxy variable which handles the lvalue behavior for the subroutine (fetch, store, etc.). You declare an lvalue subroutine with the is rw property:

```
sub storage is rw {...}

storage() = 5;
```

An lvalue sub can return an ordinary variable which acts as a proxy, return the return value from another lvalue sub, or it can return a tied proxy variable defined within the sub:

```
my sub assignable is rw {
    my $proxy is Proxy(
        FETCH => {...},
        STORE => {...},
        ...
    );
    return $proxy;
}
```

This example defines an lvalue sub named assignable. It creates a proxy variable tied to a Proxy class that defines FETCH and STORE tie methods on the fly.

# Macros

Macros are a powerful way of manipulating source code at compile time. Macros must be declared before they're called. A call to a macro routine executes as soon as it's parsed. The parser substitutes the return value from the macro into the parse tree in place of the macro call. If a macro returns undef, it makes no entry in the parse tree. So, the macro disappear takes a single string argument and returns undef. Any call to disappear is replaced at compile time with nothing, just as if it were commented out.

```
macro disappear (Str $thinair) {
    return;
}
```

```
...
```

```
disappear("Some text you'll never see");
```

If a macro returns a string, the string is parsed as Perl source code, and the resulting parse tree replaces the macro call. So, anywhere the macro twice is called, it is replaced at compile time by a for modifier:

```
macro twice {
    return "for 1..2";
}
```

```
...
```

```
print "\n" twice;      # same as:  print "\n" for 1..2;
```

If a macro returns a block, that block is parsed as a closure, and the resulting parse tree replaces the macro call. So, when the reverse_numeric macro is called, the parser substitutes the block { $^b <=> $^a } in place of the call:

```
macro reverse_numeric {
    return { $^b <=> $^a };
}
```

```
...
```

```
sort reverse_numeric, @values;
```

If a macro returns a parse tree, the parser substitutes it directly for the macro call. The returned tree may be the original parse tree, a modified parse tree, or a manufactured parse tree.

By default, a call to a macro is parsed just like an ordinary subroutine call, so it can take no arguments or a comma-separated list of arguments. But, macros can also modify the way their arguments are parsed, by adding an is parsed trait. The trait takes a rule as an argument, and will parse whatever code follows using that rule instead of the normal rule for parsing subroutine arguments. So, the macro funky essentially translates a "ValSpeak" subroutine call into an ordinary Perl subroutine call. It takes a single string argument, which it parses as a sequence of word-forming characters, surrounded by the strings "like" and ", you know". (For more on rules, see Chapter 7.) It then returns a block that will call the plain subroutine with the single argument passed to funky.

```
macro funky (Str $whatever)
  is parsed (/:w like (\w+), you know/)
  {
  return { plain($whatever); };
  }

  ...

  funky like whatever, you know
```

# CHAPTER 6

# Objects

Objects are encapsulated chunks of data and functionality. Over the years a host of concepts have sprung up around objects, such as data abstraction, code reuse, encapsulation, single and multiple inheritance, composition, delegation, mixins, polymorphism, and multiple dispatch. Every language with object-oriented syntax selects a subset of these ideas and combines them in different ways. With Perl 6 we want to provide a cleaner and simpler syntax for working with objects, but we also want to support a larger set of object-oriented ideas. Does that sound impossible? The solution is a classically Perl-ish one: make the easy things easy and the hard things possible.

With the release of Apocalypse 12, the syntax in this chapter is fairly solid, though it's still likely to change somewhat before the final implementation. This chapter is only an introduction to the concepts. For complete coverage you should read the Apocalypse itself.

## Using Objects

You can declare a class in one of two ways. The most familiar syntax for class declaration ends in a semicolon. The rest of the file after the declaration defines the class. With this syntax there can be only one class or module declaration in a file.

```
class Heart::Gold;
# class definition follows
...
```

The other syntax for class declaration wraps the definition in a block. You can have as many of these as you like in a file, and even embed one class within the block of another.

```
class Heart::Gold {
    # class definition enclosed
```

```
    ...
}
```

With a file definition, all code that follows the class declaration is defined in the Heart::Gold namespace. With a block definition, everything within the block is defined in the class's namespace.

To create a new object from a class, simply call its new method. The default new method in the universal base class Object creates and initializes an object.

```
$ship = Heart::Gold.new(length => 150);
```

There's a shortcut for typed variables so you don't have to give the name of the class twice:

```
my Heart::Gold $ship .= new(length => 150);
```

# Classes

Classes are the "cookie cutters" that build objects. Just as a module groups subroutines in a package, a class groups methods in a package. Classes can also contain subroutines, submethods, and multimethods. However, classes are significantly different from modules, primarily because they construct objects. Objects don't just define functionality, they also hold data. In Perl 5 objects were simply hashes (or arrays, or...) bestowed with special powers by bless. Perl 6 objects can still be simple blessed data structures, but the default is now an object that hides the details of its internal representation—a true opaque object.

## Attributes

Attributes are the data at the core of an opaque object. Other languages have called them instance variables, data members, or instance attributes. Attributes are declared with the has keyword, and generally have a "." after the sigil:

```
class Heart::Gold {
    has int $.length;
    has int $.height is rw;
    has @.cargo;
    has %.crew;
    ...
}
```

Attributes aren't directly accessible outside the class, but inside the class they act just like ordinary variables:

```
print $.length;
$.length = 140;
```

Attributes also automatically generate their own accessor method with the same name as the attribute. Accessor methods are accessible inside or outside the class. By default, accessors are read-only, but the is rw property marks an accessor as read/write.

```
$value = $obj.height; # returns the value of $.height
$obj.height = 90;      # sets the value of $.height
```

# Methods

Methods are similar to subroutines, but different enough to merit their own keyword, method. The most obvious differences are that they're invoked on an object (or class), and they pass their invocant (that is, the object or class on which they were invoked) as an implicit argument. The invocant is marked off from the other parameters in the list by a colon:

```
method initiate_drive ($self: $power, $tea) {
    ...
}
```

Methods topicalize their invocant, so it's always accessible as $_, even if the method doesn't include it in the parameter list. This is particularly handy since any method called without an explicit object defaults to $_:

```
method shut_down ($drive) {
    if .safe {
        .powerdown($drive);
    }
    return .status;
}
```

Method declarations support the same syntax as subroutines for optional, named, variadic, and typed parameters, default values for parameters, properties on parameters, and return values. Method calls support positional and named argument passing just like subroutines. (See Chapter 5 for more details on this syntax.)

You can call a method in one of two ways. The standard method call is connected to the object with the . operator:

```
$ship.shut_down($infinity);
```

An *indirect object* call is an alternative to the standard method call. This syntax looks like an ordinary subroutine call, except that the invocant is separated from the other arguments by a colon:

```
shut_down($ship: $infinity);
```

The parentheses are optional unless the method call is ambiguous without them:

```
shut_down $ship: $infinity;
```

## Inheritance

Any class can inherit methods from another class using the is keyword in the class declaration. You may have noticed that this is the same keyword as compile-time properties. The fact that a class inherits from some other class is really just a trait of the inheriting class.

```
use Ship;
class Heart::Gold is Ship {
    ....
}
```

Any class can inherit from multiple parent classes:

```
class Heart::Gold is Ship is Improbable {
    ....
}
```

Within a derived class, inherited attributes are accessible only through their accessor methods:

```
class Ship {
    has $.height;
    has $.length;
    ...
}

class Heart::Gold is Ship {
    method dimensions ($self:){
        print "$self.length x $self.height \n";
    }
}
```

## Construction, Initialization, and Destruction

The default new method provided by the Object base class constructs and initializes opaque objects. It does this by calling bless, which calls the CREATE and BUILDALL methods. The CREATE method constructs an opaque object. The BUILDALL method calls the initializers for all inherited classes and finally the class's own initializer. BUILDALL actually calls the parent's BUILDALL method, which calls its parent's BUILDALL method, etc. The initializer for each class is BUILD. The default BUILD initializes the attributes of the object with named arguments to new, matching the name of the argument to the name of the attribute.

There are a number of ways to change the default object construction and initialization behavior. If you override new so that it passes a data structure as the first argument to bless, it will construct a traditional blessed hash (or array, or...) object instead of calling CREATE to construct an opaque object:

```
$class.bless({answer => '42'});
```

If you override the CREATE method you can alter the way objects are constructed. If you override the BUILDALL method you can change how the initializers for inherited classes are called. If you override the BUILD method you can change how the current class initializes objects and their attributes. Overriding BUILD will be common. Overriding CREATE and BUILDALL will be rare, since their default behavior is designed to handle everything from the simple opaque object to inheriting from classes written in other languages.

Object destruction traverses the inheritance hierarchy in the reverse order of object initialization. Objects are created from least derived to most derived and destroyed from most derived to least derived. The DESTROYALL method first calls the DESTROY method of the current class, and then calls the DESTROYALL method of the parent class (which calls its own DESTROY and then its own parent's DESTROYALL, etc). You will rarely need to define a DESTROY method, since the interpreter handles memory deallocation. It can be useful for class-specific cleanup, like closing a socket or filehandle.

## Lexically Scoped Classes

Classes in Perl 6 are first class entities with entries in symbol tables or lexical scratchpads.* This means classes can be lexically scoped, just like variables or subroutines:

```
my class Infinite::Improbablity {
    ...
}

$drive = Infinite::Improbability.new();
```

A lexical class works just like any other class, but is accessible by name only within the lexical scope where it's defined.

## Anonymous Classes

You can also define anonymous classes and create objects from them:

```
$class = class {
```

---

* If you're curious, :: is the sigil for classes and packages, though it's rarely needed in code.

```
    ...
}
$object = $class.new( );
```

A class's block is a closure, just like every other block, so it has access to variables from its defining scope, no matter where it's actually used.

# Roles

A role is a reusable unit of class code. Much like a module exports subroutines into your program or another module, a role exports methods and attributes into a class. If your first thought on reading this is "Isn't that just inheritance?", then welcome to a whole new world. Inheritance is one way to reuse code, but many relationships other than isa are possible. Various languages pick an alternative and provide syntax for it: Ruby has *mixins*, Java has *interfaces*, and some versions of Smalltalk have *traits*. Perl *roles* go a bit beyond all of them.

You define a role using the role keyword:

```
role Hitchhiker {...}
```

You pull a role into a class using the does keyword:

```
class Arthur does Hitchhiker {...}
```

Roles cannot instantiate objects directly. To create an object that makes use of a role, you make a new object from a class that uses that role:

```
$person = Arthur.new(...);
```

## Composition

Like classes, roles can define both attributes and methods:

```
role Hitchhiker {
  has $.towel;
  method thumb_ride ($self: $ship) {...}
  ...
}
```

Unlike classes, when you pull a role's methods and attributes into a class they aren't maintained in an inheritance hierarchy to be searched later. Instead, they are composed into the class almost as if they had been defined in that class. All methods defined in the role are accessible in the composed class, even if they wouldn't be inherited. All attributes defined in the role are accessible in the composed class by their direct $.name, not just by their accessor method.*

One advantage of composition is that classes can reuse behavior, even if they have no connection that would justify an inheritance relation. Suppose you want to define two classes: Arthur and Ford. Arthur inherits from Human and has all the behaviors and qualities of a human creature. Ford, on the other hand, has the behaviors and qualities of a creature from Betelgeuse:

```
class Arthur is Human does Hitchhiker {...}
class Ford is Betelgeusian does Hitchhiker {...}
```

Inheritance makes sense in this case—the inherited classes are core, defining characteristics of the resulting class. But the Hitchhiker role isn't a defining part of Ford and Arthur—they weren't always hitchhikers. The role just adds some useful behavior to the class.

## Mixins

In some situations you may want to add a role at run time instead of at compile time. Perhaps you want to choose different roles based on how the object is used, or perhaps the role's behavior shouldn't be available until part-way through the life of an object. The same does keyword adds roles at run time, but operates on an object instead of a class. In this example, Arthur starts as an ordinary human, and only adds the Hitchhiker role later in life (after the Vogons destroy his home planet):

```
class Arthur is Human {...}

$person = Arthur.new;
$person.live_quietly until $vogon_ship.arrive;

$person does Hitchhiker;
$person.thumb_ride($vogon_ship);
```

## Interfaces

An *interface* is a reusable unit that defines what methods a class should support, but doesn't provide any implementations for those methods. In Perl 6, interfaces are just roles that define only method stubs and no attributes. This example defines an interface for products shipped by the Sirius Cybernetics corporation:

```
role Sirius::Cybernetics {
    method share {...}
```

---

* Though you'll probably want to use the accessor methods anyway, based on the principles of encapsulation and ease of refactoring.

---

```
    method enjoy {...}
}
```

No matter whether the product is an elevator, a nutrimatic machine, or an automatic door, it must support the share and enjoy methods. Now, since these products are so very different, none will implement the methods in quite the same way, but you're guaranteed the products will be able to "Share and Enjoy" in one way or another (generally in an irritating way).

## Conflicts

Since a class pulls in roles by composition instead of inheritance, a conflict results when two roles both have a method with the same name. So, the Hitchhiker and Writer roles both define a lunch_break method (lunch breaks being vitally important in both the publishing and footslogging industries):

```
role Hitchhiker {
    method lunch_break {
        .suck($.towel);
        .drink($old_janx);
    }
    ...
}

role Writer {
    method lunch_break {
        my $restaurant = Jolly::Nice::Restaurant.new;
        .dine($restaurant);
    }
    ...
}
```

If the Ford class does the Writer role as well as the Hitchhiker role, which kind of lunch break should he take? Since roles are composed without hierarchy or priority, both methods are equally valid choices. Rather than randomly selecting an implementation for you, Perl 6 simply requires you to choose one. There are several ways to do this. One is to define a method of the same name in the class itself. This method might simply call the method from one of the roles:

```
class Ford does Hitchhiker does Writer {
    method lunch_break { .Writer::lunch_break(@_); }
}
```

Or the method might select between the possible implementations based on one of the arguments or some condition in the object. This example checks the string value returned by the .location method to find out which lunch break is appropriate:

```
class Ford does Hitchhiker does Writer {
    method lunch_break ($self: $arg) {
```

```
        given (.location) {
            when "Megadodo Office" { $self.Writer::lunch_break($arg); }
            when "Ship Cargo Hold" { $self.Hitchhiker::lunch_break($arg); }
        }
    }
}
```

You can also get a finer-grained control over method conflict resolution using delegation syntax (explained in the next section). This example renames Hitchhiker's lunch_break method to snack in the composed class:

```
class Ford does Hitchhiker handles :snack«lunch_break» does Writer {...}
```

# Delegation

Delegation is yet another possible relationship between an object and another body of code. Rather than pull methods into a class, you call methods in another object as if they were methods of the class. In Perl 6, delegation can be done in either a class or a role. A delegated object is simply an attribute defined in the class or role. The handles keyword specifies which methods of the delegated object will act as methods of the class. This example declares that any calls to the thumb_ride method on an object with the Hitchhiker role, will actually call the method on its $.thumb attribute:

```
role Hitchhiker {
    ...
    has Electronic::Thumb $.thumb handles 'thumb_ride';
    ...
}
```

The handles keyword accepts many variations in the syntax to delegate methods. You can pass it an array reference of multiple method names:

```
has Electronic::Thumb $.thumb handles ['thumb_ride', 'sub_etha'];
```

or a quoted list:

```
has Electronic::Thumb $.thumb handles «thumb_ride sub_etha»;
```

A pair in place of a string method name gives the method a different name in the class. This example declares a method named hitch in the class, but any calls to it are delegated to the thumb_ride method on the $.thumb object:

```
has Electronic::Thumb $.thumb handles :hitch«thumb_ride»;
```

If the method name is given as a pattern, it's a wildcard delegation and all methods that match that pattern will be delegated to the attribute. This example delegates all methods that start with "thumb" to $.thumb:

```
has Electronic::Thumb $.thumb handles /^thumb/;
```

If the method name is a substitution, it does wildcard method renaming. This example would delegate a method call to hitch_ride to a method named thumb_ride in $.thumb:

```
has Electronic::Thumb $.thumb handles (s/^hitch/thumb/);
```

# Private and Public

By default, all methods and attribute accessors are *public* methods, so they can be called anywhere. You can also declare *private* methods or accessors, which can be called only within the class where they're defined, or from certain trusted classes. A private method is declared with a colon at the start of the name:

```
method :inaccessible ($self: $value) {...}
```

A private attribute is declared with a colon in place of the dot (.) in the name:

```
has $:hidden;
```

You call a private method or accessor with a colon in the call:

```
$object.:hidden(42);
```

The attribute variable ($:name or $.name) is never accessible outside the class, whether the attribute is public or private.

At first glance this might look like nothing more than the "encapsulation by convention" of Perl 5. It's actually much more than that. The colon implicitly sets a private trait on the method or attribute. The encapsulation is enforced by the interpreter. An external call to a private method will fail as if the method simply didn't exist. External queries to the package symbol table for private methods also fail.

Only public methods are inherited by a derived class, but inherited public methods can call private methods from their own class. Private methods and attributes in a role are private to the composed class, as if they were defined in that class.

The one loophole in private methods is that a class can declare that it trusts certain other classes to allow those classes to access its private methods. Roles cannot declare a trusted class. In this example, the Friendly class declares that it trusts the Zaphod class:

```
class Friendly {
    trusts Zaphod; # probably a bad idea, really
}
```

# Subroutines

You can define ordinary subroutines within a class or role. They cannot be invoked on an object with the $object.methodname syntax and will never pass an implicit invocant argument. They aren't inherited but can be pulled in with role composition. They're mainly useful for utility code internal to the class:

```
class Answer::Young;

has $.answer;
...
sub is_valid ($value) {
    return 1 if 10 < $value < 42;
}
...
method set_answer ($new) {
    $.answer = $new if is_valid($new);
}
```

Subroutines may be exported if the class also functions as a module.

# Submethods

A submethod is declared like a method, but behaves more like a sub in that it's not inherited but can be pulled in with a role. Submethods are useful for inheriting interface without inheriting implementation—you can override a method from a parent class without inflicting the changes on any child classes.

The Frogstar::A class defines a set of methods and attributes for the Frogstar Scout robots:

```
class Frogstar::A {
    has Laser::Beam    $.beam;
    has Antimatter::Ray $.ray;
    has Electron::Ram  $.ram;
    ...
    method zap   ($target) { $.beam.fire($target); }
    method shoot ($target) { $.ray.fire($target); }
    method smash ($target) { $.ram.fire($target); }
    ...
}
```

In addition to methods for navigation, propulsion, etc., the Frogstar Scouts boast an astounding number of destructive methods (as is to be expected). The Frogstar::B class inherits all of Frogstar::A's methods and attributes, and also adds its own additional weaponry. Instead of defining a new

---

method for the Zenon Emitter, the Frogstar Scout B overrides the smash method to use the emitter:

```
class Frogstar::B is Frogstar::A {
    has Zenon::Emitter $.emitter;
    submethod smash ($target) { $.emitter.fire($target); }
}
```

It still smashes the target, only faster, as you might expect from a newer model. Since the overridden method was declared as a submethod, it has no effect on the Frogstar Scout C, which inherits from Frogstar::B:

```
class Frogstar::C is Frogstar::B {...}
...
$fighter = Frogstar::C.new(...);
$fighter.smash($floor); # uses the Electron::Ram
```

# Multiple Dispatch

In the previous chapter, we mentioned multi subroutines. The multi keyword actually applies to any code object: subroutines, methods, or submethods. As we said before, multi allows you to define multiple, different routines all with the same name but different signatures. This example dispatches to a variant of the lunch method depending on the types of the arguments:

```
multi method lunch (Lunching::Friar $who, Megadodo::Office $location) {
    print "Jolly nice restaurant.";
}

multi method lunch (Hitchhiker $who, Cargo::Hold $location) {
    print "Towel again.";
}
```

A member of the Lunching Friars of Voondon must always eat at a nice restaurant when he visits the offices of Megadodo Publications. A hitchhiker in a cargo hold, however, will just have to settle for the nutrient solution soaked into the corner of his towel.

A call to a multimethod has the same syntax as a call to a subroutine—the name of the routine followed by a list of arguments:

```
lunch($zaphod, $where);
```

This call searches outward through its lexical, package, and global scopes for a matching name. If it finds a nonmulti sub it makes an ordinary subroutine call. Otherwise, it generates a list of multi subs, methods, or submethods with that name and dispatches to the closest matching signature. (For more complete details on the dispatch process, see Apocalypse 12.)

You can also call a multimethod with an ordinary single-dispatch method call:

```
$zaphod.lunch($where);
```

In this case, the call will only failover to multiple dispatch if it can't find a suitable method to call under single dispatch to $zaphod.

## Operator Overloading

Operator overloading makes use of multiple dispatch. An operator is just a subroutine with special call syntax. Operators define the kind of syntax they use as part of their name: prefix, postfix, infix, circumfix, etc. This example overloads two operators that use the + symbol—one prefix operator and one infix operator:

```
multi sub *prefix:+ (Time $a) {...}        # $x = +$y;
multi sub *infix:+ (Time $a, Time $b) {...} # $x = $y + $z;
```

These operators are declared as multi subs with global scope, as most operators will be in Perl 6 (global is specified by the leading * in the name). They're multi, so it's easy to add new behavior for new types of operands. They're global so that any operation anywhere with the defined operand types will find the right multi variant of the operator.

# CHAPTER 7

# Grammars and Rules

Perl 6 "regular expressions" are so far beyond the formal definition of regular expressions that we decided it was time for a more meaningful name.[*] We now call them "rules." Perl 6 rules bring the full power of recursive descent parsing to the core of Perl, but are comfortably useful even if you don't know anything about recursive descent parsing. In the usual case, all you'll ever need to know is that rules are patterns for matching text.

## Using Rules

Rules are a language within a language, with their own syntax and conventions. At the highest level, though, they're just another set of Perl constructs. So the first thing to learn about rules is the Perl "glue" code for creating and using them.

### Immediate Matches

The simplest way to create and use a rule is an immediate match. A rule defined with the m// operator always immediately matches. Substitutions, defined with the s/// operator also immediately match. A rule defined with the // operator immediately matches when it's in void, Boolean, string, or numeric context, or the argument of the smart-match operator (~~).

```
if ($string ~~ m/\w+/)      {...}
if ($string ~~ s/\w+/word/) {...}
if ($string ~~ /\w+/)       {...}
```

---

[*] Regular expressions describe regular languages, and consist of three primitives and a limited set of operations (three or so, depending on the formulation). So even Perl 5 "regular expressions" weren't formal regular expressions.

You can substitute other delimiters, such as #...#, [...], and {...}, for the standard /.../, though ?...? and (...) are not valid delimiters:

```
if ($string ~~ s[\w+][word]) {...}
```

## Deferred Matches

Sometimes you want a little more flexibility than an immediate match. The rx// operator defines an anonymous rule that can be executed later.

```
$digits = rx/\d+/;
```

The simple // operator also defines an anonymous rule in all contexts other than void, Boolean, string, or numeric, or as an argument of ~~:

```
$digits = /\d+/; # store rule
```

You can use the unary context forcing operators, +, ?, and ~, to force the // operator to match immediately in a context where it ordinarily wouldn't. For a Boolean value of success or failure, force Boolean context with ?//. For a count of matches, force numeric context with +//. For the matched string value, force string context with ~//.

```
$truth  = ?/\d+/;       # match $_ and return success
$count  = +/(\d+\s+)*/; # match $_ and return count
$string = ~/^\w+/;      # match $_ and return string
```

Another option for deferred matches is a rule block. The rule keyword defines a named or anonymous rule, in much the same way that sub declares a subroutine or method declares a method. But the code within the block of a rule is rule syntax, not Perl syntax.

```
$digits = rule {\d+};

rule digits {\d+}
```

To match a named or anonymous rule, call it as a subrule within another rule. Subrules, whether they're named rules or a variable containing an anonymous rule, are enclosed in assertion delimiters <...>. You can read more about assertions in "Assertions" later in this chapter.

```
$string ~~ /\d+/;
# same as
$string ~~ /<$digits>/;
$string ~~ /<digits>/;
```

Table 7-1 summarizes the basic Perl syntax for defining rules.

*Table 7-1. Rules*

| Syntax | Meaning |
| --- | --- |
| m/.../ | Match a pattern (immediate execution). |
| s/.../.../ | Perform a substitution (immediate execution). |
| rx/.../ | Define an anonymous rule (deferred execution). |
| /.../ | Immediately match or define an anonymous rule, depending on the context. |
| rule {...} | Define an anonymous rule. |
| rule name {...} | Define a named rule. |

# Grammars

A grammar is a collection of rules, in much the same way that a class is a collection of methods. In fact, grammars are classes, they're just classes that inherit from the universal base class Rule. This means that grammars can inherit from other grammars, and that they define a namespace for their rules.

```
grammar Hitchhikers {
    rule name {Zaphod|Ford|Arthur}

    rule id    {\d+}

    ...
}
```

Any rule in the current grammar or in one of its parents can be called directly, but a rule from an external grammar needs to have its package specified:

```
if $newsrelease ~~ /<Hitchhikers.name>/ {
    send_alert($1);
}
```

Grammars are especially useful for complex text or data parsing.

# Building Blocks

Every language has a set of basic components (words or parts of words) and a set of syntax rules for combining them. The "words" in rules are literal characters (or symbols), some metacharacters (or metasymbols), and escape sequences, while the combining syntax includes other metacharacters, quantifiers, bracketing characters, and assertions.

# Metacharacters

The "word"-like metacharacters are ., ^, ^^, $, and $$. The . matches any single character, even a newline character. Actually, what it matches by default is a Unicode grapheme, but you can change that behavior with a pragma in your code, or a modifier on the rule. (We'll discuss modifiers in "Modifiers" later in this chapter.) The ^ and $ metacharacters are zero-width matches on the beginning and end of a string. They each have doubled alternates ^^ and $$ that match at the beginning and end of every line within a string.

The |, &, \, #, and := metacharacters are all syntax structure elements. The | is an alternation between two options. The & matches two patterns simultaneously (the patterns must be the same length). The \ turns literal characters into metacharacters (the escape sequences) or turns metacharacters into literal characters. The # marks a comment to the end of the line. Whitespace insensitivity (the old /x modifier) is on by default, so you can start a comment at any point on any line in a rule. Just make sure you don't comment out the symbol that terminates the rule. The := binds a hypothetical variable to the result of a subrule or grouped pattern. Hypotheticals are covered in "Hypothetical Variables" later in this chapter.

The metacharacters ( ), [ ], { }, and <> are bracketing pairs. The pairs always have to be balanced within the rule, unless they are literal characters (escaped with a \). The brackets ( ) and [ ] group patterns to match as a single atom. They're often used to capture a result, mark the boundaries of an alternation, or mark a group of patterns with a quantifier, among other things. Parentheses (( )) are capturing, and square brackets ([ ]) are noncapturing. The { } brackets define a section of Perl code (a closure) within a rule. These closures are always a successful zero-width match, unless the code explicitly calls the fail function. The < ... > brackets mark assertions, which handle a variety of constructs including character classes and user-defined quantifiers. Assertions are covered in "Assertions" later in this chapter.

Table 7-2 summarizes the basic set of metacharacters.

*Table 7-2. Metacharacters*

| Symbol | Meaning |
| --- | --- |
| . | Match any single character, including a newline. |
| ^ | Match the beginning of a string. |
| $ | Match the end of a string. |
| ^^ | Match the beginning of a line. |
| $$ | Match the end of a line. |

Table 7-2. Metacharacters (continued)

| Symbol | Meaning |
|---|---|
| \| | Match alternate patterns (OR). |
| & | Match multiple patterns (AND). |
| \ | Escape a metacharacter to get a literal character, or escape a literal character to get a metacharacter. |
| # | Mark a comment (to the end of the line). |
| := | Bind the result of a match to a hypothetical variable. |
| ( ... ) | Group patterns and capture the result. |
| [ ... ] | Group patterns without capturing. |
| { ... } | Execute a closure (Perl 6 code) within a rule. |
| < ... > | Match an assertion. |

# Escape Sequences

The escape sequences are literal characters acting as metacharacters, marked with the \ escape. Some escape sequences represent single characters that are difficult to represent literally, like \t for tab, or \x[ ... ] for a character specified by a hexadecimal number. Some represent limited character classes, like \d for digits or \w for word characters. Some represent zero-width positions in a match, like \b for a word boundary. With all the escape sequences that use brackets, ( ), { }, and <> work in place of [ ].

Note that since an ordinary variable now interpolates as a literal string by default, the \Q escape sequence is rarely needed.

Table 7-3 shows the escape sequences for rules.

Table 7-3. Escape sequences

| Escape | Meaning |
|---|---|
| \o[ ... ] | Match a character given in octal (brackets optional). |
| \b | Match a word boundary. |
| \B | Match when not on a word boundary. |
| \c[ ... ] | Match a named character or control character. |
| \C[ ... ] | Match any character except the bracketed named or control character. |
| \d | Match a digit. |
| \D | Match a nondigit. |
| \e | Match an escape character. |
| \E | Match anything but an escape character. |
| \f | Match the form feed character. |

*Table 7-3. Escape sequences (continued)*

| Escape | Meaning |
|---|---|
| \F | Match anything but a form feed. |
| \n | Match a (logical) newline. |
| \N | Match anything but a (logical) newline. |
| \h | Match horizontal whitespace. |
| \H | Match anything but horizontal whitespace. |
| \L[ . . . ] | Everything within the brackets is lowercase. |
| \Q[ . . . ] | All metacharacters within the brackets match as literal characters. |
| \r | Match a return. |
| \R | Match anything but a return. |
| \s | Match any whitespace character. |
| \S | Match anything but whitespace. |
| \t | Match a tab. |
| \T | Match anything but a tab. |
| \U[ . . . ] | Everything within the brackets is uppercase. |
| \v | Match vertical whitespace. |
| \V | Match anything but vertical whitespace. |
| \w | Match a word character (Unicode alphanumeric plus "_"). |
| \W | Match anything but a word character. |
| \x[ . . . ] | Match a character given in hexadecimal (brackets optional). |
| \X[ . . . ] | Match anything but the character given in hexadecimal (brackets optional). |

# Quantifiers

Quantifiers specify the number of times an atom (a single character, meta-character, escape sequence, grouped pattern, assertion, etc.) will match.

The numeric quantifiers use assertion syntax. A single number (<3>) requires exactly that many matches. A numeric range quantifier (<3..5>) succeeds if the number of matches is between the minimum and maximum numbers. A range with three trailing dots (<2...>) is shorthand for <$n$..Inf> and matches as many times as possible.

Each quantifier has a minimal alternate form, marked with a trailing ?, that matches the shortest possible sequence first.

Table 7-4 shows the built-in quantifiers.

*Table 7-4. Quantifiers*

| Maximal | Minimal | Meaning |
|---|---|---|
| * | *? | Match 0 or more times. |
| + | +? | Match 1 or more times. |
| ? | ?? | Match 0 or 1 times. |
| <n> | <n>? | Match exactly n times. |
| <n..m> | <n..m>? | Match at least n and no more than m times. |
| <n...> | <n...>? | Match at least n times. |

# Assertions

Generally, an assertion simply states that some condition or state is true and the match fails when that assertion is false. Many different constructs with many different purposes use assertion syntax.

Assertions match named and anonymous rules, arrays, or hashes containing anonymous rules, and subroutines or closures that return anonymous rules. You have to enclose a variable in assertion delimiters to get it to interpolate as an anonymous rule or rules. A bare scalar in a pattern interpolates as a literal string, while a scalar variable in assertion brackets interpolates as an anonymous rule. A bare array in a pattern matches as a series of alternate literal strings, while an array in assertion brackets interpolates as a series of alternate anonymous rules. In the simplest case, a bare hash in a pattern matches a word (\w+) and tries to find that word as one of its keys,* while a hash in assertion brackets does the same, but then also matches the associated value as an anonymous rule.

A bare closure in a pattern always matches (unless it calls fail), but a closure in assertion brackets <{ ... }> must return an anonymous rule, which is immediately matched.

An assertion with parentheses <( ... )> is similar to a bare closure in a pattern in that it allows you to include straight Perl code within a rule. The difference is that <( ... )> evaluates the return value of the closure in Boolean context. The match succeeds if the return value is true and fails if the return value is false.

Assertions match character classes, both named and enumerated. A named rule character class is often more accurate than an enumerated character class. For example, <[a-zA-Z]> is commonly used to match alphabetic characters,

---

* The effect is much as if it matched the keys as a series of alternates, but you're guaranteed to match the longest possible key, instead of just the first one it hits in random order.

but generally, what's really needed is the built-in rule <alpha>, which matches the full set of Unicode alphabetic characters.

Table 7-5 shows the syntax for assertions.

*Table 7-5. Assertions*

| Syntax | Meaning |
|---|---|
| <...> | Generic assertion delimiter. |
| <!...> | Negate any assertion. |
| <*name*> | Match a named rule or character class. |
| <[...]> | Match an enumerated character class. |
| <-...> | Complement a character class (named or enumerated). |
| <"..."> | Match a literal string (interpolated at match time). |
| <'...'> | Match a literal string (not interpolated). |
| <(...)> | Boolean assertion. Execute a closure and match if it returns a true result. |
| <$scalar> | Match an anonymous rule. |
| <@array> | Match a series of anonymous rules as alternates. |
| <%hash> | Match a key from the hash, then its value (which is an anonymous rule). |
| <&sub( )> | Match an anonymous rule returned by a sub. |
| <{code}> | Match an anonymous rule returned by a closure. |
| <.> | Match any logical grapheme, including combining character sequences. |

# Modifiers

Modifiers alter the meaning of the pattern syntax. The standard position for modifiers is at the beginning of the rule, right after the m, s, or rx, or after the name in a named rule. Modifiers cannot attach to the outside of a bare /.../. For example:

```
m:i/marvin/ # case insensitive
rule names :i { marvin | ford | arthur }
```

The single-character modifiers can be grouped, but the others must be separated by a colon:

```
m:wig/ zaphod /                          # OK
m:words:ignorecase:globally / zaphod / # OK
m:wordsignorecaseglobally / zaphod /    # Not OK
```

Most of the modifiers can also go inside the rule, attached to the rule delimiters or to grouping delimiters. Internal modifiers are lexically scoped to their enclosing delimiters, so you get a temporary alteration of the pattern:

```
m/:w I saw [:i zaphod] / # only 'zaphod' is case insensitive
```

The repetition modifiers (:*N*x, :*N*th, :once, :globally, and :exhaustive) and the continue modifier (:cont) can't be lexically scoped, because they alter the return value of the entire rule.

The :*N*x modifier matches the rule a counted number of times. If the modifier expects more matches than the string has, the match fails. It has an alternate form :x(*N*), which can take a variable in place of the number.

The :once modifier on a rule only allows it to match once. The rule will not match again until you call the .reset method on the rule object.

The :globally modifier matches as many times as possible. The :exhaustive modifier also matches as many times as possible, but in as many different ways as possible.

The :*N*th modifier preserves one result from a particular counted match. If the rule matches fewer times than the modifier expects, the match fails. It has several alternate forms. One form—:th(*N*)—can take a variable in place of the number. The other forms—:*N*st, :*N*nd, and :*N*rd—are for cases where it's more natural to write :1st, :2nd, :3rd than it is to write :1th, :2th, :3th. Either way is valid, so pick the one that's most comfortable for you.

By default, rules ignore literal whitespace within the pattern. The :w modifier makes rules sensitive to literal whitespace, but in an intelligent way. Any cluster of literal whitespace acts like an explicit \s+ when it separates two identifiers and \s* everywhere else.

There are no modifiers to alter whether the matched string is treated as a single line or multiple lines. That's why the "beginning of string" and "end of string" metasymbols have "beginning of line" and "end of line" counterparts.

Table 7-6 shows the current list of modifiers.

*Table 7-6. Modifiers*

| Short | Long | Meaning |
| --- | --- | --- |
| :i | :ignorecase | Case-insensitive match. |
| :I | | Case-sensitive match (on by default). |
| :c | :cont | Continue where the previous match on the string left off. |
| :w | :words | Literal whitespace in the pattern matches as \s+ or \s*. |
| :W | | Turn off intelligent whitespace matching (return to default). |
| | :*N*x/:x(*N*) | Match the pattern N times. |
| | :*N*th/:nth(*N*) | Match the Nth occurrence of a pattern. |
| | :once | Match the pattern only once. |

*Table 7-6. Modifiers (continued)*

| Short | Long | Meaning |
|---|---|---|
| :g | :globally | Match the pattern as many times as possible, but only possibilities that don't overlap |
| :e | :exhaustive | Match every possible occurrence of a pattern, even overlapping possibilities. |
| | :u0 | . is a byte. |
| | :u1 | . is a Unicode codepoint. |
| | :u2 | . is a Unicode grapheme. |
| | :u3 | . is language dependent. |
| | :p5 | The pattern uses Perl 5 regex syntax. |

# Built-in Rules

A number of named rules are provided by default, including a complete set of POSIX-style classes, and Unicode property classes. The list isn't fully defined yet, but Table 7-7 shows a few you're likely to see.

*Table 7-7. Built-in rules*

| Rule | Meaning |
|---|---|
| <alpha> | Match a Unicode alphabetic character. |
| <digit> | Match a Unicode digit. |
| <sp> | Match a single-space character (the same as \s). |
| <ws> | Match any whitespace (the same as \s+). |
| <null> | Match the null string. |
| <prior> | Match the same thing as the previous match. |
| <before ...> | Zero-width lookahead. Assert that you're *before* a pattern. |
| <after ...> | Zero-width lookbehind. Assert that you're *after* a pattern. |
| <prop ...> | Match any character with the named property. |
| <replace(...)> | Replace everything matched so far in the rule or subrule with the given string (under consideration). |

The <null> rule matches a zero-width string (so it's always true) and <prior> matches whatever the most recent successful rule matched. These replace the two behaviors of the Perl 5 null pattern //, which is no longer valid syntax for rules.

# Backtracking Control

Backtracking is triggered whenever part of the pattern fails to match. You can also explicitly trigger backtracking by calling the `fail` function within a closure. Table 7-8 shows some metacharacters and built-in rules relevant to backtracking.

*Table 7-8. Backtracking controls*

| Operator | Meaning |
|---|---|
| : | Don't retry the previous atom; fail to the next earlier atom. |
| :: | Don't backtrack over this point; fail out of the closest enclosing group (( . . . ), [ . . . ], or the rule delimiters). |
| ::: | Don't backtrack over this point; fail out of the current rule or subrule. |
| <commit> | Don't backtrack over this point; fail out of the entire match (even from within a subrule). |
| <cut> | Like <commit>, but also cuts the string matched. The current matching position at this point becomes the new beginning of the string. |

# Hypothetical Variables

Hypothetical variables are a powerful way of building up data structures from within a match. Ordinary captures with ( ) store the result of the captures in $1, $2, etc. The values stored in these variables will be kept if the match is successful, but thrown away if the match fails (hence the term "hypothetical"). The numbered capture variables are accessible outside the match, but only within the immediate surrounding lexical scope:

```
"Zaphod Beeblebrox" ~~ m:w/ (\w+) (\w+) /;

print $1; # prints Zaphod
```

You can also capture into any user-defined variable with the binding operator :=. These variables must already be defined in the lexical scope surrounding the rule:

```
my $person;
"Zaphod's just this guy." ~~ / ^ $person := (\w+) /;
print $person; # prints Zaphod
```

Repeated matches can be captured into an array:

```
my @words;
"feefifofum" ~~ / @words := (f<-[f]>+)* /;
# @words contains ("fee", "fi", "fo", "fum")
```

Pairs of repeated matches can be captured into a hash:

```
my %customers;
$records ~~ m:w/ %customers := [ <id> =
<name> \n]* /;
```

If you don't need the captured value outside the rule, use a $? variable instead. These are only directly accessible within the rule:

```
"Zaphod saw Zaphod" ~~ m:w/ $?name := (\w+) \w+ $?name/;
```

A match of a named rule stores the result in a $? variable with the same name as the rule. These variables are also accessible only within the rule:

```
"Zaphod saw Zaphod" ~~ m:w/ <name> \w+ $?name /;
```

# CHAPTER 8

# Parrot Internals

This chapter details the architecture and internal workings of Parrot, the interpreter behind Perl 6. Parrot is a register-based, bytecode-driven, object-oriented, multithreaded, dynamically typed, self-modifying, asynchronous interpreter. Though that's an awful lot of buzzwords, the design fits together remarkably well.

## Core Design Principles

Three main principles drive the design of Parrot—speed, abstraction, and stability.

*Speed* is a paramount concern. Parrot absolutely must be as fast as possible, since the engine effectively imposes an upper limit on the speed of any program running on it. It doesn't matter how efficient your program is or how clever your program's algorithms are if the engine it runs on limps along. While Parrot can't make a poorly written program run fast, it could make a well-written program run slowly, a possibility we find entirely unacceptable.

Speed encompasses more than just raw execution time. It extends to resource usage. It's irrelevant how fast the engine can run through its bytecode if it uses so much memory in the process that the system spends half its time swapping to disk. Although we're not averse to using resources to gain speed benefits, we try not to use more than we need, and to share what we do use.

*Abstraction* indicates that things are designed such that there's a limit to what anyone needs to keep in their head at any one time. This is very important because Parrot is conceptually very large, as you'll see when you read the rest of the chapter. There's a lot going on, too much to keep the whole thing in mind at once. The design is such that you don't have to remember what everything does, and how it all works. This is true regardless of whether you're writing code that runs on top of Parrot or working on one of its internal subsystems.

Parrot also uses abstraction boundaries as places to cheat for speed. As long as it *looks* like an abstraction is being completely fulfilled, it doesn't matter if it actually *is* being fulfilled, something we take advantage of in many places within the engine. For example, variables are required to be able to return a string representation of themselves, and each variable type has a "give me your string representation" function we can call. That lets each class have custom stringification code, optimized for that particular type. The engine has no idea what goes on beneath the covers and doesn't care—it just knows to call that function when it needs the string value of a variable. Objects are another good case in point—though they look like nice, clean black boxes on the surface, under the hood we cheat profoundly.

*Stability* is important for a number of reasons. We're building the Parrot engine to be a good backend for many language compilers to target. We must maintain a stable interface so compiled programs can continue to run as time goes by. We're also working hard to make Parrot a good interpreter for embedded languages, so we must have a stable interface exposed to anyone who wants to embed us. Finally, we want to avoid some of the problems that Perl 5 has had over the years that forced C extensions written to be recompiled after an upgrade. Recompiling C extensions is annoying during the upgrade and potentially fraught with danger. Such backward-incompatible changes have sometimes been made to Perl itself.

## Parrot's Architecture

The Parrot system is divided into four main parts, each with its own specific task. Figure 8-1 shows the parts, and the way source code and control flows through Parrot. Each of the four parts of Parrot are covered briefly here, and the features and parts of the interpreter are covered in more detail in later sections.

The flow starts with source code, which is passed into the parser module. The parser processes that source into a form that the compiler module can handle. The compiler module takes the processed source and emits byte-code, which Parrot can directly execute. That bytecode is passed into the optimizer module, which processes the bytecode and produces bytecode that should be faster than what the compiler emitted. Finally, the bytecode is handed off to the interpreter module, which interprets the bytecode. Since

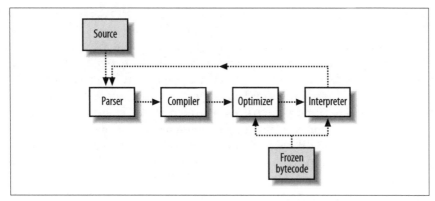

*Figure 8-1. Parrot's flow*

compilation and execution are so tightly woven in Perl, the control may well end up back at the parser to parse more code.

Parrot's compiler module also has the capability to freeze bytecode to disk and read that frozen bytecode back again, bypassing the parser and compilation phases entirely. The bytecode can be directly executed, or handed to the optimizer to work on before execution. This may happen if you've loaded in a precompiled library and want Parrot to optimize the combination of your code and the library code. The bytecode loader is interesting in its own right, and also warrants a small section.

## Parser

The parser module is responsible for taking source code in and turning it into an Abstract Syntax Tree (AST). An AST is a digested form of the program, one that's much more amenable to manipulation. In some systems, this task is split into two parts—the lexing and the parsing—but since the tasks are so closely bound, Parrot combines them into a single module.

Lexing (or tokenizing) turns a stream of characters into a stream of tokens. It doesn't assign any meaning to those tokens—that's the job of the parser—but it is smart enough to see that $a = 1 + 2; is composed of 6 tokens ($, a, =, 1, +, and 2).

Parsing is the task of taking the tokens that the lexer has found and assigning some meaning to them. Sometimes the parsed output can be directly executed.

Parsing can be a chore, as anyone who's done it before knows. In some cases it can be downright maddening—Perl 5's parser has over ten thousand lines of C code. Utility programs such as *lex* and *yacc* are often used to automate the generation of parser code. Perl 5 itself uses a *yacc*-processed grammar to handle some of the task of parsing Perl code.* Rather than going with a custom-built parser for each language, Parrot provides a general-purpose parser built on top of Perl 6's grammar engine, with hooks for calling out to special-purpose code where necessary. Perl 6 grammars are designed to be powerful enough to handle parsing Perl, so it made good sense to leverage the engine as a general-purpose parser. Parrot provides some utility code to transform a *yacc* grammar into a Perl 6 grammar, so languages that already use *yacc* can be moved over to Parrot's parser with a minimum amount of fuss. This allows you to use a *yacc* grammar instead of a Perl 6 grammar to describe the language being parsed, both because many languages already have their grammars described with *yacc* and because a *yacc* grammar is sometimes a more appropriate way to describe things.

Parrot does support independent parsers for cases where the Perl 6 grammar engine isn't the appropriate choice. A language might already have an existing parser available, or different techniques might be in order. The Perl 5 parsing engine may get embedded this way, as it's easier to embed a quirky existing parser than it is to recreate all the quirks in a new parser.

## Compiler

The compiler module takes the AST that the parser generates and turns it into code that the interpreter engine can execute. This translation is very straightforward. It involves little more than flattening the AST and running the flattened tree though a series of substitutions.

The compiler is the least interesting part of Parrot. It transforms one machine representation of your program—the AST that the parser generated—into another machine representation of your program—the bytecode that the interpreter needs. It's little more than a simple, rule-based filter module, albeit one that's necessary for Parrot to understand your source code.

For many languages, the parser and compiler are essentially a single unit. Like the parser, the compiler is pluggable, so you can load in your own compiler. When not using the Perl 6 grammar engine, the compiler and parser modules will usually be loaded together. Parrot itself comes with two compiler modules for Parrot assembly and Parrot Intermediate Representation

---

* *yacc* can handle only part of the task, though. As the saying goes, "The task of parsing Perl is divided between *lex*, *yacc*, smoke, and mirrors."

(PIR) (see Chapter 11). It's likely many compilers will actually emit either assembly or PIR code, rather than directly emitting bytecode.

## Optimizer

The optimizer module takes the AST that the parser generated and the byte-code that the compiler generated, and transforms the bytecode to make it run faster.

Optimizing code for dynamic languages such as Perl, Python, and Ruby is an interesting task. The languages are so dynamic that the optimizer can't be sure how a program will actually run. For example, the code:

```
$a = 0;
for (1..10000) {
    $a++;
}
```

looks straightforward enough. The variable $a starts at 0, is incremented 10,000 times, and has an end value of 10000. A standard optimizer would turn that code into the single line:

```
$a = 10000;
```

and remove the loop entirely. Unfortunately, that's not necessarily appropriate for Perl. $a could easily be tied, perhaps representing the position of some external hardware. If incrementing the variable 10,000 times smoothly moves a stepper motor from 0 to 10,000 in increments of 1, just assigning a value of 10000 to the variable might whip the motor forward in one step, damaging the hardware. A tied variable might also keep track of the number of times it has been accessed or modified. Either way, optimizing the loop away changes the semantics of the program in ways the original programmer didn't want.

Because of the potential for active or tied data, especially for languages as dynamically typed as Perl, optimizing is a nontrivial task. Other languages, such as C or Pascal, are more statically typed and lack active data, so an aggressive optimizer is in order for them. Breaking out the optimizer into a separate module allows us to add in optimizations piecemeal without affecting the compiler. There's a lot of exciting work going into the problem of optimizing dynamic languages, and we fully expect to take advantage of it where we can.

Optimization is potentially an expensive operation, another good reason to have it in a separate module. Spending 10 seconds optimizing a program that will run in 5 seconds is a huge waste of time when using Perl's traditional compile-and-go model—optimizing the code will make the program run slower. On the other hand, spending 10 seconds to optimize a program makes sense if you save the optimized version to disk and use it over and over again. Even if you save only 1 second per program run, it doesn't take long for the 10-second optimization time to pay off. The default is to optimize heavily when freezing bytecode to disk and lightly when running directly, but this can be changed with a command-line switch.

Perl 5, Python, and Ruby all lack a robust optimizer (outside their regular expression engines), so any optimizations we add will increase their performance. This, we feel, is a good thing.

## Interpreter

The interpreter module is the part of the engine that executes the generated bytecode. Calling it an interpreter is something of a misnomer, since Parrot's core includes both a traditional bytecode interpreter module as well as a high-performance JIT engine, but you can consider that an implementation detail.

All the interesting things happen inside the interpreter, and the remainder of the chapter is dedicated to the interpreter and the functions it provides. It's not out of line to consider the interpreter as the real core of Parrot, and to consider the parser, compiler, and optimizer as utility modules whose ultimate purpose is to feed bytecode to the interpreter.

## Bytecode Loader

The bytecode loader isn't part of our block diagram, but it is interesting enough to warrant brief coverage.

The bytecode loader handles loading in bytecode that's been frozen to disk. The Parrot bytecode loader is clever enough to handle loading in Parrot bytecode regardless of the sort of system that it was saved on, so we have cross-platform portability. You can generate bytecode on a 32-bit x86 system and load it up on a 64-bit Alpha or SPARC system without any problems.

The bytecode loading system also has a heuristic engine built into it, so it can identify the bytecode format it's reading. This means Parrot can not only tell what sort of system Parrot bytecode was generated on so it can properly process it, but also allows it to identify bytecode generated for other bytecode driven systems, such as .NET, the JVM, and the Z-machine.[*]

---

[*] The Z-machine is the interpreter for Infocom text adventures, such as Zork and The Lurking Horror.

In addition to loading in bytecode, the loader is sufficiently clever to recognize source files for any language that has a registered compiler. It loads and compiles that source as if it were frozen bytecode.

Together with Parrot's loadable opcode library system (something we'll talk about later), this gives Parrot the capability to load in foreign bytecode formats and transform them into something Parrot can execute. With a sophisticated enough loader, Parrot can load and execute Java and .NET bytecode and present Java and .NET library code to languages that generate native Parrot bytecode. This is something of a happy accident. The original purpose of the architecture was to allow Parrot to load and execute Z-machine bytecode, but happy accidents are the best kind.

# The Interpreter

The interpreter is the engine that actually runs the code emitted by the parser, compiler, and optimizer modules. The Parrot execution engine is a virtual CPU done completely in software. We've drawn on research in CPU and interpreter design over the past forty years to try and build the best engine to run dynamic languages.

That emphasis on dynamic languages is important. We are not trying to build the fastest C, Forth, Lisp, or Prolog engine. Each class of languages has its own quirks and emphasis, and no single engine will handle all the different types of languages well. Trying to design an engine that works equally well for all languages will get you an engine that executes all of them poorly.

That doesn't mean that we've ignored languages outside our area of primary focus—far from it. We've worked hard to make sure that we can accommodate as many languages as possible without compromising the performance of our core language set. We feel that even though we may not run Prolog or Scheme code as fast as a dedicated engine would, the flexibility Parrot provides to mix and match languages more than makes up for that.

Parrot's core design is that of a register rich CISC CPU, like many of the CISC machines of the past, such as the VAX, Motorola 68000, and IBM System/3x0. Many of Parrot's basic instructions perform complex operations. It also bears some resemblance to modern RISC CPUs such as the IBM Power series and Intel Alpha,* as it does all its operations on data in registers. Using a core design similar to older systems gives us decades of compiler research

---

* Formerly HP, formerly Compaq, formerly Digital Alpha.

to draw on. Most compiler research since the early 1970s deals with targeting register systems of one sort or another.

Using a register architecture as the basis for Parrot goes against the current trends in virtual machines, which favor stack-based approaches. Although a stack approach is simpler to implement, a register system provides a richer set of semantics. It's also just more pleasant for us assembly old-timers to write code for. Combined with the decades of sophisticated compiler research, we feel that it's the correct design decision.

# Registers

Parrot has four basic types of registers: PMC, string, integer, and floating-point, one for each of the core data types in Parrot. PMCs, short for Parrot Magic Cookies, are the structures that represent high-level variables such as arrays, hashes, scalars, and objects. We separate the register types for ease of implementation, garbage collection, and space efficiency. Since PMCs and strings are garbage-collectable entities, restricting what can access them— strings in string registers and PMCs in PMC registers—makes the garbage collector a bit faster and simpler. Having integers and floats in separate register sets makes sense from a space standpoint, since floats are normally larger than integers.

The current Parrot architecture provides 32 of each register type, for a total of 128 registers. Though this may seem like overkill, compensating for running out of registers can be a significant speed hit, so it's in our best interests to make sure it happens rarely. Thirty-two is a good compromise between performance and memory usage.

# Stacks

Parrot has seven separate stacks, each with a specific purpose. The four register sets each have their own stack for quickly saving register contents. There is a separate stack dedicated to saving and restoring individual integers, which the regular expression system uses heavily. The control stack keeps track of control information, exception handlers, and other such things. Finally, the general-purpose typed stack stores individual values.

The backing stacks for the register sets are somewhat special. Operations on the register stacks don't act on single registers. The engine pushes and pops entire register sets in one operation. This may seem somewhat unusual, but it makes the primary use of these stacks—to save registers across function calls—very fast. A save or restore operation is essentially a single memory copy operation, something that's highly optimized just about everywhere.* The integer stack is specifically designed to hold integers. Since it doesn't have to be general-purpose, integer stack operations can be faster than operations on the general-purpose stack—a speed gain the regular expression code makes use of. Regular expressions make heavy use of integer code, as they move back and forth within strings, and make heavy use of the integer stack to manage backtracking information.

The control stack is private to the interpreter, so user code can't directly access it. The interpreter engine uses it to manage exception handlers, return locations for function calls, and track other internal data. User code can inspect the stack through Parrot's introspective features.

Finally, the general-purpose stack is used to save and restore individual registers. It's a typed stack, so it doesn't allow you to do things like push an integer register onto the stack and pop the value into a string register. For compiled code, this stack is used if a routine needs more than 32 registers of the same type. The extra values are pushed on and popped off the stack in an operation called register spilling. This stack is also used when Parrot runs code designed for a stack machine such as the JVM or .NET. Stack-based code is less efficient than register-based code, but we can still run it.

All of Parrot's stacks are segmented—they're composed of a set of stack pieces instead of a single chunk of memory. Segmenting has a small performance impact, but it allows us to make better usage of available memory. Traditional stacks are composed of a single chunk of memory, since this makes it faster to read from and write to the stack. Usually, when you run off the end of that chunk of memory your program crashes. To avoid this, most systems allocate a large stack. This isn't much of a problem if you have only a single stack, but it doesn't work well in today's multithreaded world, where each thread has to have its own stack.

Another pleasant benefit of segmenting the stacks is that it makes supporting coroutines and continuations much easier. It is much easier to save off part of a segmented stack. Combined with Parrot's copy-on-write features, this makes for efficient continuations and coroutines. It may not be a feature that many folks will use, but it's a pleasant fall-out from other things.

Interestingly, while Parrot's stacks look and act like stacks in all but the most extreme circumstances, they're really trees. Each subroutine (and potentially each block, as they're occasionally the same thing) gets a fresh stack frame, linked to the stack of its caller. Those stack frames will be

* The SPARC processor, for example, has a cache-friendly memory copy as a core operation.

cleaned up by the garbage collector when there are no outstanding references to them, though it's not guaranteed to happen immediately.

# Strings

Text data is deceptively complex, so Parrot has strings as a fundamental data type. We do this out of sheer practicality. We know strings are complex and error-prone, so we implement them only once. All languages that target Parrot can share the same implementation, and don't have to make their own mistakes.

The big problem with text is the vast number of human languages and the variety of conventions around the world for dealing with it. Long ago, 7-bit ASCII with 127 characters was sufficient. Computers were limited and mostly used in English, regardless of the user's native language. These heavy restrictions were acceptable because the machines of the day were so limited that any other option was too slow. Also, most people using computers at the time were fluent in English either as their native language or a comfortable second language.

That day passed quite a few years ago. Many different ways of representing text have sprung up, from the various multibyte Japanese and Chinese representations—designed for languages with many thousands of characters—to a half dozen or so European representations, which take only a byte but disagree on what characters fit into that byte. The Unicode consortium has been working for years on the Unicode standard to try and unify all the different schemes, but full unification is still years away, if it ever happens.

In the abstract, strings are a series of integers with meaning attached to them, but getting from real-world data to abstract integers isn't as simple as you might want. There are three important things associated with string data—encoding, character set, and language—and Parrot's string system knows how to deal with them.

A string's *encoding* says how to turn data from a stream of bytes to a stream of characters represented by integers. Something like ASCII data is simple to deal with, since each character is a single byte, and characters range in value from 0 to 255. UTF-8, one of the Unicode encodings, is more complex—a single character can take anywhere from one to six bytes.

The *character set* for a string tells Parrot what each of the integers actually represents. Parrot won't get too far if it doesn't know that 65 is a capital "A" in an ASCII or Unicode character stream, for example.

Finally, the *language* for a string determines how the string behaves in some contexts. Different languages have different rules for sorting and case-folding characters. Whether an accented character keeps its accent when upper-cased or lowercased depends on the language that the string came from.

The capability of translating strings from one encoding to another and one character set to another, and to determine when it's needed, is built into Parrot. The I/O and regular expression systems fully exploit Parrot's core string capabilities, so any language that uses Parrot's built-in string functionality gets this for free. Since properly implementing even a single system like Unicode is fraught with peril, this makes the job of people writing languages that target Parrot (including Perl 6) much easier.

While Parrot provides these facilities, languages aren't required to make use of them. Perl 6, for example, generally mandates that all strings will be treated as if they are Unicode. In this case Parrot's multilingual capabilities mainly act as filters to translate to and from Unicode. Parrot presents all the data as if it were Unicode, but only translates non-Unicode data to Unicode in situations where your program may notice.

Unicode is Parrot's character set of last resort when it needs one. We use IBM's ICU Unicode library to do all the heavy lifting, since writing a properly done Unicode library is a nontrivial undertaking. It makes more sense to use a well-tested and debugged library than it does to try and reimplement Unicode again.

## Variables

Variables are a fundamental construct in almost all computer languages.[*] With low-level languages such as C, variables are straightforward—they are either basic hardware constructs like a 32-bit integer, a 64-bit IEEE floating-point number, or the address of some location in memory, or they're a structure containing basic hardware constructs. Exchanging variables between low-level languages is simple because all the languages operate on essentially the same things.

Once you get to higher-level languages, variables get more interesting. Object-oriented (OO) languages have the concept of the object as a fundamental construct, but no two OO languages seem to agree on exactly how objects should behave or how they should be implemented. Then there are higher-level languages like Perl, with complex constructs like hashes, arrays, and polymorphic scalars as fundamental constructs.

---

[*] With the exception of functional languages, though they can be useful there as well.

The first big issue that Parrot had to face was implementing these constructs. The second was doing it in a way that allowed Perl code to use Ruby objects, Ruby code to use Python objects, and Lisp code to use both. Parrot's solution is the PMC, or Parrot Magic Cookie.

A PMC is an abstract variable and a base data type—the same way that integers and floating-point numbers are base data types for hardware CPUs. The languages we're working to support—Perl, Python, and Ruby—have base variables that are far more complex than just an integer or floating-point number. If we want them to exchange any sort of real data, they must have a common base variable type. Parrot provides that with the PMC construct. Each language can build on this common base. More importantly, each language can make sure that their variables behave properly regardless of which language is using them.

When you think about it, there is a large list of things that a variable should be able to do. You should, for example, be able to load or store a value, add or subtract it from another variable, call a method or set a property on it, get its integer or floating-point representation, and so on. What we did was make a list of these functions and make them mandatory.

Each PMC has a virtual table (vtable) attached to it. This table of function pointers is fixed—the list of functions, and where they are in the table, is the same for each PMC. All the common operations a program might perform on a variable—as well as all the operators that might be overloaded for a PMC—have vtable entries.

## Bytecode

Like any CPU, software, or hardware, Parrot needs a set of instructions to tell it what to do. For hardware, this is a stream of executable code or machine language. For Parrot, this is bytecode. Calling it bytecode isn't strictly accurate, since the individual instructions are 32 bits each rather than 8 bits each, but since it's the common term for most other virtual machines, it's the term we use.

Each instruction—also known as an *opcode*—tells the interpreter engine what to do. Some opcodes are very low level, such as the one to add two integers together. Others are significantly more complex, like the opcode to take a continuation.

Parrot's bytecode is designed to be directly executable. The code on disk can be run by the interpreter without needing any translation. This gets us a number of benefits. Loading is much faster, of course, since we don't have to do much (if any) processing on the bytecode as it's loaded. It also means we can use special operating system calls that map a file directly into the memory space of a process. Because of the way this is handled by the operating system,* the bytecode file will be loaded into the system's memory only once, no matter how many processes use the file. This can save a significant amount of real RAM on server systems. Files loaded this way also get their parts loaded on demand. Since we don't need to process the bytecode in any way to execute it, if you map in a large bytecode library file, only those bits of the file your program actually executes will get read in from disk. This can save a lot of time.

Parrot creates bytecode in a format optimized for the platform it's built on, since the common case by far is executing bytecode that's been built on the system you're using. This means that floating-point numbers are stored in the current platform's native format, integers are in the native size, and both are stored in the byte order for the current platform. Parrot does have the capability of executing bytecode that uses 32-bit integers and IEEE floating-point numbers on any platform, so you can build and ship bytecode that can be run by anyone with a Parrot interpreter.

If you do use a bytecode file that doesn't match the current platform's requirements (perhaps the integers are a different size), Parrot automatically translates the bytecode file as it reads it in. In this case, Parrot does have to read in the entire file and process it. The sharing and load speed benefits are lost, but it's a small price to pay for the portability. Parrot ships with a utility to turn a portable bytecode file into a native format bytecode file if the overhead is too onerous.

# I/O, Events, and Threads

Parrot has comprehensive support for I/O, threads, and events. These three systems are interrelated, so we'll treat them together. The systems we talk about in this section are less mature than other parts of the engine, so they may change by the time we roll out the final design and implementation.

## I/O

Parrot's base I/O system is fully asynchronous I/O with callbacks and per-request private data. Since this is massive overkill in many cases, we have a plain vanilla synchronous I/O layer that your programs can use if they don't need the extra power.

---

* Conveniently, this works the same way for all the flavors of Unix, Windows, and VMS.

Asynchronous I/O is conceptually pretty simple. Your program makes an I/O request. The system takes that request and returns control to your program, which keeps running. Meanwhile, the system works on satisfying the I/O request. When the request is satisfied, the system notifies your program in some way. Since there can be multiple requests outstanding, and you can't be sure exactly what your program will be doing when a request is satisfied, programs that make use of asynchronous I/O can be complex.

Synchronous I/O is even simpler. Your program makes a request to the system and then waits until that request is done. There can be only one request in process at a time, and you always know what you're doing (waiting) while the request is being processed. It makes your program much simpler, since you don't have to do any sort of coordination or synchronization.

The big benefit of asynchronous I/O systems is that they generally have a much higher throughput than a synchronous system. They move data around much faster—in some cases three or four times faster. This is because the system can be busy moving data to or from disk while your program is busy processing data that it got from a previous request.

For disk devices, having multiple outstanding requests—especially on a busy system—allows the system to order read and write requests to take better advantage of the underlying hardware. For example, many disk devices have built-in track buffers. No matter how small a request you make to the drive, it always reads a full track. With synchronous I/O, if your program makes two small requests to the same track, and they're separated by a request for some other data, the disk will have to read the full track twice. With asynchronous I/O, on the other hand, the disk may be able to read the track just once, and satisfy the second request from the track buffer.

Parrot's I/O system revolves around a request. A request has three parts: a buffer for data, a completion routine, and a piece of data private to the request. Your program issues the request, then goes about its business. When the request is completed, Parrot will call the completion routine, passing it the request that just finished. The completion routine extracts out the buffer and the private data, and does whatever it needs to do to handle the request. If your request doesn't have a completion routine, then your program will have to explicitly check to see if the request was satisfied.

Your program can choose to sleep and wait for the request to finish, essentially blocking. Parrot will continue to process events while your program is waiting, so it isn't completely unresponsive. This is how Parrot implements synchronous I/O—it issues the asynchronous request, then immediately waits for that request to complete.

The reason we made Parrot's I/O system asynchronous by default was sheer pragmatism. Network I/O is all asynchronous, as is GUI programming, so we knew we had to deal with asynchrony in some form. It's also far easier to make an asynchronous system pretend to be synchronous than it is the other way around. We could have decided to treat GUI events, network I/O, and file I/O all separately, but there are plenty of systems around that demonstrate what a bad idea that is.

## Events

An event is a notification that something has happened: the user has manipulated a GUI element, an I/O request has completed, a signal has been triggered, or a timer has expired. Most systems these days have an event handler,* because handling events is so fundamental to modern GUI programming. Unfortunately, the event handling system is not integrated, or poorly integrated, with the I/O system, leading to nasty code and unpleasant workarounds to try and make a program responsive to network, file, and GUI events simultaneously. Parrot presents a unified event handling system, integrated with its I/O system, which makes it possible to write cross-platform programs that work well in a complex environment.

Parrot's events are fairly simple. An event has an event type, some event data, an event handler, and a priority. Each thread has an event queue, and when an event happens it's put into the right thread's queue (or the default thread queue in those cases where we can't tell which thread an event was destined for) to wait for something to process it.

Any operation that would potentially block drains the event queue while it waits, as do a number of the cleanup opcodes that Parrot uses to tidy up on scope exit. Parrot doesn't check each opcode for an outstanding event for pure performance reasons, as that check gets expensive quickly. Still, Parrot generally ensures timely event handling, and events shouldn't sit in a queue for more than a few milliseconds unless event handling has been explicitly disabled.

When Parrot does extract an event from the event queue, it calls that event's event handler, if it has one. If an event doesn't have a handler, Parrot instead looks for a generic handler for the event type and calls it instead. If for some reason there's no handler for the event type, Parrot falls back to the generic event handler, which throws an exception when it gets an event it doesn't know how to handle. You can override the generic event handler if you want

* Often two or three, which is something of a problem.

Parrot to do something else with unhandled events, perhaps silently discarding them instead.

Because events are handled in mainline code, they don't have the restrictions commonly associated with interrupt-level code. It's safe and acceptable for an event handler to throw an exception, allocate memory, or manipulate thread or global state safely. Event handlers can even acquire locks if they need to, though it's not a good idea to have an event handler blocking on lock acquisition.

Parrot uses the priority on events for two purposes. First, the priority is used to order the events in the event queue. Events for a particular priority are handled in a FIFO manner, but higher-priority events are always handled before lower-priority events. Parrot also allows a user program or event handler to set a minimum event priority that it will handle. If an event with a priority lower than the current minimum arrives, it won't be handled, instead it will sit in the queue until the minimum priority level is dropped. This allows an event handler that's dealing with a high-priority event to ignore lower-priority events.

User code generally doesn't need to deal with prioritized events, so programmers should adjust event priorities with care. Adjusting the default priority of an event, or adjusting the current minimum priority level, is a rare occurrence. It's almost always a mistake to change them, but the capability is there for those rare occasions where it's the correct thing to do.

## Signals

Signals are a special form of event, based on the Unix signal mechanism. Parrot presents them as mildly special, as a remnant of Perl's Unix heritage, but under the hood they're not treated any differently from any other event.

The Unix signaling mechanism is something of a mash, having been extended and worked on over the years by a small legion of undergrad programmers. At this point, signals can be divided into two categories, those that are fatal, and those that aren't.

Fatal signals are things like SIGKILL, which unconditionally kills a process, or SIGSEGV, which indicates that the process has tried to access memory that isn't part of your process. There's no good way for Parrot to catch these signals, so they remain fatal and will kill your process. On some systems it's possible to catch some of the fatal signals, but Parrot code itself operates at too high a level for a user program to do anything with them—they must be handled with special-purpose code written in C or some other low-level language.

Parrot itself may catch them in special circumstances for its own use, but that's an implementation detail that isn't exposed to a user program.

Nonfatal signals are things such as SIGCHLD, indicating that a child process has died, or SIGINT, indicating that the user has pressed ^C on the keyboard. Parrot turns these signals into events and puts them in the event queue. Your program's event handler for the signal will be called as soon as Parrot gets to the event in the queue, and your code can do what it needs to with it.

SIGALRM, the timer expiration signal, is treated specially by Parrot. Generated by an expiring alarm( ) system call, this signal is normally used to provide timeouts for system calls that would otherwise block forever, which is very useful. The big downside to this is that on most systems there can only be one outstanding alarm( ) request, and while you can get around this somewhat with the setitimer call (which allows up to three pending alarms) it's still quite limited.

Since Parrot's I/O system is fully asynchronous and never blocks—even what looks like a blocking request still drains the event queue—the alarm signal isn't needed for this. Parrot instead grabs SIGALRM for its own use, and provides a fully generic timer system which allows any number of timer events, each with their own callback functions and private data, to be outstanding.

## Threads

Threads are a means of splitting a process into multiple pieces that execute simultaneously. It's a relatively easy way to get some parallelism without too much work. Threads don't solve all the parallelism problems your program may have. Sometimes multiple processes on a single system, multiple processes on a cluster, or processes on multiple separate systems are better. But threads do present a good solution for many common cases.

All the resources in a threaded process are shared between threads. This is simultaneously the great strength and great weakness of threads. Easy sharing is fast sharing, making it far faster to exchange data between threads or access shared global data than to share data between processes on a single system or on multiple systems. Easy sharing is dangerous, though, since without some sort of coordination between threads it's easy to corrupt that shared data. And, because all the threads are contained within a single process, if any one of them fails for some reason the entire process, with all its threads, dies.

With a low-level language such as C, these issues are manageable. The core data types, integers, floats, and pointers are all small enough to be handled atomically. Composite data can be protected with mutexes, special structures that a thread can get exclusive access to. The composite data elements that need protecting can each have a mutex associated with them, and when a thread needs to touch the data it just acquires the mutex first. By default there's very little data that must be shared between threads, so it's relatively easy, barring program errors, to write thread-safe code if a little thought is given to the program structure.

Things aren't this easy for Parrot, unfortunately. A PMC, Parrot's native data type, is a complex structure, so we can't count on the hardware to provide us atomic access. That means Parrot has to provide atomicity itself, which is expensive. Getting and releasing a mutex isn't really that expensive in itself. It has been heavily optimized by platform vendors because they want threaded code to run quickly. It's not free, though, and when you consider that running flat-out Parrot does one PMC operation per 100 CPU cycles, even adding an additional 10 cycles per operation can slow down Parrot by 10%.

For any threading scheme, it's important that your program isn't hindered by the platform and libraries it uses. This is a common problem with writing threaded code in C, for example. Many libraries you might use aren't thread-safe, and if you aren't careful with them your program will crash. Although we can't make low-level libraries any safer, we can make sure that Parrot itself won't be a danger. There is very little data shared between Parrot interpreters and threads, and access to all the shared data is done with coordinating mutexes. This is invisible to your program, and just makes sure that Parrot itself is thread-safe.

When you think about it, there are really three different threading models. In the first one, multiple threads have no interaction among themselves. This essentially does with threads the same thing that's done with processes. This works very well in Parrot, with the isolation between interpreters helping to reduce the overhead of this scheme. There's no possibility of data sharing at the user level, so there's no need to lock anything.

In the second threading model, multiple threads run and pass messages back and forth between each other. Parrot supports this as well, via the event mechanism. The event queues are thread-safe, so one thread can safely inject an event into another thread's event queue. This is similar to a multiple-process model of programming, except that communication between threads is much faster, and it's easier to pass around structured data.

In the third threading model, multiple threads run and share data between themselves. Although Parrot can't guarantee that data at the user level remains consistent, it can make sure that access to shared data is at least safe. We do this with two mechanisms.

First, Parrot presents an advisory lock system to user code. Any piece of user code running in a thread can lock a variable. Any attempt to lock a variable that another thread has locked will block until the lock is released. Locking a variable only blocks other lock attempts. It does *not* block plain access. This may seem odd, but it's the same scheme used by threading systems that obey the POSIX thread standard, and has been well tested in practice.

Second, Parrot forces all shared PMCs to be marked as such, and all access to shared PMCs must first acquire that PMC's private lock. This is done by installing an alternate vtable for shared PMCs, one that acquires locks on all its parameters. These locks are held only for the duration of the vtable function, but ensure that the PMCs affected by the operation aren't altered by another thread while the vtable function is in progress.

# Objects

Perl 5, Perl 6, Python, and Ruby are all OO languages in some form or other, so Parrot has to have core support for objects and classes. Unfortunately, all these languages have somewhat different object systems, which made the design of Parrot's object system somewhat tricky.[*] It turns out that if you draw the abstraction lines in the right places, support for the different systems is easily possible. This is especially true if you provide core support for things like method dispatch, which the different object systems can use and override.

## Generic Object Interfacing

Parrot's object system is very simple—in fact, a PMC only has to handle method calls to be considered an object. Just handling methods covers well over 90% of the object functionality that most programs use, since the vast majority of object access is via method calls. This means user code that does the following:

```
object = some_constructor(1, 2, "foo");
object.bar(12);
```

---

[*] As we write this, it's still in progress, though it should be done by the time this book is in print.

will work just fine, no matter what language the class that backs DEFANGED_ object is written in, if DEFANGED_object even has a class backing it. It could be Perl 5, Perl 6, Python, Ruby, or even Java, C#, or Common Lisp; it doesn't matter.

Objects may override other functionality as well. For example, Python objects use the basic PMC property mechanism to implement object attributes. Both Python and Perl 6 mandate that methods and properties share the same namespace, with methods overriding properties of the same name.

## Parrot Objects

When we refer to Parrot objects we're really talking about Parrot's default base object system. Any PMC can have methods called on it and act as an object, and Parrot is sufficiently flexible to allow for alternate object systems, such as the one Perl 5 uses. However, in this section, we're talking about what we provide in our standard object system. Parrot's standard object system is pretty traditional—it's a class-based system with multiple inheritance, interface declarations, and slot-based objects.

Each object is a member of a class, which defines how the object behaves. Each class in an object's hierarchy can have one or more attributes—that is, named slots that are guaranteed to be in each object of that class. The names are all class-private so there's no chance of collision. Objects are essentially little fixed-sized arrays that know what class they belong to. Most of the "smarts" for an object lives in that object's class. Parrot allows you to add attributes at runtime to a class. If you do, then all objects with that class in their inheritance hierarchy will get the new attribute added into it. Though this is potentially expensive, it's a very useful feature for languages that may extend a class at runtime.

Parrot uses a multiple inheritance scheme for classes. Each class can have two or more parent classes, and each of those classes can have multiple parents. A class has control over how methods are searched for, but the default search is a left-most, depth-first search, the same way that Perl 5 does it. Individual class implementers may change this if they wish, but only the class an object is instantiated into controls the search order. Parrot also fully supports correct method redispatch, so a method may properly call the next method in the hierarchy even in the face of multiple parents. One limitation we place on inheritance is that a class is instantiated in the hierarchy only once, no matter how many times it appears in class and parent class inheritance lists.

Each class has its own vtable, which all objects of that class share. This means that with the right vtable methods every object can behave like a basic PMC type in addition to an object. For unary operations such as load or store, the default class vtable first looks for the appropriately named method in the class hierarchy. For binary operators such as addition and subtraction, it first looks in the multimethod dispatch table. This is only the default, and individual languages may make different choices. Objects that implement the proper methods can also act as arrays or hashes.

Finally, Parrot implements an interface declaration scheme. You may declare that a class does one or more named interfaces, and later query objects at runtime to see if they implement an interface. This doesn't put any methods in a class. For that you need to either inherit from a class that does or implement them by hand. All it does is make a declaration of what your class does. Interface declarations are inheritable as well, so if one of your parent classes declares that it implements an interface then your class will as well. This is used in part to implement Perl 6's roles.

## Mixed Class-Type Support

The final piece of Parrot's object system is the support for inheriting from classes of different types. This could be a Perl 6 class inheriting from a Perl 5 class, or a Ruby class inheriting from a .NET class. It could even involve inheriting from a fully compiled language such as C++ or Objective C, if proper wrapping is established.* As we talked about earlier, as long as a class either descends from the base Parrot class or has a small number of required properties, Parrot can subclass it. This potentially goes both ways, as any class system that knows how to subclass from Parrot's base class can inherit from it.

Allowing classes to inherit from other classes of a different base type does present some interesting technical issues. The inheritance isn't 100% invisible, though you have to head off into the corner cases to find the cracks. It's an important feature to design into Parrot, so we can subclass Perl 5 style classes, and they can subclass Parrot classes. Being able to subclass C++ and Objective C classes is a potential bonus. Python, Ruby, and Perl 6 all share a common (but hidden) base class in Parrot's base object type, so they can inherit from each other without difficulty.

---

* DEFANGED_Objective C is particularly simple, as it has a fully introspective class system that allows for run-time class creation. Inheritance can go both ways between it and Parrot.

# Advanced Features

Since the languages Parrot targets (like Perl and Ruby) have sophisticated concepts as core features, it's in Parrot's best interest to have core support for them. This section covers some (but not all) of these features.

## Garbage Collection

It's expected that modern languages have garbage collection built in. The programmer shouldn't have to worry about explicitly cleaning up after dead variables, or even identifying them. For interpreted languages, this requires support from the interpreter engine, so Parrot provides that support.

Parrot has two separate allocation systems built into it. Each allocation system has its own garbage collection scheme. Parrot also has some strict rules over what can be referenced and from where. This allows it to have a more efficient garbage collection system.

The first allocation system is responsible for PMC and string structures. These are fixed-sized objects that Parrot allocates out of arenas, which are pools of identically sized things. Using arenas makes it easy for Parrot to find and track them, and speeds up the detection of dead objects.

Parrot's dead object detection system works by first running through all the arenas and marking all strings and PMCs as dead. It then runs through the stacks and registers, marking all strings and PMCs they reference as alive. Next, it iteratively runs through all the live PMCs and strings and marks everything they reference as alive. Finally, it sweeps through all the arenas looking for newly dead PMCs and strings, which it puts on the free list. At this point, any PMC that has a custom destruction routine, such as an object with a DESTROY method, has its destruction routine called. The dead object detector is triggered whenever Parrot runs out of free objects, and can be explicitly triggered by running code. Often a language compiler will force a dead object sweep when leaving a block or subroutine.

Parrot's memory allocation system is used to allocate space for the contents of strings and PMCs. Allocations don't have a fixed size; they come from pools of memory that Parrot maintains. Whenever Parrot runs out of memory in its memory pools, it makes a compacting run—squeezing out unused sections from the pools. When it's done, one end of each pool is entirely actively used memory, and the other end is one single chunk of free memory. This makes allocating memory from the pools faster, as there's no need to walk a free list looking for a segment of memory large enough to satisfy the request for memory. It also makes more efficient use of memory, as there's less overhead than in a traditional memory allocation system.

Splitting memory pool compaction from dead object detection has a nice performance benefit for Perl and languages like it. For most Perl programs, the interpreter allocates and reallocates far more memory for string and variable contents than it does actual string and variable structures. The structures are reused over and over as their contents change. With a traditional single-collector system, each time the interpreter runs out of memory it has to do a full scan for dead objects and compact the pools after. With a split system, Parrot can just sweep through the variables it thinks are live and compact their contents. This does mean that Parrot will sometimes move data for variables and strings that are really dead because it hasn't found that out yet. That expense is normally much less than the expense of doing a full tracing run to find out which variables are actually dead.

Parrot's allocation and collection systems have some compromises that make interfacing with low-level code easier. The structure that describes a PMC or string is guaranteed not to move over the lifetime of the string or variable. This allows C code to store pointers to variables in internal structures without worrying that what they're referencing may move. It also means that the garbage collection system doesn't have to worry about updating pointers that C code might hold, which it would have to do if PMC or string structures could move.

## Multimethod Dispatching

Multimethod dispatching (also known as signature-based dispatching) is a powerful technique that uses the parameters of a function or method call to help decide at runtime which function or method Parrot should call. This is one of the new features being built into Perl 6. It allows you to have two or more subroutines or methods with the same name that differ only in the types of their arguments.

In a standard dispatch system, each subroutine or method name must be unique within a namespace. Attempting to create a second routine with the same name either throws an error or overlays the original one. This is certainly straightforward, but in some circumstances it leads to code that looks like:

```
sub foo {
    my ($self, $arg) = @_;
    if ($arg->isa("Foo")) {
        # Do something with a Foo arg
    } elsif ($arg->isa("Bar")) {
```

```
        # Do something with a Bar arg
    } elsif ($arg->isa("Baz")) {
        # Do something with a Baz arg
    } else {
        #...
    }
}
```

This method effectively dispatches both on the type of the object and on the type of the argument to the method. This sort of thing is common, especially in operator overloading functions. Manually checking the types of the arguments to select an action is both error-prone and difficult to extend. Multimethod dispatch solves this problem.

With multimethod dispatch, there can be more than one method or subroutine with the same name as long as each variant has different parameters in its declaration. When code calls a method or subroutine that participates in multiple dispatch, the system chooses the variant that most closely matches the types of the parameters in the call.

One very notable thing about subs and methods that do multimethod dispatch is that the named subroutines and methods live outside of any namespace. By default, when searching for a method or subroutine, Parrot first looks for an explict sub or method of that name in the current namespace (or the inheritance hierarchy of an object), then for the default subroutine or method (AUTOLOAD or its equivalent) in the inheritance hierarchy, and only when those fail will it look for a multimethod dispatch version of the subroutine or method. Since Parrot allows individual PMC classes to control how their dispatching is done, this sequence may be changed on a per-class basis if need be.

Parrot itself makes heavy use of multimethod dispatch, with most of the core PMC classes using it to provide operator overloading. The only reason we don't use it for all our operator dispatching is that some of the languages we're interested in require a left-side wins scheme. It's so heavily used for operator overloading, in fact, that we actually have two separate versions of multiple dispatch built into Parrot, one specially tailored to operator overloading and a more general version for normal subroutine and method dispatch.

## Continuations

Continuations are possibly the most powerful high-level flow control construct. Originating with lambda calculus, and built into Lisp over thirty years ago, continuations can be thought of as a closure for control flow. They not only capture their lexical scope, which gets restored when they're invoked, but also capture their call stack, so when they're invoked it's as if you never left the spot where they were created. Like closures, though, while they capture the variables in scope when the continuation is taken, they don't capture the values of the variables. When you invoke a continuation it's not like rolling back a transaction.

Continuations are phenomenally powerful, and have the undeserved reputation of being bizarre and mind-warping things. This turns out not to be the case. Originally we put continuations into Parrot to support Ruby, which has them. This decision turned out to be fortuitous.

In a simple call/return system, which many languages use, when you make a subroutine call the return address is pushed onto a stack somewhere. When the subroutine is done it takes the address off the stack and returns there. This is a simple and straightforward operation, and quite fast. The one disadvantage is that with a secure system the calling routine needs to preserve any information that is important before making the call and restore it on return.

An alternative calling scheme is called Continuation Passing Style (CPS). With CPS, rather than pushing a return address onto the stack you create a return continuation and pass that into the subroutine as a parameter. When the subroutine is done it invokes the return continuation, effectively returning to the caller with the caller's environment automatically restored. This includes not only things like the call stack and lexical variables, but also meta-information like security credentials.

When we were originally designing Parrot we'd planned on the simpler call/ return style, with the caller preserving everything important before the call, and restoring it afterwards. Three things soon became clear: we were saving and restoring a lot of individual pieces; we were going to have to add new pieces in the future; and there wasn't any difference between what we were doing for a call and what we were doing for a continuation, except that the call was a lot more manual.

The future-proofing was what finally made the decision. Parrot is making a strong guarantee of backward compatibility, which means that code compiled to Parrot bytecode once we've released will run safely and unchanged on all future version of Parrot. If we require all the individual pieces of the environment (registers, lexical pads, nested namespaces, opcode libraries, stack pointers, exception handlers, and assorted things) to be saved manually for a subroutine call, it means that we can't add any new pieces in the future, as then old code would no longer work properly. We briefly toyed with the idea of an opcode to package up the entire environment in one go.

Then we realized that package was a continuation, and as such we might as well just go all the way and use them.

As a result, Parrot implements a full CPS system internally, and uses it for all subroutine and method calls. We also have the simpler call/return style of flow control available for languages that don't need the heavier-weight call system, as well as for compilers to use for internal processing and optimization. We do go to some lengths to hide the continuations. PIR code, for example, allows compiler writers to create subroutines and methods (and calls to them) that conform to Parrot's CPS mechanism without ever touching continuations directly. We then have the benefits of what appears to be a simple calling scheme, secure future-proofing, and the full power of continuations for languages that want them.

## Coroutines

A coroutine is a subroutine or method that can suspend itself partway through, then later pick up where it left off. This isn't quite the same thing as a continuation, though it may seem so at first. Coroutines are often used to implement iterators and generators, as well as threads on systems that don't have native threading support. Since they are so useful, and since Perl 6 and Python provide them either directly or as generators, Parrot has support for them built in.

Coroutines present some interesting technical challenges. Calling into an existing coroutine requires reestablishing not only the lexical state and potentially the hypothetical state of variables, but also the control state for just the routine. In the presence of exceptions they're a bit more complex than plain subroutines and continuations, but they're still very useful things, and as such we've given them our full support.

# Conclusion

We've touched on much of Parrot's core functionality, but certainly not all. We hope we've given you enough of a feel for how Parrot works to expand your knowledge with the Parrot documentation and source.

# CHAPTER 9

# Parrot Assembly Language

Parrot assembly (PASM) is an assembly language written for Parrot's virtual CPU. PASM has an interesting mix of features. Because it's an assembly language, it has many low-level features, such as flow control based on branches and jumps, and direct manipulation of values in the software registers and on the stacks. Basic register operations or branches are generally a single CPU instruction.* On the other hand, because it's designed to implement dynamic high-level languages, it has support for many advanced features, such as lexical and global variables, objects, garbage collection, continuations, coroutines, and much more.

## Getting Started

The first step before you start playing with PASM code is to get a copy of the source code and compile it. There is some information on this in "Use the source" in Chapter 2. For more information and updates, see *http:// www.parrotcode.org* and the documentation in the distributed code.

The basic steps are:†

```
$ perl Configure.pl
$ make
$ make test
```

Once you've compiled Parrot, create a small test file in the main *parrot* directory. We'll call it *fjord.pasm*.

```
print "He's pining for the fjords.\n"
end
```

---

* This means the JIT run-time has a performance of up to one PASM instruction per processor cycle.

† Not all operating systems have *make*. Check the documentation for instructions for systems that aren't Unix-based.

*.pasm* is the standard extension for Parrot assembly language source files. Now you can run this file with:

```
$ ./parrot fjord.pasm
```

And watch the result of the program execution. Instead of executing the program immediately, you could also compile it to bytecode:

```
$ ./parrot --output fjord.pbc fjord.pasm
```

You specify the name of the output bytecode file with the --output (or -o) switch. *.pbc* is the standard extension for Parrot bytecode. To execute the compiled bytecode, run it through the *parrot* interpreter:

```
$ ./parrot fjord.pbc
```

That's all there is to it.

# Basics

PASM has a simple syntax. Each statement stands on its own line. Statements begin with a Parrot instruction code (commonly referred to as an "opcode"). Arguments follow the opcode, separated by commas:

```
[label] opcode dest, source, source ...
```

If the opcode returns a result, it is stored in the first argument. Sometimes the first register is both a source value and the destination of the result. The arguments are either registers or constants, though only source arguments can be constants:

```
LABEL:
    print "The answer is: "
    print 42
    print "\n"
    end                     # halt the interpreter
```

A label names a line of code so other instructions can refer to it. Label names consist of letters, numbers, and underscores. Simple labels are often all caps to make them stand out more clearly. A label definition is simply the name of the label followed by a colon. It can be on its own line:

```
LABEL:
    print "Norwegian Blue\n"
```

or before a statement on the same line:

```
LABEL: print "Norwegian Blue\n"
```

Comments are marked with the hash sign (#) and continue to the end of the line.

POD (plain old documentation) markers are ignored by Parrot. An equals sign in the first column marks the start of a POD block, and a =cut marks the end of a POD block.

```
=head1
...
=cut
```

## Constants

Integer constants are signed integers.* Integer constants can have a positive (+) or negative (-) sign in front. Binary integers are preceded by 0b or 0B, and hexadecimal integers are preceded by 0x or 0X:

```
print 42         # integer constant
print 0x2A       # hexadecimal integer
print 0b1101     # binary integer
print -0b101     # binary integer with sign
```

Floating-point constants can also be positive or negative. Scientific notation provides an exponent, marked with e or E (the sign of the exponent is optional):

```
print 3.14159    # floating point constant
print 1.e6       # scientific notation
print -1.23e+45
```

String constants are wrapped in single or double quotation marks. Quotation marks inside the string must be escaped by a backslash. Other special characters also have escape sequences. These are the same as for Perl 5's qq( ) operator: \t (tab), \n (newline), \r (return), \f (form feed), \\ (literal slash), \" (literal double quote), etc.

```
print "string\n"    # string constant with escaped newline
print "\\"          # a literal backslash
print 'that\'s it'  # escaped single quote
print 'a\n'         # three chars: 'a', a backslash, and a 'n'
```

## Working with Registers

Parrot is a register-based virtual machine. It has four types of register sets with 32 registers in each set. The types are integers, floating-point numbers, strings, and PMCs (Parrot Magic Cookies). Register names consist of a capital letter

---

* The size of integers is defined when Parrot is configured. It's typically 32 bits on 32-bit machines (a range of −231 to +231−1) and twice that size on 64-bit processors.

indicating the register set and the number of the register, between 0 and 31. For example:

```
I0    integer register #0
N11   number or floating point register #11
S2    string register #2
P31   PMC register #31
```

Integer and number registers hold values, while string and PMC registers contain pointers to allocated memory for a string header or a PMC.

The length of strings is limited only by your system's virtual memory and by the size of integers on the particular platform. Parrot can work with strings of different character types and encodings. It automatically converts string operands with mixed characteristics to Unicode.* PMCs are Parrot's low-level objects. They can represent data of any arbitrary type. The operations (methods) for each PMC class are defined in a fixed vtable, which is a structure containing function pointers that implement each operation.

### Register assignment

The most basic operation on registers is assignment using the set opcode:

```
set I0, 42        # set integer register #0 to the integer value 42
set N3, 3.14159   # set number register #3 to an approximation of π
set I1, I0        # set register I1 to what I0 contains
set I2, N3        # truncate the floating point number to an integer
```

PASM uses registers where a high-level language would use variables. The exchange opcode swaps the contents of two registers of the same type:

```
exchange I1, I0   # set register I1 to what I0 contains
                  # and set register I0 to what I1 contains
```

As we mentioned before, string and PMC registers are slightly different because they hold a pointer instead of directly holding a value. Assigning one string register to another:

```
set S0, "Ford"
set S1, S0
set S0, "Zaphod"
print S1                  # prints "Ford"
end
```

doesn't make a copy of the string; it makes a copy of the pointer. Just after set S1, S0, both S0 and S1 point to the same string. But assigning a constant string to a string register allocates a new string. When "Zaphod" is assigned to S0, the pointer changes to point to the location of the new string, leaving

---

* This conversion isn't fully implemented yet.

the old string untouched. So strings act like simple values on the user level, even though they're implemented as pointers.

Unlike strings, assignment to a PMC doesn't automatically create a new object; it only calls the PMC's vtable method for assignment. So, rewriting the same example using a PMC has a completely different result:

```
new P0, .PerlString
set P0, "Ford"
set P1, P0
set P0, "Zaphod"
print P1              # prints "Zaphod"
end
```

The new opcode creates an instance of the .PerlString class. The class's vtable methods define how the PMC in P0 operates. The first set statement calls P0's vtable method set_string_native, which assigns the string "Ford" to the PMC. When P0 is assigned to P1:

```
set P1, P0
```

it copies the pointer, so P1 and P0 are both aliases to the same PMC. Then, assigning the string "Zaphod" to P0 changes the underlying PMC, so printing P1 or P0 prints "Zaphod".*

## PMC object types

Internally, PMC types are represented by positive integers, and built-in types by negative integers. PASM provides two opcodes to deal with types. Use typeof to look up the name of a type from its integer value or to look up the named type of a PMC. Use find_type to look up the integer value of a named type.

When the source argument is a PMC and the destination is a string register, typeof returns the name of the type:

```
new P0, .PerlString
typeof S0, P0        # S0 is "PerlString"
print S0
print "\n"
end
```

In this example, typeof returns the type name "PerlString".

When the source argument is a PMC and the destination is an integer register, typeof returns the integer representation of the type:

```
new P0, .PerlString
typeof I0, P0        # I0 is 36
```

---

* Contrast this with assign (in "PMC Assignment" later in this chapter).

```
print I0
print "\n"
end
```

This example returns the integer representation of PerlString, which is 36.

When typeof's source argument is an integer, it returns the name of the type represented by that integer:

```
set I1, -100
typeof S0, I1              # S0 is "INTVAL"
print S0
print "\n"
end
```

In this example typeof returns the type name "INTVAL" because the integer representation of a built-in integer value is –100.

The source argument to find_type is always a string containing a type name, and the destination register is always an integer. It returns the integer representation of the type with that name:

```
find_type I1, "PerlString"  # I1 is 36
print I1
print "\n"
find_type I2, "INTVAL"      # I2 is -100
print I2
print "\n"
end
```

Here, the name "PerlString" returns 36, and the name "INTVAL" returns –100.

All Parrot classes inherit from the class default, which has the type number 0. The default class provides some default functionality, but mainly throws exceptions when the default variant of a method is called (meaning the subclass didn't define the method). Type number 0 returns the type name "illegal", since no object should ever be created from the default class:

```
find_type I1, "fancy_super_long_double" # I1 is 0
print I1
print "\n"
typeof S0, I1                            # S0 is "illegal"
print S0
print "\n"
end
```

The type numbers are not fixed values. They change whenever a new class is added to Parrot or when the class hierarchy is altered. An include file containing an enumeration of PMC types (*runtime/parrot/include/pmctypes.pasm*) is generated during the configuration of the Parrot source tree. Internal data types and their names are specified in *runtime/parrot/include/datatypes.pasm*.

You can generate a complete and current list of valid PMC types by running this command within the main Parrot source directory:

```
$ perl classes/pmc2c2.pl --tree classes/*.pmc
```

which produces output like:

```
Array
    default
Boolean
    PerlInt
        perlscalar
            scalar
                default
Closure
    Sub
        default
...
```

The output traces the class hierarchy for each class: Boolean inherits from PerlInt, which is derived from the abstract perlscalar, scalar, and default classes (abstract classes are listed in lowercase). The actual classnames and their hierarchy may have changed by the time you read this.

### Type morphing

The classes PerlUndef, PerlInt, PerlNum, and PerlString implement Perl's polymorphic scalar behavior. Assigning a string to a number PMC morphs it into a string PMC. Assigning an integer value morphs it to a PerlInt, and assigning undef morphs it to PerlUndef:

```
new P0, .PerlString
set P0, "Ford\n"
print P0            # prints "Ford\n"
set P0, 42
print P0            # prints 42
print "\n"
typeof S0, P0
print S0            # prints "PerlInt"
print "\n"
end
```

P0 starts as a PerlString, but when set assigns it an integer value 42 (replacing the old string value "Ford"), it changes type to PerlInt.

## Math Operations

PASM has a full set of math instructions. These work with integers, floating-point numbers, and PMCs that implement the vtable methods of a numeric object. Most of the major math opcodes have two- and three-argument forms:

```
add I0, I1              # I0 += I1
add I10, I11, I2        # I10 = I11 + I2
```

The three-argument form of add stores the sum of the last two registers in the first register. The two-argument form adds the first register to the second and stores the result back in the first register.

The source arguments can be Parrot registers or constants, but they must be compatible with the type of the destination register. Generally, "compatible" means that the source and destination have to be the same type, but there are a few exceptions:

```
sub I0, I1, 2           # I0 = I1 - 2
sub N0, N1, 1.5         # N0 = N1 - 1.5
```

If the destination register is an integer register, like I0, the other arguments must be integer registers or integer constants. A floating-point destination, like N0, usually requires floating-point arguments, but many math opcodes also allow the final argument to be an integer. Opcodes with a PMC destination register may take an integer, floating-point, or PMC final argument:

```
mul P0, P1              # P0 *= P1
mul P0, I1
mul P0, N1
mul P0, P1, P2          # P0 = P1 * P2
mul P0, P1, I2
mul P0, P1, N2
```

Operations on a PMC are implemented by the vtable method of the destination (in the two-argument form) or the left-source argument (in the three argument form). The result of an operation is entirely determined by the PMC. A class implementing imaginary number operations might return an imaginary number, for example.

We won't list every math opcode here, but we'll list some of the most common ones. You can get a complete list in "PASM Opcodes" in Chapter 11.

### Unary math opcodes

The unary opcodes have either a destination argument and a source argument, or a single argument as destination and source. Some of the most common unary math opcodes are inc (increment), dec (decrement), abs (absolute value), neg (negate), and fact (factorial):

```
abs N0, -5.0  # the absolute value of -5.0 is 5.0
fact I1, 5    # the factorial of 5 is 120
inc I1        # 120 incremented by 1 is 121
```

## Binary math opcodes

Binary opcodes have two source arguments and a destination argument. As we mentioned before, most binary math opcodes have a two-argument form in which the first argument is both a source and the destination. Parrot provides add (addition), sub (subtraction), mul (multiplication), div (division), and pow (exponent) opcodes, as well as two different modulus operations. mod is Parrot's implementation of modulus, and cmod is the % operator from the C library. It also provides gcd (greatest common divisor) and lcm (least common multiple).

```
div I0, 12, 5    # I0 = 12 / 5
mod I0, 12, 5    # I0 = 12 % 5
```

## Floating-point operations

Although most of the math operations work with both floating-point numbers and integers, a few require floating-point destination registers. Among these are ln (natural log), log2 (log base 2), log10 (log base 10), and exp ($e^x$), as well as a full set of trigonometric opcodes such as sin (sine), cos (cosine), tan (tangent), sec (secant), cosh (hyperbolic cosine), tanh (hyperbolic tangent), sech (hyperbolic secant), asin (arc sine), acos (arc cosine), atan (arc tangent), asec (arc secant), exsec (exsecant), hav (haversine), and vers (versine). All angle arguments for the trigonometric functions are in radians:

```
sin N1, N0
exp N1, 2
```

The majority of the floating-point operations have a single source argument and a single destination argument. Even though the destination must be a floating-point register, the source can be either an integer or floating-point number.

The atan opcode also has a three-argument variant that implements C's atan2( ):

```
atan N0, 1, 1
```

# Working with Strings

The string operations work with string registers and with PMCs that implement a string class.

Most operations on string registers generate new strings in the destination register. Some operations have an optimized form that modifies an existing string in place. These are denoted by an _r suffix, as in substr_r.

String operations on PMC registers require all their string arguments to be PMCs.

## Concatenating strings

Use the concat opcode to concatenate strings. With string register or string constant arguments, concat has both a two-argument and a three-argument form. The first argument is a source and a destination in the two-argument form:

```
set S0, "ab"
concat S0, "cd"     # S0 has "cd" appended
print S0            # prints "abcd"
print "\n"

concat S1, S0, "xy" # S1 is the string S0 with "xy" appended
print S1            # prints "abcdxy"
print "\n"
end
```

The first concat concatenates the string "cd" onto the string "ab" in S0. It generates a new string "abcd" and changes S0 to point to the new string. The second concat concatenates "xy" onto the string "abcd" in S0 and stores the new string in S1.

For PMC registers, concat has only a three-argument form with separate registers for source and destination:

```
new P0, .PerlString
new P1, .PerlString
new P2, .PerlString
set P0, "ab"
set P1, "cd"
concat P2, P0, P1
print P2            # prints abcd
print "\n"
end
```

Here, concat concatenates the strings in P0 and P1 and stores the result in P2.

## Repeating strings

The repeat opcode repeats a string a certain number of times:

```
set S0, "x"
repeat S1, S0, 5  # S1 = S0 x 5
print S1          # prints "xxxxx"
print "\n"
end
```

In this example, repeat generates a new string with "x" repeated five times and stores a pointer to it in S1.

## Length of a string

The length opcode returns the length of a string in characters. This won't be the same as the length in bytes for multibyte encoded strings:

```
set S0, "abcd"
length I0, S0            # the length is 4
print I0
print "\n"
end
```

Currently, length doesn't have an equivalent for PMC strings, but it probably will be implemented in the future.

## Substrings

The simplest version of the substr opcode takes four arguments: a destination register, a string, an offset position, and a length. It returns a substring of the original string, starting from the offset position (0 is the first character) and spanning the length:

```
substr S0, "abcde", 1, 2      # S0 is "bc"
```

This example extracts a two-character string from "abcde" at a one-character offset from the beginning of the string (starting with the second character). It generates a new string, "bc", in the destination register S0.

When the offset position is negative, it counts backward from the end of the string. So an offset of −1 starts at the last character of the string.

substr also has a five-argument form, where the fifth argument is a string to replace the substring. This modifies the second argument and returns the removed substring in the destination register.

```
set S1, "abcde"
substr S0, S1, 1, 2, "XYZ"
print S0                 # prints "bc"
print "\n"
print S1                 # prints "aXYZde"
print "\n"
end
```

This replaces the substring "bc" in S1 with the string "XYZ", and returns "bc" in S0.

When the offset position in a replacing substr is one character beyond the original string length, substr appends the replacement string just like the concat opcode. If the replacement string is an empty string, the characters are just removed from the original string.

When you don't need to capture the replaced string, there's an optimized version of substr that just does a replace without returning the removed substring.

```
set S1, "abcde"
substr S1, 1, 2, "XYZ"
print S1                     # prints "aXYZde"
print "\n"
end
```

The PMC versions of substr are not yet implemented.

## Chopping strings

The chopn opcode removes characters from the end of a string. It takes two arguments: the string to modify and the count of characters to remove.

```
set S0, "abcde"
chopn S0, 2
print S0        # prints "abc"
print "\n"
end
```

This example removes two characters from the end of S0. If the count is negative, that many characters are kept in the string.

```
set S0, "abcde"
chopn S0, -2
print S0        # prints "ab"
print "\n"
end
```

This keeps the first two characters in S0 and removes the rest. chopn also has a three-argument version that stores the chopped string in a separate destination register, leaving the original string untouched:

```
set S0, "abcde"
chopn S1, S0, 1
print S1        # prints "abcd"
print "\n"
end
```

## Copying strings

The clone opcode makes a deep copy of a string or PMC. Instead of just copying the pointer, as normal assignment would, it recursively copies the string or object underneath.

```
new P0, .PerlString
set P0, "Ford"
clone P1, P0
set P0, "Zaphod"
print P1        # prints "Ford"
end
```

This example creates an identical, independent clone of the PMC in P0 and puts a pointer to it in P1. Later changes to P0 have no effect on P1.

With simple strings, the copy created by clone, as well as the results from substr, are copy-on-write (COW). These are rather cheap in terms of memory usage because the new memory location is only created when the copy is assigned a new value. Cloning is rarely needed with ordinary string registers since they always create a new memory location on assignment.

### Converting characters

The chr opcode takes an integer value and returns the corresponding character as a one-character string, while the ord opcode takes a single character string and returns the integer that represents that character in the string's encoding:

```
chr S0, 65          # S0 is "A"
ord I0, S0          # I0 is 65
```

ord has a three-argument variant that takes a character offset to select a single character from a multicharacter string. The offset must be within the length of the string:

```
ord I0, "ABC", 2    # I0 is 67
```

A negative offset counts backward from the end of the string, so −1 is the last character:

```
ord I0, "ABC", -1   # I0 is 67
```

### Formatting strings

The sprintf opcode generates a formatted string from a series of values. It takes three arguments: the destination register, a string specifying the format, and an ordered aggregate PMC (like a PerlArray) containing the values to be formatted. The format string and the destination register can be either strings or PMCs:

```
sprintf S0, S1, P2
sprintf P0, P1, P2
```

The format string is similar to the one for C's sprintf function, but with some extensions for Parrot data types. Each format field in the string starts with a % and ends with a character specifying the output format. The output format characters are listed in Table 9-1.

*Table 9-1. Format characters*

| Format | Meaning |
| --- | --- |
| %c | A character |
| %d | A decimal integer |
| %i | A decimal integer |
| %u | An unsigned integer |
| %o | An octal integer |
| %x | A hex integer, preceded by (0x when # is specified) |
| %X | A hex integer with a capital X (when # is specified) |
| %b | A binary integer, preceded by 0b (when # is specified) |
| %B | A binary integer with a capital B (when # is specified) |
| %p | A pointer address in hex |
| %f | A floating-point number |
| %e | A floating-point number in scientific notation (displayed with a lowercase e). |
| %E | The same as %e, but displayed with an uppercase E |
| %g | The same as either %e or %f, whichever fits best. |
| %G | The same as %g, but displayed with an uppercase E |
| %s | A string |

Each format field can be specified with several options: *flags*, *width*, *precision*, and *size*. The format flags are listed in Table 9-2.

*Table 9-2. Format flags*

| Flag | Meaning |
| --- | --- |
| 0 | Pad with zeros. |
| <space> | Pad with spaces. |
| + | Prefix numbers with a sign. |
| - | Align left. |
| # | Prefix a leading 0 for octal, 0x for hex, or force a decimal point. |

The *width* is a number defining the minimum width of the output from a field. The *precision* is the maximum width for strings or integers, and the number of decimal places for floating-point fields. If either *width* or *precision* is an asterisk (*), it takes its value from the next argument in the PMC.

The *size* modifier defines the type of the argument the field takes. The flags are listed in Table 9-3.

*Table 9-3. Size flags*

| Character | Meaning |
|-----------|---------|
| h | Short or float |
| l | Long |
| H | Huge value (long long or long double) |
| v | INTVAL or FLOATVAL |
| O | opcode_t |
| P | PMC |
| S | String |

The values in the aggregate PMC must have a type compatible with the specified *size*.

Here's a short illustration of string formats:

```
new P2, .PerlArray
new P0, .PerlInt
set P0, 42
push P2, P0
new P1, .PerlNum
set P1, 10
push P2, P1
sprintf S0, "int %#Px num %+2.3Pf\n", P2
print S0     # prints "int 0x2a num +10.000"
print "\n"
end
```

The first eight lines create a `PerlArray` with two elements: a `PerlInt` and a `PerlNum`. The format string of the `sprintf` has two format fields. The first, `%#Px`, takes a PMC argument from the aggregate (`P`) and formats it as a hexadecimal integer (`x`), with a leading `0x` (`#`). The second format field, `%+2.3Pf`, takes a PMC argument (`P`) and formats it as a floating-point number (`f`), with a minimum of two whole digits and a maximum of three decimal places (`2.3`) and a leading sign (`+`).

The test files *t/op/string.t* and *t/src/sprintf.t* have many more examples of format strings.

### Testing for substrings

The `index` opcode searches for a substring within a string. If it finds the substring, it returns the position where the substring was found as a character offset from the beginning of the string. If it fails to find the substring, it returns −1:

```
index I0, "Beeblebrox", "eb"
print I0                      # prints 2
```

```
print "\n"
index I0, "Beeblebrox", "Ford"
print I0                    # prints -1
print "\n"
end
```

index also has a four-argument version, where the fourth argument defines an offset position for starting the search:

```
index I0, "Beeblebrox", "eb", 3
print I0                    # prints 5
print "\n"
end
```

This finds the second "eb" in "Beeblebrox" instead of the first, because the search skips the first three characters in the string.

## Joining strings

The join opcode joins the elements of an array PMC into a single string. The second argument separates the individual elements of the PMC in the final string result.

```
new P0, .PerlArray
push P0, "hi"
push P0, 0
push P0, 1
push P0, 0
push P0, "parrot"
join S0, "__", P0
print S0                    # prints "hi__0__1__0__parrot"
end
```

This example builds a PerlArray in P0 with the values "hi", 0, 1, 0, and "parrot". It then joins those values (separated by the string "__") into a single string, and stores it in S0.

## Splitting strings

Splitting a string yields a new array containing the resulting substrings of the original string. Since regular expressions aren't implemented yet, the current implementation of the split opcode just splits individual characters, much like Perl 5's split with an empty pattern.

```
split P0, "", "abc"
set P1, P0[0]
print P1                    # 'a'
set P1, P0[2]
print P1                    # 'c'
end
```

This example splits the string "abc" into individual characters and stores them in an array in P0. It then prints out the first and third elements of the array. For now, the split pattern (the second argument to the opcode) is ignored except for a test to make sure that its length is zero.

# I/O Operations

The I/O subsystem has at least one set of significant revisions ahead, so you can expect this section to change. It's worth an introduction, though, because the basic set of opcodes is likely to stay the same, even if their arguments and underlying functionality change.

### Open and close a file

The open opcode opens a file for access. It takes three arguments: a destination register, the name of the file, and a modestring. It returns a ParrotIO object on success and a PerlUndef object on failure. The ParrotIO object hides operating-system-specific details.

```
open P0, "people.txt", "<"
```

The modestring specifies whether the file is opened in read-only (<), write-only (>), read/write (+<), or append mode (>>).

The close opcode closes a ParrotIO object:

```
close P0        # close a PIO
```

### Output operations

We already saw the print opcode in several examples above. The one-argument form prints a register or constant to stdout. It also has a two-argument form: the first argument is the ParrotIO object where the value is printed.

```
print P0, "xxx"        # print to PIO in P0
```

The getstdin, getstdout, and getstderr opcodes return ParrotIO objects for the stdio streams:

```
getstdin P0
gestdout P0
getstderr P0
```

Printing to stderr has a shortcut:

```
printerr "troubles"
getstderr P10
print P10, "troubles"        # same
```

### Reading from files

The read opcode reads a specified number of bytes from stdin or from a ParrotIO object:

```
read S0, I0          # read from stdin up to I0 bytes into S0
read S0, P0, I0      # read from the PIO in P0 up to I0 bytes
```

readline is a variant of read that works with ParrotIO objects. It reads a whole line at a time, terminated by the newline character:

```
getstdin P0
readline S0, P0      # read a line from stdin
```

The seek opcode sets the current file position on a ParrotIO object. It takes four arguments: a destination register, a ParrotIO object, an offset, and a flag specifying the origin point:

```
seek I0, P0, I1, I2
```

In this example, the position of P0 is set by an offset (I1) from an origin point (I2). 0 means the offset is from the start of the file, 1 means the offset is from the current position, and 2 means the offset is from the end of the file. The return value (in I0) is 0 when the position is successfully set and −1 when it fails. seek also has a five-argument form that seeks with a 64-bit offset, constructed from two 32-bit arguments.

## Logical and Bitwise Operations

The logical opcodes evaluate the truth of their arguments. They're often used to make decisions on control flow. Logical operations are implemented for integers and PMCs. Numeric values are false if they're 0 and true otherwise. Strings are false if they're the empty string or a single character "0" and true otherwise. PMCs are true when their get_bool vtable method returns a nonzero value.

The and opcode returns the second argument if it's false and the third argument otherwise:

```
and I0, 0, 1  # returns 0
and I0, 1, 2  # returns 2
```

The or opcode returns the second argument if it's true and the third argument otherwise:

```
or I0, 1, 0  # returns 1
or I0, 0, 2  # returns 2

or P0, P1, P2
```

Both and and or are short-circuiting. If they can determine what value to return from the second argument, they'll never evaluate the third. This is significant only for PMCs, as they might have side effects on evaluation.

The xor opcode returns the second argument if it is the only true value, returns the third argument if it is the only true value, and returns false if both values are true or both are false:

```
xor I0, 1, 0  # returns 1
xor I0, 0, 1  # returns 1
xor I0, 1, 1  # returns 0
xor I0, 0, 0  # returns 0
```

The not opcode returns a true value when the second argument is false, and a false value if the second argument is true:

```
not I0, I1
not P0, P1
```

The bitwise opcodes operate on their values a single bit at a time. band, bor, and bxor return a value that is the logical AND, OR, or XOR of each bit in the source arguments. They each take a destination register and two source registers. They also have two-argument forms where the destination is also a source. bnot is the logical NOT of each bit in a single-source argument.

```
bnot I0, I1
band P0, P1
bor I0, I1, I2
bxor P0, P1, I2
```

The bitwise opcodes also have string variants for AND, OR, and XOR: bors, bands, and bxors. These take string register or PMC string source arguments and perform the logical operation on each byte of the strings to produce the final string.

```
bors S0, S1
bands P0, P1
bors S0, S1, S2
bxors P0, P1, I2
```

The bitwise string opcodes only have meaningful results when they're used with simple ASCII strings because the bitwise operation is done per byte.

The logical and arithmetic shift operations shift their values by a specified number of bits:

```
shl I0, I1, I2    # shift I1 left by count I2 giving I0
shr I0, I1, I2    # arithmetic shift right
lsr P0, P1, P2    # logical shift right
```

# Working with PMCs

In most of the examples we've shown so far, PMCs just duplicate the functionality of integers, numbers, and strings. They wouldn't be terribly useful if that's all they did, though. PMCs offer several advanced features, each with its own set of operations.

## Aggregates

PMCs can define complex types that hold multiple values. These are commonly called "aggregates." The most important feature added for aggregates is keyed access. Elements within an aggregate PMC can be stored and retrieved by a numeric or string key. PASM also offers a full set of operations for manipulating aggregate data types.

Since PASM is intended to implement Perl, the two most fully featured aggregates already in operation are arrays and hashes. Any aggregate defined for any language could take advantage of the features described here.

### Arrays

The `PerlArray` PMC is an ordered aggregate with zero-based integer keys. The syntax for keyed access to a PMC puts the key in square brackets after the register name:

```
new P0, .PerlArray   # obtain a new array object
set P0, 2            # set its length
set P0[0], 10        # set first element to 10
set P0[1], I31       # set second element to I31
set I0, P0[0]        # get the first element
set I1, P0           # get array length
```

A key on the destination register of a set operation sets a value for that key in the aggregate. A key on the source register of a set returns the value for that key. If you set P0 without a key, you set the length of the array, not one of its values.* And if you assign the `PerlArray` to an integer, you get the length of the array.

By the time you read this, the syntax for getting and setting the length of an array may have changed. The change would separate array allocation (how much storage the array provides) from the actual element count. The currently proposed syntax uses set to set or retrieve the allocated size of an

---

* `PerlArray` is an autoextending array, so you never need to set its length. Other array types may require the length to be set explicitly.

array, and an elements opcode to set or retreive the count of elements stored in the array.

```
set P0, 100        # allocate store for 100 elements
elements P0, 5     # set element count to 5
set I0, P0         # obtain current allocation size
elements I0, P0    # get element count
```

Some other useful instructions for working with arrays are push, pop, shift, and unshift (you'll find them in "PASM Opcodes" in Chapter 11).

## Hashes

The PerlHash PMC is an unordered aggregate with string keys:

```
new P1, .PerlHash    # generate a new hash object
set P1["key"], 10    # set key and value
set I0, P1["key"]    # obtain value for key
set I1, P1           # number of entries in hash
```

The exists opcode tests whether a keyed value exists in an aggregate. It returns 1 if it finds the key in the aggregate and returns 0 if it doesn't. It doesn't care if the value itself is true or false, only that the key has been set:

```
new P0, .PerlHash
set P0["key"], 0
exists I0, P0["key"] # does a value exist at "key"
print I0             # prints 1
print "\n"
end
```

The delete opcode is also useful for working with hashes: it removes a key/value pair.

## Iterators

Iterators extract values from an aggregate PMC. You create an iterator by creating a new Iterator PMC, and passing the array to new as an additional parameter:

```
new P1, .Iterator, P2
```

The include file *iterator.pasm* defines some constants for working with iterators. The .ITERATE_FROM_START and .ITERATE_FROM_END constants are used to select whether an array iterator starts from the beginning or end of the array. The shift opcode extracts values from the array. An iterator PMC is true as long as it still has values to be retrieved (tested by unless in the following):

```
.include "iterator.pasm"
    new P2, .PerlArray
    push P2, "a"
    push P2, "b"
    push P2, "c"
```

```
        new P1, .Iterator, P2
        set P1, .ITERATE_FROM_START

iter_loop:
    unless P1, iter_end
    shift P5, P1
    print P5                            # prints "a", "b", "c"
    branch iter_loop
iter_end:
    end
```

Hash iterators work similarly to array iterators, but they extract keys. With hashes it's only meaningful to iterate in one direction, since they don't define any order for their keys.

```
    .include "iterator.pasm"
        new P2, .PerlHash
        set P2["a"], 10
        set P2["b"], 20
        set P2["c"], 30
        new P1, .Iterator, P2
        set P1, .ITERATE_FROM_START_KEYS

iter_loop:
    unless P1, iter_end
    shift S5, P1                        # one of the keys "a", "b", "c"
    set I9, P2[S5]
    print I9                            # prints e.g. 20, 10, 30
    branch iter_loop
iter_end:
    end
```

## Data structures

Arrays and hashes can hold any data type, including other aggregates. Accessing elements deep within nested data structures is a common operation, so PASM provides a way to do it in a single instruction. Complex keys specify a series of nested data structures, with each individual key separated by a semicolon:

```
    new P0, .PerlHash
    new P1, .PerlArray
    set P1[2], 42
    set P0["answer"], P1
    set I1, 2
    set I0, P0["answer";I1]     # $i = %hash{"answer"}[2]
    print I0
    print "\n"
    end
```

This example builds up a data structure of a hash containing an array. The complex key P0["answer";I1] retrieves an element of the array within the hash. You can also set a value using a complex key:

```
set P0["answer";0], 5    # %hash{"answer"}[0] = 5
```

The individual keys are integers or strings, or registers with integer or string values.

## PMC Assignment

We mentioned before that set on two PMCs simply aliases them both to the same object, and that clone creates a complete duplicate object. But if you just want to assign the value of one PMC to another PMC, you need the assign opcode:

```
new P0, .PerlInt
new P1, .PerlInt
set P0, 42
set P2, P0
assign P1, P0      # note: P1 has to exist already
inc P0
print P0           # prints 43
print "\n"
print P1           # prints 42
print "\n"
print P2           # prints 43
print "\n"
end
```

This example creates two PerlInt PMCs: P0 and P1. It gives P0 a value of 42. It then uses set to give the same value to P2, but uses assign to give the value to P1. When P0 is incremented, P2 also changes, but P1 doesn't. The destination register for assign must have an existing object of the right type in it, since assign doesn't create a new object (as with clone) or reuse the source object (as with set).

## Properties

PMCs can have additional values attached to them as "properties" of the PMC. What these properties do is entirely up to the language being implemented. Perl 6 uses them to store extra information about a variable: whether it's a constant, if it should always be interpreted as a true value, etc.

The setprop opcode sets the value of a named property on a PMC. It takes three arguments: the PMC to be set with a property, the name of the property, and a PMC containing the value of the property. The getprop opcode returns the value of a property. It also takes three arguments: the PMC to store the property's value, the name of the property, and the PMC from which the property value is to be retrieved:

```
new P0, .PerlString
set P0, "Zaphod"
new P1, .PerlInt
set P1, 1
setprop P0, "constant", P1    # set a property on P0
getprop P3, "constant", P0    # retrieve a property on P0
print P3                      # prints 1
print "\n"
end
```

This example creates a PerlString object in P0, and a PerlInt object with the value 1 in P1. setprop sets a property named "constant" on the object in P0 and gives the property the value in P1.* getprop retrieves the value of the property "constant" on P0 and stores it in P3.

Properties are kept in a separate hash for each PMC. Property values are always PMCs, but only references to the actual PMCs. Trying to fetch the value of a property that doesn't exist returns a PerlUndef.

delprop deletes a property from a PMC:

```
delprop P1, "constant"  # delete property
```

You can also return a complete hash of all properties on a PMC with prophash:

```
prophash P0, P1        # set P0 to the property hash of P1
```

# Flow Control

Although it has many advanced features, at heart PASM is an assembly language. All flow control in PASM—as in most assembly languages—is done with branches and jumps.

Branch instructions transfer control to a relative offset from the current instruction. The rightmost argument to every branch opcode is a label, which the assembler converts to the integer value of the offset. You can also branch on a literal integer value, but there's rarely any need to do so. The simplest branch instruction is branch:

```
branch L1              # branch 4
print "skipped\n"
```

---

* The "constant" property is ignored by PASM, but is significant to the Perl 6 code running on top of it.

```
L1:
    print "after branch\n"
    end
```

This example unconditionally branches to the location of the label L1, skipping over the first print statement.

Jump instructions transfer control to an absolute address. The jump opcode doesn't calculate an address from a label, so it's used together with set_addr:

```
    set_addr I0, L1
    jump I0
    print "skipped\n"
    end
L1:
    print "after jump\n"
    end
```

The set_addr opcode takes a label or an integer offset and returns an absolute address.

You've probably noticed the end opcode as the last statement in many examples above. This terminates the execution of the current run loop. Terminating the main bytecode segment (the first run loop) stops the interpreter. Without the end statement, execution just falls off the end of the bytecode segment, with a good chance of crashing the interpreter.

## Conditional Branches

Unconditional jumps and branches aren't really enough for flow control. What you need to implement the control structures of high-level languages is the ability to select different actions based on a set of conditions. PASM has opcodes that conditionally branch based on the truth of a single value or the comparison of two values. The following example has if and unless conditional branches:

```
    set I0, 0
    if I0, TRUE
    unless I0, FALSE
    print "skipped\n"
    end
TRUE:
    print "shouldn't happen\n"
    end
FALSE:
    print "the value was false\n"
    end
```

if branches if its first argument is a true value, and unless branches if its first argument is a false value. In this case, the if doesn't branch because I0 is false, but the unless does branch. The comparison branching opcodes compare two values and branch if the stated relation holds true. These are eq (branch when equal), ne (when not equal), lt (when less than), gt (when greater than), le (when less than or equal), and ge (when greater than or equal). The two compared arguments must be the same register type:

```
set I0, 4
set I1, 4
eq I0, I1, EQUAL
print "skipped\n"
end
EQUAL:
print "the two values are equal\n"
end
```

This compares two integers, I0 and I1, and branches if they're equal. Strings of different character sets or encodings are converted to Unicode before they're compared. PMCs have a cmp vtable method. This gets called on the left argument to perform the comparison of the two objects.

The comparison opcodes don't specify if a numeric or string comparison is intended. The type of the register selects for integers, floats, and strings. With PMCs, the vtable method cmp or is_equal of the first argument is responsible for comparing the PMC meaningfully with the other operand. If you need to force a numeric or string comparison on two PMCs, use the alternate comparison opcodes that end in the _num and _str suffixes.

```
eq_str P0, P1, label    # always a string compare
gt_num P0, P1, label    # always numerically
```

Finally, the eq_addr opcode branches if two PMCs or strings are actually the same object (have the same address), and the is_null opcode branches if a PMC is NULL (has no assigned address):

```
eq_addr P0, P1, same_pmcs_found
is_null P2, the_pmc_is_null
```

## Iteration

PASM doesn't define high-level loop constructs. These are built up from a combination of conditional and unconditional branches. A *do while*–style loop can be constructed with a single conditional branch:

```
set I0, 0
set I1, 10
REDO:
inc I0
print I0
print "\n"
lt I0, I1, REDO
end
```

This example prints out the numbers 1 to 10. The first time through, it executes all statements up to the lt statement. If the condition evaluates as true (I0 is less than I1) it branches to the REDO label and runs the three statements in the loop body again. The loop ends when the condition evaluates as false.

Conditional and unconditional branches can build up quite complex looping constructs, as follows:

```
# loop ($i=1; $i<=10; $i++) {
#    print "$i\n";
# }
loop_init:
  set I0, 1
  branch loop_test
loop_body:
  print I0
  print "\n"
  branch loop_continue
loop_test:
  le I0, 10, loop_body
  branch out
loop_continue:
  inc I0
  branch loop_test
out:
  end
```

This example emulates a counter-controlled loop like Perl 6's loop keyword or C's for. The first time through the loop it sets the initial value of the counter in loop_init, tests that the loop condition is met in loop_test, and then executes the body of the loop in loop_body. If the test fails on the first iteration, the loop body will never execute. The end of loop_body branches to loop_continue, which increments the counter and then goes to loop_test again. The loop ends when the condition fails, and it branches to out. The example is more complex than it needs to be just to count to 10, but it nicely shows the major components of a loop.

# Stacks and Register Frames

Parrot provides 32 registers of each type: integer, floating-point number, string, and PMC. This is a generous number of registers, but it's still too restrictive for the average use. You can hardly limit your code to 32 integers at a time. This is especially true when you start working with subroutines and need a way to store the caller's values and the subroutine's values. So, Parrot also provides stacks for storing values outside the 32 registers. Parrot has seven basic stacks, each used for a different purpose: the user stack, the control stack, the pad stack, and the four register-backing stacks.

## User Stack

The user stack, also known as the general-purpose stack, stores individual values. The two main opcodes for working with the user stack are save, to push a value onto the stack, and restore, to pop one off the stack:

```
save 42      # push onto user stack
restore I1   # pop off user stack
```

The one argument to save can be either a constant or a register. The user stack is a typed stack, so restore will only pop a value into a register of the same type as the original value:

```
save 1
set I0, 4
restore I0
print I0      # prints 1
end
```

If that restore were restore N0 instead of an integer register, you'd get an exception, "Wrong type on top of stack!"

A handful of other instructions are useful for manipulating the user stack. rotate_up rotates a given number of elements on the user stack to put a different element on the top of the stack. The depth opcode returns the number of entries currently on the stack. The entrytype opcode returns the type of the stack entry at a given depth, and lookback returns the value of the element at the given depth without popping the element off the stack:

```
save 1
save 2.3
set S0, "hi\n"
save S0
save P0
entrytype I0, 0
print I0        # prints 4 (PMC)
entrytype I0, 1
print I0        # prints 3 (STRING)
entrytype I0, 2
print I0        # prints 2 (FLOATVAL)
entrytype I0, 3
print I0        # prints 1 (INTVAL)
print "\n"
depth I2        # get entries
print I2        # prints 4
print "\n"
lookback S1, 1  # get entry at depth 1
print S1        # prints "hi\n"
```

```
depth I2       # unchanged
print I2       # prints 4
print "\n"
end
```

This example pushes four elements onto the user stack: an integer, a floating-point number, a string, and a PMC. It checks the entrytype of all four elements and prints them out. It then checks the depth of the stack, gets the value of the second element with a lookback, and checks that the number of elements hasn't changed.

## Control Stack

The control stack, also known as the call stack, stores return addresses for subroutines called by bsr and exception handlers. There are no instructions for directly manipulating the control stack.

## Register Frames

The final set of stacks are the register backing stacks. Parrot has four backing stacks, one for each type of register. Instead of saving and restoring individual values, the backing stacks work with register frames. Each register frame is the full set of 32 registers for one type. Each frame is separated into two halves: the bottom half (registers 0–15) and the top half (registers 16–32). Some opcodes work with full frames while others work with half-frames. The backing stacks are commonly used for saving the contents of all the registers (or just the top half of each frame) before a subroutine call, so they can be restored when control returns to the caller.

PASM has five opcodes for storing full register frames, one for each register type and one that saves all four at once:

```
pushi          # copy I-register frame
pushn          # copy N-register frame
pushs          # copy S-register frame
pushp          # copy P-register frame
saveall        # copy all register frames
```

Each pushi, pushn, pushs, or pushp pushes a register frame containing all the current values of one register type onto the backing stack of that type. saveall simply calls pushi, pushn, pushs, and pushp.

PASM also has five opcodes to restore full register frames. Again, it has one for each register type and one that restores all four at once:

```
popi           # restore I-register frame
popn           # restore N-register frame
pops           # restore S-register frame
```

```
popp                # restore P-register frame
restoreall          # restore all register frames
```

The popi, popn, pops, and popp opcodes pop a single register frame off a particular stack and replace the values in all 32 registers of that type with the values in the restored register frame. restoreall calls popi, popn, pops, and popp, restoring every register of every type to values saved earlier.

Saving a register frame to the backing stack doesn't alter the values stored in the registers; it simply copies the values:

```
set I0, 1
print I0            # prints 1
pushi               # copy away I0..I31
print I0            # unchanged, still 1
inc I0
print I0            # now 2
popi                # restore registers to state of previous pushi
print I0            # old value restored, now 1
print "\n"
end
```

This example sets the value of I0 to 1 and stores the complete set of integer registers. Before I0 is incremented, it has the same value as before the pushi.

In "Working with Registers" earlier in this chapter, we mentioned that string and PMC registers hold pointers to the actual objects. When string or PMC register frames are saved, only the pointers are copied, not the actual contents of the strings or PMCs. The same is true when string or PMC register frames are restored:

```
set S0, "hello"          # set S0 to "hello"
pushs
substr S0, 0, 5, "world" # alter the string in S0
set S0, "test"           # set S0 to a new string
pops                     # restores the first string pointer
print S0                 # prints "world"
end
```

In this example, we first use the pushs opcode to copy the string pointer to the string register frame stack. This gives us two pointers to the same underlying string, with one currently stored in S0, and the other saved in the string register frame stack. If we then use substr to alter the contents of the string, both pointers will now point to the altered string, and so restoring our original pointer using pops does not restore the original string value.

Each of the above pushX and popX opcodes has a variant that will save or restore only the top or bottom half of one register set or all the register sets:

```
pushtopi            # save I16..I31
popbottoms          # restore S0..S15
savetop             # save regs 16-31 in each frame
restoretop          # restore regs 16-31 in each frame
```

PASM also has opcodes to clear individual register frames: cleari, clearn, clears, and clearp. These reset the numeric registers to 0 values and the string and PMC registers to null pointers, which is the same state that they have when the interpreter first starts.

The user stack can be useful for holding onto some values that would otherwise be obliterated by a restoreall:

```
# ... coming from a subroutine
save I5     # Push some registers
save I6     # holding the return values
save N5     # of the sub.
restoreall  # restore registers to state before calling subroutine
restore N0  # pop off last pushed
restore I0  # pop 2nd
restore I1  # and so on
```

# Lexicals and Globals

So far, we've been treating Parrot registers like the variables of a high-level language. This is fine, as far as it goes, but it isn't the full picture. The dynamic nature and introspective features of languages like Perl make it desirable to manipulate variables by name, instead of just by register or stack location. These languages also have global variables, which are visible throughout the entire program. Storing a global variable in a register would either tie up that register for the lifetime of the program or require unwieldy manipulation of the user stack.

Parrot provides structures for storing both global and lexically scoped named variables. Lexical and global variables must be PMC values. PASM provides instructions for storing and retrieving variables from these structures so the PASM opcodes can operate on their values.

## Globals

Global variables are stored in a PerlHash, so every variable name must be unique. PASM has two opcodes for globals, store_global and find_global:

```
new P10, .PerlInt
set P10, 42
store_global "$foo", P10
# ...
find_global P0, "$foo"
print P0                       # prints 42
end
```

The first two statements create a PerlInt in the PMC register P10 and give it the value 42. In the third statement, store_global stores that PMC as the named global variable $foo. At some later point in the program, find_global retrieves the PMC from the global variable by name, and stores it in P0 so it can be printed.

The store_global opcode only stores a reference to the object. If we add an increment statement:

```
inc P10
```

after the store_global, it increments the stored global, printing 43. If that's not what you want, you can clone the PMC before you store it. Leaving the global variable as an alias does have advantages, though. If you retrieve a stored global into a register and modify it as follows:

```
find_global P0, "varname"
inc P0
```

the value of the stored global is directly modified, so you don't need to call store_global again.

The two-argument forms of store_global and find_global store or retrieve globals from the outermost namespace (what Perl users will know as the "main" namespace). A simple flat global namespace isn't enough for most languages, so Parrot also needs to support hierarchical namespaces for separating packages (classes and modules in Perl 6). The three-argument versions of store_global and find_global add an argument to select a nested namespace:

```
store_global "Foo", "var", P0 # store P0 as var in the Foo namespace
find_global P1, "Foo", "var"  # get Foo::var
```

Eventually, the global opcodes will have variants that take a PMC to specify the namespace, but the design and implementation of these aren't finished yet.

## Lexicals

Lexical variables are stored in a lexical scratchpad. There's one pad for each lexical scope. Every pad has both a hash and an array, so elements can be stored either by name or by numeric index. Parrot stores the scratchpads for nested lexical scopes in a pad stack.

### Basic instructions

The instructions for manipulating lexical scratchpads are new_pad to create a new pad, store_lex to store a variable in a pad, find_lex to retrieve a variable from a pad, push_pad to push a pad onto the pad stack, and pop_pad to remove a pad from the stack:

```
new_pad 0              # create and push a pad with depth 0
new P0, .PerlInt       # create a variable
set P0, 10             # assign value to it
store_lex 0, "$foo", P0 # store the var at depth 0 by name
# ...
find_lex P1, 0, "$foo"  # get the var into P1
print P1
print "\n"             # prints 10
pop_pad                # remove pad
end
```

The first statement creates a new scratchpad and pushes it onto the pad stack. It's created with depth 0, which is the outermost lexical scope. The next two statements create a new PMC object in P0, and give it a value. The store_lex opcode stores the object in P0 as the named variable $foo in the scratchpad at depth 0. At some later point in the program, the find_lex opcode retrieves the value of $foo in the pad at depth 0 and stores it in the register P1 so it can be printed. At the very end, pop_pad removes the pad from the pad stack.

The new_pad opcode has two forms, one that creates a new scratchpad and stores it in a PMC, and another that creates a new scratchpad and immediately pushes it onto the pad stack. If the pad were stored in a PMC, you would have to push it onto the pad stack before you could use it:

```
new_pad P10, 0             # create a new pad in P10
push_pad P10               # push it onto the pad stack
```

In a simple case like this, it really doesn't make sense to separate out the two instructions, but you'll see later in "Subroutines" why it's valuable to have both.

The store_lexand find_lex opcodes can take an integer index in place of a name for the variable:

```
store_lex 0, 0, P0 # store by index
# ...
find_lex P1, 0     # retrieve by index
```

With an index, the variable is stored in the scratchpad array, instead of the scratchpad hash.

### Nested scratchpads

To create a nested scope, you create another scratchpad with a higher depth number and push it onto the pad stack. The outermost scope is always depth 0, and each nested scope is one higher. The pad stack won't allow you to push on a scratchpad that's more than one level higher than the current depth of the top of the stack:

```
new_pad 0                    # outer scope
new_pad 1                    # inner scope
new P0, .PerlInt
set P0, 10
store_lex -1, "$foo", P0     # store in top pad
new P1, .PerlInt
set P1, 20
store_lex -2, "$foo", P1     # store in next outer scope
find_lex P2, "$foo"          # find in all scopes
print P2                     # prints 10
print "\n"
find_lex P2, -1, "$foo"      # find in top pad
print P2                     # prints 10
print "\n"
find_lex P2, -2, "$foo"      # find in next outer scope
print P2                     # prints 20
print "\n"
pop_pad
pop_pad
end
```

The first two statements create two new scratchpads, one at depth 0 and one at depth 1, and push them onto the pad stack. When store_lex and find_lex have a negative number for the depth specifier, they count backward from the top pad on the stack, so −1 is the top pad, and −2 is the second pad back. In this case, the pad at depth 1 is the top pad, and the pad at depth 0 is the second pad. So:

```
store_lex -1, "$foo", P0    # store in top pad
```

stores the object in P0 as the named variable $foo in the pad at depth 1. Then:

```
store_lex -2, "$foo", P1    # store in next outer scope
```

stores the object in P1 as the named variable $foo in the pad at depth 0.

A find_lex statement with no depth specified searches every scratchpad in the stack from the top of the stack to the bottom:

```
find_lex P2, "$foo"         # find in all scopes
```

Both pad 0 and pad 1 have variables named $foo, but only the value from the top pad is returned. store_lex also has a version with no depth specified, but it only works if the named lexical has already been created at a particular depth. It searches the stack from top to bottom and stores the object in the first lexical it finds with the right name.

The peek_pad instruction retrieves the top entry on the pad stack into a PMC register, but doesn't pop it off the stack.

# Subroutines

Subroutines and methods are the basic building blocks of larger programs. At the heart of every subroutine call are two fundamental actions: it has to store the current location so it can come back to it, and it has to transfer control to the subroutine. The bsr opcode does both. It pushes the address of the next instruction onto the control stack, and then branches to a label that marks the subroutine:

```
print "in main\n"
bsr _sub
print "and back\n"
end
_sub:
    print "in sub\n"
    ret
```

At the end of the subroutine, the ret instruction pops a location back off the control stack and goes there, returning control to the caller. The jsr opcode pushes the current location onto the call stack and jumps to a subroutine. Just like the jump opcode, it takes an absolute address in an integer register, so the address has to be calculated first with the set_addr opcode:

```
print "in main\n"
set_addr I0, _sub
jsr I0
print "and back\n"
end
_sub:
    print "in sub\n"
    ret
```

## Calling Conventions

A bsr or jsr is fine for a simple subroutine call, but few subroutines are quite that simple. The biggest issues revolve around register usage. Parrot has 32 registers of each type, and the caller and the subroutine share the same set of registers. How does the subroutine keep from destroying the caller's values? More importantly, who is responsible for saving and restoring registers? Where are arguments for the subroutine stored? Where are the subroutine's return values stored? A number of different answers are possible. You've seen how many ways Parrot has of storing values. The critical point is that the caller and the called subroutine have to agree on all the answers.

## Reserved registers

A very simple system would be to declare that the caller uses registers through 15, and the subroutine uses 16–31. This works in a small program with light register usage. But what about a subroutine call from within another subroutine or a recursive call? The solution doesn't extend to a large scale.

## Callee saves

Another possibility is to make the subroutine responsible for saving the caller's registers:

```
    set I0, 42
    save I0            # pass args on stack
    bsr _inc           # j = inc(i)
    restore I1         # restore args from stack
    print I1
    print "\n"
    end
_inc:
    saveall            # preserve all registers
    restore I0         # get argument
    inc I0             # do all the work
    save I0            # push return value
    restoreall         # restore caller's registers
    ret
```

This example stores arguments to the subroutine and return values from the subroutine on the user stack. The first statement in the _inc subroutine is a saveall to save all the caller's registers onto the backing stacks, and the last statement before the return restores them.

One advantage of this approach is that the subroutine can choose to save and restore only the register frames it actually uses, for a small speed gain. The example above could use pushi and popi instead of saveall and restoreall because it uses only integer registers. One disadvantage is that it doesn't allow optimization of tail calls, where the last statement of a recursive subroutine is a call to itself.

## Parrot-calling conventions

Internal subroutines can use whatever calling convention serves them best. Externally visible subroutines and methods need stricter rules. Since these routines may be called as part of an included library or module and even from a different high-level language, it's important to have a consistent interface.

Under the Parrot-calling conventions the caller is responsible for preserving its own registers. The first 11 arguments of each register type are passed in Parrot registers, as are several other pieces of information. Register usage for subroutine calls is listed in Table 9-4.

*Table 9-4. Calling and return conventions*

| Register | Usage |
|---|---|
| P0 | Subroutine/method object |
| P1 | Return continuation if applicable |
| P2 | Object for a method call (invocant) or NULL for a subroutine call |
| P3 | Array with overflow parameters/return values |
| S0 | Fully qualified method name, if it's a method call |
| I0 | True for prototyped parameters |
| I1 | Number of integer arguments/return results |
| I2 | Number of string arguments/return results |
| I3 | Number of PMC arguments/return results |
| I4 | Number of float arguments/return results |
| I5 ... I15 | First 11 integer arguments/return results |
| N5 ... N15 | First 11 float arguments/return results |
| S5 ... S15 | First 11 string arguments/return results |
| P5 ... P15 | First 11 PMC arguments/return results |

If there are more than 11 arguments or return values of one type for the subroutine, overflow parameters are passed in an array in P3. Subroutines without a prototype pass all their arguments or return values in P registers and if needed in the overflow array.*

The _inc subroutine from above can be rewritten as a prototyped subroutine:

```
set I16, 42          # use local regs from 16..31
newsub P0, .Sub, _inc # create a new Sub object
set I5, I16          # first integer argument
set I0, 1            # prototype used
set I1, 1            # one integer argument
null I2             # no string arguments
null I3             # no PMC arguments
null I4             # no numeric arguments
null P2             # no object (invocant)
pushtopi            # preserve top I register frame
invokecc            # call function object in P0
poptopi             # restore registers
```

* Prototyped subroutines have a defined signature.

```
      print I5
      print "\n"
      # I16 is still valid here, whatever the subroutine did
      end

      .pcc_sub _inc:
      inc I5                        # do all the work
      set I0, 1                     # prototyped return
      set I1, 1                     # one retval in I5
      null I2                       # nothing else
      null I3
      null I4
      invoke P1                     # return from the sub
```

Instead of using a simple bsr, this set of conventions uses a subroutine object. There are several kinds of subroutine-like objects, but Sub is a class for PASM subroutines.

The .pcc_sub directive defines globally accessible subroutine objects. The _inc function above can be found as:

```
      find_global P20, "_inc"
```

Subroutine objects of all kinds can be called with the invoke opcode. With no arguments, it calls the subroutine in P0, which is the standard for the Parrot-calling conventions. There is also an invoke Px instruction for calling objects held in a different register.

The invokecc opcode is like invoke, but it also creates and stores a new return continuation in P1. When the called subroutine invokes this return continuation, it returns control to the instruction after the function call. This kind of call is known as Continuation Passing Style (CPS).

In a simple example like this, it isn't really necessary to set up all the registers to obey to the Parrot-calling conventions. But when you call into library code, the subroutine is likely to check the number and type of arguments passed to it. So it's always a good idea to follow the full conventions. This is equally true for return values. The caller might check how many arguments the subroutine really returned.

Setting all these registers for every subroutine call might look wasteful at first glance, and it does increase the size of the bytecode, but you don't need to worry about execution time: the JIT system executes each register setup opcode in one CPU cycle.

# Native Call Interface

A special version of the Parrot-calling conventions are used by the Native Call Interface (NCI) for calling subroutines with a known prototype in shared libraries. This is not really portable across all libraries, but it's worth a short example. This is a simplified version of the first test in *t/pmc/nci.t*:

```
loadlib P1, "libnci"        # get library object for a shared lib
print "loaded\n"
dlfunc P0, P1, "nci_dd", "dd" # obtain the function object
print "dlfunced\n"
set I0, 1                   # prototype used - unchecked
set N5, 4.0                 # first argument
invoke                      # call nci_dd
ne N5, 8.0, nok_1           # the test functions returns 2*arg
print "ok 1\n"
end
nok_1:
    ...
```

This example shows two new instructions: loadlib and dlfunc. The loadlib opcode obtains a handle for a shared library. It searches for the shared library in the current directory, in *runtime/parrot/dynext*, and in a few other configured directories. It also tries to load the provided filename unaltered and with appended extensions like *.so* or *.dll*. Which extensions it tries depends on the operating system on which Parrot is running.

The dlfunc opcode gets a function object from a previously loaded library (second argument) of a specified name (third argument) with a known function signature (fourth argument). The function signature is a string where the first character is the return value and the rest of the parameters are the function parameters. The characters used in NCI function signatures are listed in Table 9-5.

*Table 9-5. Function signature letters*

| Character | Register set | C type |
| --- | --- | --- |
| v | - | void (no return value) |
| c | I | char |
| s | I | short |
| i | I | int |
| l | I | long |
| f | N | float |
| d | N | double |
| t | S | char * |
| p | P | void * (or other pointer) |
| I | - | Parrot_Interp * interpreter |
| C | - | A callback function pointer |
| D | - | A callback function pointer |

Table 9-5. Function signature letters (continued)

| Character | Register set | C type |
|-----------|--------------|--------|
| Y | P | The subroutine into which C or D calls |
| Z | P | The argument for Y |

For more information on callback functions, read the documentation in *docs/pdds/pdd16_native_call.pod* and *docs/pmc/struct.pod*.

# Closures

A closure is a subroutine that retains values from the lexical scope where it was defined, even when it's called from an entirely different scope. The closure shown here is equivalent to this Perl 5 code snippet:

```
#   sub foo {
#       my ($n) = @_;
#       sub {$n += shift}
#   }
#   my $closure = foo(10);
#   print &$closure(3), "\n";
#   print &$closure(20), "\n";

# call _foo
newsub P16, .Sub, _foo   # new subroutine object at address _foo
new P17, .PerlInt        # value for $n
set P17, 10              # we use local vars from P16 ...
set P0, P16              # the subroutine
set P5, P17              # first argument
pushtopp                 # save registers
invokecc                 # call foo
poptopp                  # restore registers
set P18, P5              # the returned closure

# call _closure
new P19, .PerlInt        # argument to closure
set P19, 3
set P0, P18              # the closure
set P5, P19              # one argument
pushtopp                 # save registers
invokecc                 # call closure(3)
poptopp
print P5                 # prints 13
print "\n"

# call _closure
set P19, 20              # and again
set P5, P19
set P0, P18
pushtopp
```

```
    invokecc                # call closure(20)
    poptopp
    print P5                # prints 33
    print "\n"
    end

_foo:
    new_pad 0               # push a new pad
    store_lex -1, "$n", P5  # store $n
    newsub P5, .Closure, _closure
                            # P5 has the lexical "$n" in the pad
    invoke P1               # return

_closure:
    find_lex P16, "$n"      # invoking the closure pushes the lexical pad
                            # of the closure on the pad stack
    add P16, P5             # $n += shift
    set P5, P16             # set return value
    invoke P1               # return
```

That's quite a lot of PASM code for such a little bit of Perl 5 code, but anonymous subroutines and closures hide a lot of magic under that simple interface. The core of this example is that when the new subroutine is created in _foo with:

```
newsub P5, .Closure, _closure
```

it inherits and stores the current lexical scratchpad—the topmost scratchpad on the pad stack at the time. Later, when _closure is invoked from the main body of code, the stored pad is automatically pushed onto the pad stack. So, all the lexical variables that were available when _closure was defined are available when it's called.

## Coroutines

As we mentioned in Chapter 8, coroutines are subroutines that can suspend themselves and return control to the caller—and then pick up where they left off the next time they're called, as if they never left.

In PASM, coroutines are subroutine-like objects:

```
newsub P0, .Coroutine, _co_entry
```

The Coroutine object has its own user stack, register frame stacks, control stack, and pad stack. The pad stack is inherited from the caller. The coroutine's control stack has the caller's control stack prepended, but is still distinct. When the coroutine invokes itself, it returns to the caller and restores the caller's context (basically swapping all stacks). The next time the coroutine is invoked, it continues to execute from the point at which it previously returned:

```
new_pad 0                # push a new lexical pad on stack
new P0, .PerlInt         # save one variable in it
set P0, 10
store_lex -1, "var", P0

newsub P0, .Coroutine, _cor
                         # make a new coroutine object
saveall                  # preserve environment
invoke                   # invoke the coroutine
restoreall
print "back\n"
saveall
invoke                   # invoke coroutine again
restoreall
print "done\n"
pop_pad
end

_cor:
    find_lex P1, "var"   # inherited pad from caller
    print "in cor "
    print P1
    print "\n"
    inc P1               # var++
    saveall
    invoke               # yield( )
    restoreall
    print "again "
    branch _cor          # next invocation of the coroutine
```

This prints out the result:

```
in cor 10
back
again in cor 11
done
```

The invoke inside the coroutine is commonly referred to as *yield*. The coroutine never ends. When it reaches the bottom, it branches back up to _cor and executes until it hits invoke again.

The interesting part about this example is that the coroutine yields in the same way that a subroutine is called. This means that the coroutine has to preserve its own register values. This example uses saveall but it could have only stored the registers the coroutine actually used. Saving off the registers like this works because coroutines have their own register frame stacks.

# Continuations

A continuation is a subroutine that gets a complete copy of the caller's context, including its own copy of the call stack. Invoking a continuation starts or restarts it at the entry point:

```
new P1, .PerlInt
set P1, 5

newsub P0, .Continuation, _con
_con:
  print "in cont "
  print P1
  print "\n"
  dec P1
  unless P1, done
  invoke                     # P0
done:
  print "done\n"
  end
```

This prints:

```
in cont 5
in cont 4
in cont 3
in cont 2
in cont 1
done
```

# Evaluating a Code String

This isn't really a subroutine operation, but it does produce a code object that can be invoked. In this case, it's a bytecode segment object.

The first step is to get an assembler or compiler for the target language:

```
compreg P1, "PASM"
```

Within the Parrot interpreter there are currently three registered languages: PASM, PIR, and PASM1. The first two are for Parrot assembly language and Parrot intermediate represention code. The third is for evaluating single statements in PASM. Parrot automatically adds an end opcode at the end of PASM1 strings before they're compiled.

This example places a bytecode segment object into the destination register P0 and then invokes it with invoke:

```
compreg P1, "PASM1"          # get compiler
set S1, "in eval\n"
compile P0, P1, "print S1"
invoke                       # eval code P0
```

```
print "back again\n"
end
```

You can register a compiler or assembler for any language inside the Parrot core and use it to compile and invoke code from that language. These compilers may be written in PASM or reside in shared libraries.

```
compreg "MyLanguage", P10
```

In this example the compreg opcode registers the subroutine-like object P10 as a compiler for the language "MyLanguage". See *examples/compilers* and *examples/japh/japh16.pasm* for an external compiler in a shared library.

# Exceptions and Exception Handlers

Exceptions provide a way of calling a piece of code outside the normal flow of control. They are mainly used for error reporting or cleanup tasks, but sometimes exceptions are just a funny way to branch from one code location to another one. The design and implementation of exceptions in Parrot isn't complete yet, but this section will give you an idea where we're headed.

Exceptions are objects that hold all the information needed to handle the exception: the error message, the severity and type of the error, etc. The class of an exception object indicates the kind of exception it is.

Exception handlers are derived from continuations. They are ordinary subroutines that follow the Parrot-calling conventions, but are never explicitly called from within user code. User code pushes an exception handler onto the control stack with the set_eh opcode. The system calls the installed exception handler only when an exception is thrown (perhaps because of code that does division by zero or attempts to retrieve a global that wasn't stored.)

```
newsub P20, .Exception_Handler, _handler
set_eh P20              # push handler on control stack
null P10               # set register to null
find_global P10, "none"  # may throw exception
clear_eh               # pop the handler off the stack
...

_handler:              # if not, execution continues here
    is_null P10, not_found   # test P10
    ...
```

This example creates a new exception handler subroutine with the newsub opcode and installs it on the control stack with the set_eh opcode. It sets the P10 register to a null value (so it can be checked later) and attempts to retrieve the global variable named none. If the global variable is found, the next statement (clear_eh) pops the exception handler off the control stack and normal execution continues. If the find_global call doesn't find none, it throws an exception by pushing an exception object onto the control stack. When Parrot sees that it has an exception, it pops it off the control stack and calls the exception handler _handler.

The first exception handler in the control stack sees every exception thrown. The handler has to examine the exception object and decide whether it can handle it (or discard it) or whether it should rethrow the exception to pass it along to an exception handler deeper in the stack. The rethrow opcode is only valid in exception handlers. It pushes the exception object back onto the control stack so Parrot knows to search for the next exception handler in the stack. The process continues until some exception handler deals with the exception and returns normally, or until there are no more exception handlers on the control stack. When the system finds no installed exception handlers it defaults to a final action, which normally means it prints an appropriate message and terminates the program.

When the system installs an exception handler, it creates a return continuation with a snapshot of the current interpreter context. If the exception handler just returns (that is, if the exception is cleanly caught) the return continuation restores the control stack back to its state when the exception handler was called, cleaning up the exception handler and any other changes that were made in the process of handling the exception.

Exceptions thrown by standard Parrot opcodes (like the one thrown by find_global above or by the throw opcode) are always resumable, so when the exception handler function returns normally it continues execution at the opcode immediately after the one that threw the exception. Other exceptions at the run-loop level are also generally resumable.

```
new P10, Exception          # create new Exception object
set P10["_message"], "I die" # set message attribute
throw P10                    # throw it
```

Exceptions are designed to work with the Parrot-calling conventions. Since the return addresses of bsr subroutine calls and exception handlers are both pushed onto the control stack, it's generally a bad idea to combine the two.

# Events

An event is a notification that something has happened: a timer expired, an I/O operation finished, a thread sent a message to another thread, or the user pressed Ctrl-C to interrupt program execution.

What all of these events have in common is that they arrive asynchronously. It's generally not safe to interrupt program flow at an arbitrary point and continue at a different position, so the event is placed in the interpreter's task queue. The run-loop code regularly checks whether an event needs to be handled. Event handlers may be an internal piece of code or a user-defined event handler subroutine.

Events are still experimental in Parrot, so the implementation and design is subject to change.

# Timers

Timer objects are the replacement for Perl 5's alarm handlers. They are also a significant improvement. Timers can fire once or repeatedly, and multiple timers can run independently. The precision of a timer is limited by the operating system on which Parrot runs, but it is always more fine-grained then a whole second. The final syntax isn't yet fixed, so please consult the documentation for examples.

# Signals

Signal handling is related to events. When Parrot gets a signal it needs to handle from the operating system, it converts that signal into an event and broadcasts it to all running threads. Each thread independently decides if it's interested in this signal and, if so, how to respond to it.

```
    newsub P20, .Exception_Handler, _handler
    set_eh P20                   # establish signal handler
    print "send SIGINT:\n"
    sleep 2                      # press ^C after you saw start
    print "no SIGINT\n"
    end
_handler:
    .include "signal.pasm"       # get signal definitions
    print "caught "
    set I0, P5["_type"]          # if _type is negative, the ...
    neg I0, I0                   # ... negated type is the signal
    ne I0, .SIGINT, nok
    print "SIGINT\n"
nok:
    end
```

This example creates a signal handler and pushes it on to the control stack. It then prompts the user to send a SIGINT from the shell (this is usually Ctrl-C, but it varies in different shells), and waits for two seconds. If the user doesn't send a SIGINT in two seconds, the example just prints "no SIGINT" and ends. If the user does send a SIGINT, the signal handler catches it, prints out "caught SIGINT" and ends.*

# Threads

Threads allow multiple pieces of code to run in parallel. This is useful when you have multiple physical CPUs to share the load of running individual threads. With a single processor, threads still provide the feeling of parallelism, but without any improvement in execution time. Even worse, sometimes using threads on a single processor will actually slow down your program.

Still, many algorithms can be expressed more easily in terms of parallel running pieces of code and many applications profit from taking advantage of multiple CPUs. Threads can vastly simplify asynchronous programs like internet servers: a thread splits off, waits for some I/O to happen, handles it, and relinquishes the processor again when it's done.

Parrot compiles in thread support by default (at least, if the platform provides some kind of support for it). Unlike Perl 5, compiling with threading support doesn't impose any execution time penalty for a non-threaded program. Like exceptions and events, threads are still under development, so you can expect significant changes in the near future.

As outlined in the previous chapter, Parrot implements three different threading models. The following example uses the third model, which takes advantage of shared data. It uses a TQueue (thread-safe queue) object to synchronize the two parallel running threads. This is only a simple example to illustrate threads, not a typical usage of threads (no one really wants to spawn two threads just to print out a simple string).

```
find_global P5, "_th1"          # locate thread function
new P2, .ParrotThread           # create a new thread
find_method P0, P2, "thread3"   # a shared thread's entry
new P7, .TQueue                 # create a Queue object
new P8, .PerlInt                # and a PerlInt
push P7, P8                     # push the PerlInt onto queue
new P6, .PerlString            # create new string
set P6, "Js nte artHce\n"
set I3, 3                       # thread function gets 3 args
invoke                          # _th1.run(P5,P6,P7)
new P2, .ParrotThread           # same for a second thread
find_global P5, "_th2"
```

* Currently, only Linux installs a SIGINT sigaction handler, so this example won't work on other platforms.

```
    set P6, "utaohrPro akr"           # set string to 2nd thread's
    invoke                            # ... data, run 2nd thread too
    end                               # Parrot joins both

.pcc_sub _th1:                        # 1st thread function
w1: sleep 0.001                       # wait a bit and schedule
    defined I1, P7                    # check if queue entry is ...
    unless I1, w1                     # ... defined, yes: it's ours
    set S5, P6                        # get string param
    substr S0, S5, I0, 1              # extract next char
    print S0                          # and print it
    inc I0                            # increment char pointer
    shift P8, P7                      # pull item off from queue
    if S0, w1                         # then wait again, if todo
    invoke P1                         # done with string

.pcc_sub _th2:                        # 2nd thread function
w2: sleep 0.001
    defined I1, P7                    # if queue entry is defined
    if I1, w2                         # then wait
    set S5, P6
    substr S0, S5, I0, 1              # if not print next char
    print S0
    inc I0
    new P8, .PerlInt                  # and put a defined entry
    push P7, P8                       # onto the queue so that
    if S0, w2                         # the other thread will run
    invoke P1                         # done with string
```

This example creates a ParrotThread object and calls its thread3 method,
passing three arguments: a PMC for the _th1 subroutine in P5, a string argument in P6, and a TQueue object in P7 containing a single integer. Remember
from the earlier section "Parrot calling conventions" that registers 5–15 hold
the arguments for a subroutine or method call, and I3 stores the number of
arguments. The thread object is passed in P2.

This call to the thread3 method spawns a new thread to run the _th1 subroutine. The main body of the code then creates a second ParrotThread
object in P2, stores a different subroutine in P5, sets P6 to a new string value,
and then calls the thread3 method again, passing it the same TQueue object as
the first thread. This method call spawns a second thread. The main body of
code then ends, leaving the two threads to do the work.

At this point the two threads have already started running. The first thread
(_th1) starts off by sleeping for .001 seconds. It then checks if the TQueue
object contains a value. Since it contains a value when the thread is first
called, it goes ahead and runs the body of the subroutine. The first thing this
does is pull one character off a copy of the string parameter using substr
and print the character. It then increments the current position (I0) in the

string, shifts the element off the TQueue, and loops back to the w1 label and sleeps. Since the queue doesn't have any elements now, the subroutine keeps sleeping.

Meanwhile, the second thread (_th2) also starts off by sleeping for .001 seconds. It checks if the shared TQueue object contains a defined value but unlike the first thread it only continues sleeping if the queue does contain a value. Since the queue contains a value when the second thread is first called, the subroutine loops back to the w2 label and continues sleeping. It keeps sleeping until the first thread shifts the integer off the queue, then runs the body of the subroutine. The body pulls one character off a copy of the string parameter using substr, prints the character, and increments the current position in the string. It then creates a new PerlInt, pushes it onto the shared queue, and loops back to the w2 label again to sleep. The queue has an element now, so the second thread keeps sleeping, but the first thread runs through its loop again.

The two threads alternate like this, printing a character and marking the queue so the next thread can run, until there are no more characters in either string. At the end, each subroutine invokes the return continuation in P1 which terminates the thread. The interpreter waits for all threads to terminate in the cleanup phase after the end in the main body of code.

The final printed result (as you might have guessed) is:

```
Just another Parrot Hacker
```

The syntax for threads isn't carved in stone and the implementation still isn't finished but as this example shows, threads are working now and already useful.

Several methods are useful when working with threads. The join method belongs to the ParrotThread class. When it's called on a ParrotThread object, the calling code waits until the thread terminates.

```
new P2, .ParrotThread    # create a new thread
set I5, P2               # get thread ID

find_method P0, P2, "join" # get the join method...
invoke                   # ...and join (wait for) the thread
set P16, P5              # the return result of the thread
```

kill and detach are interpreter methods, so you have to grab the current interpreter object before you can look up the method object:

```
set I5, P2               # get thread ID of thread P2
getinterp P3             # get this interpreter object
find_method P0, P3, "kill" # get kill method
invoke                   # kill thread with ID I5
```

```
find_method P0, P3, "detach"
invoke                      # detach thread with ID I5
```

By the time you read this, some of these combinations of statements and much of the threading syntax above may be reduced to a simpler set of opcodes.

# Loading Bytecode

In addition to running Parrot bytecode on the command line, you can also load precompiled bytecode directly into your PASM source file. The load_bytecode opcode takes a single argument: the name of the bytecode file to load. So, if you create a file named *file.pasm* containing a single subroutine:

```
# file.pasm
.pcc_sub _sub2:              # .pcc_sub stores a global sub
    print "in sub2\n"
    invoke P1
```

and compile it to bytecode using the -o command-line switch:

```
$ parrot -o file.pbc file.pasm
```

You can then load the compiled bytecode into *main.pasm* and directly call the subroutine defined in *file.pasm*:

```
# main.pasm
_main:
    load_bytecode "file.pbc"    # compiled file.pasm
    find_global P0, "_sub2"
    invokecc
    end
```

The load_bytecode opcode also works with source files, as long as Parrot has a compiler registered for that type of file:

```
# main2.pasm
_main:
    load_bytecode "file.pasm"  # PASM source code
    find_global P0, "_sub2"
    invokecc
    end
```

Subroutines marked with @LOAD run as soon as they're loaded (before load_bytecode returns), rather than waiting to be called. A subroutine marked with @MAIN will always run first, no matter what name you give it or where you define it in the file.

```
# file3.pasm
.pcc_sub @LOAD _entry:       # mark the sub as to be run
    print "file3\n"
    invoke P1                # return
```

```
# main3.pasm
_first:                       # first is never invoked
  print "never\n"
  invoke P1

.pcc_sub @MAIN _main:         # because _main is marked as the
  print "main\n"              # MAIN entry of program execution
  load_bytecode "file3.pasm"
  print "back\n"
  end
```

This example uses both @LOAD and @MAIN. Because the _main subroutine is defined with @MAIN it will execute first even though another subroutine comes before it in the file. _main prints a line, loads the PASM source file, and then prints another line. Because _entry in *file3.pasm* is marked with @LOAD it runs before load_bytecode returns, so the final output is:

```
main
file3
back
```

# Classes and Objects

Parrot's object system is a new addition in version 0.1.0. Objects still have some rough edges (for example, you currently can't add new attributes to a class after it has been instantiated), but they're functional for basic use.

This section revolves around one complete example that defines a class, instantiates objects, and uses them. The whole example is included at the end of the section.

## Class Declaration

The newclass opcode defines a new class. It takes two arguments, the name of the class and the destination register for the class PMC. All classes (and objects) inherit from the ParrotClass PMC, which is the core of the Parrot object system.

```
newclass P1, "Foo"
```

To instantiate a new object of a particular class, you first look up the integer value for the class type with the find_type opcode, then create an object of that type with the new opcode:

```
find_type I1, "Foo"
new P3, I1
```

The new opcode also checks to see if the class defines a method named "__init" and calls it if it exists.

# Attributes

The `addattribute` opcode creates a slot in the class for an attribute (some-times known as an *instance variable*) and associates it with a name:

```
addattribute P1, ".i"           # Foo.i
```

This chunk of code from the __init method looks up the position of the first attribute, creates a `PerlInt` PMC, and stores it as the first attribute:

```
classoffset I0, P2, "Foo"    # first "Foo" attribute of object P2
new P6, .PerlInt             # create storage for the attribute
setattribute P2, I0, P6      # store the first attribute
```

The `classoffset` opcodetakes a PMC containing an object and the name of its class, and returns an integer index for the position of the first attribute. The `setattribute` opcode uses the integer index to store a PMC value in one of the object's attribute slots. This example initializes the first attribute. The second attribute would be at I0 + 1, the third attribute at I0 + 2, etc.:

```
inc I0
setattribute P2, I0, P7      # store next attribute
...
```

There is also support for named parameters with fully qualified parameter names (although this is a little bit slower than getting the class offset once and accessing several attributes by index):

```
new P6, .PerlInt
setattribute P2, "Foo\x0.i", P6   # store the attribute
```

You use the same integer index to retrieve the value of an attribute. The `getattribute` opcode takes an object and an index as arguments and returns the attribute PMC at that position:

```
classoffset I0, P2, "Foo"    # first "Foo" attribute of object P2
getattribute P10, P2, I0     # indexed get of attribute
```

or:

```
getattribute P10, P2, "Foo\x0.i"  # named get
```

To set the value of an attribute PMC, first retrieve it with `getattribute` and then assign to the returned PMC. Because PMC registers are only pointers to values, you don't need to store the PMC again after you modify its value:

```
getattribute P10, P2, I0
set P10, I5
```

# Methods

Methods in PASM are just subroutines installed in the namespace of the class. You define a method with the `.pcc_sub` directive before the label:

```
.pcc_sub _half:
  classoffset I0, P2, "Foo"
  getattribute P10, P2, I0
  set I5, P10                # get value
  div I5, 2
  invoke P1
```

This routine returns half of the value of the first attribute of the object. Method calls use the Parrot-calling conventions so they always pass the *invocant* object (often called *self*) in P2. Invoking the return continuation in P1 returns control to the caller.

The `.pcc_sub` directive automatically stores the subroutine as a global in the current namespace. The `.namespace` directive sets the current namespace:

```
.namespace [ "Foo" ]
```

If no namespace is set, or if the namespace is explicitly set to an empty string, then the subroutine is stored in the outermost namespace.

The `callmethodcc` opcode makes a method call. It follows the Parrot-calling conventions, so it expects to find the invocant object in P2, the method object in P0, etc. It adds one bit of magic, though. If you pass the name of the method in S0, `callmethodcc` looks up that method name in the invocant object and stores the method object in P0 for you:

```
set S0, "_half"        # set method name
set P2, P3             # the object
savetop                # preserve registers
callmethodcc           # create return continuation, call
restoretop
print I5               # result of method call
print "\n"
```

The `callmethodcc` opcode also generates a return continuation and stores it in P1. The `callmethod` opcode doesn't generate a return continuation, but is otherwise identical to `callmethodcc`. Just like ordinary subroutine calls, you have to preserve and restore any registers you want to keep after a method call. Whether you store individual registers, register frames, or half register frames is up to you.

## Overriding vtable functions

Every object inherits a default set of *vtable* functions from the `ParrotObject` PMC, but you can also override them with your own methods. The vtable functions have predefined names that start with a double underscore (__). The following code defines a method named __init in the Foo class that initializes the first attribute of the object with an integer:

```
.pcc_sub __init:
    classoffset I0, P2, "Foo"    # lookup first attribute position
    new P6, .PerlInt             # create storage for the attribute
    setattribute P2, I0, P6      # store the first attribute
    invoke P1                    # return
```

Ordinary methods have to be called explicitly, but the vtable functions are called implicitly in many different contexts. Parrot saves and restores registers for you in these calls. The __init method is called whenever a new object is constructed:

```
find_type I1, "Foo"
new P3, I1              # call __init if it exists
```

A few other vtable functions in the complete code example for this section are __set_integer_native, __add, __get_integer, __get_string, and __increment. The set opcode calls Foo's __set_integer_native vtable function when its destination register is a Foo object and the source register is a native integer:

```
set P3, 30             # call __set_integer_native method
```

The add opcode calls Foo's __add vtable function when it adds two Foo objects:

```
new P4, I1             # same with P4
set P4, 12
new P5, I1             # create a new store for add

add P5, P3, P4         # __add method
```

The inc opcode calls Foo's __increment vtable function when it increments a Foo object:

```
inc P3                 # __increment
```

Foo's __get_integer and __get_string vtable functions are called whenever an integer or string value is retrieved from a Foo object:

```
set I10, P5            # __get_integer
...
print P5               # calls __get_string, prints 'fortytwo'
```

## Inheritance

The subclass opcode creates a new class that inherits methods and attributes from another class. It takes three arguments: the destination register for the new class, a register containing the parent class, and the name of the new class:

```
subclass P3, P1, "Bar"
```

For multiple inheritance, the addparent opcode adds additional parents to a subclass.

```
newclass P4, "Baz"
addparent P3, P4
```

To override an inherited method, define a method with the same name in the namespace of the subclass. The following code overrides Bar's __increment method so it decrements the value instead of incrementing it:

```
.namespace [ "Bar" ]

.pcc_sub __increment:
    classoffset I0, P2, "Foo"    # get Foo's attribute slot offset
    getattribute P10, P2, I0     # get the first Foo attribute
    dec P10                      # the evil line
    invoke P1
```

Notice that the attribute inherited from Foo can be looked up only with the Foo class name, not the Bar class name. This preserves the distinction between attributes that belong to the class and inherited attributes.

Object creation for subclasses is the same as for ordinary classes:

```
find_type I1, "Bar"
new P5, I1
```

Calls to inherited methods are just like calls to methods defined in the class:

```
set P5, 42          # inherited __set_integer_native
inc P5              # overridden __increment
print P5            # prints 41 as Bar's __increment decrements
print "\n"

set S0, "_half"     # set method name
set P2, P5          # the object
savetop             # preserve registers
callmethodcc        # create return continuation, call
restoretop
print I5
print "\n"
```

# Additional Object Opcodes

The isa and can opcodes are also useful when working with objects. isa checks whether an object belongs to or inherits from a particular class. can checks whether an object has a particular method. Both return a true or false value.

```
isa I0, P3, "Foo"          # 1
isa I0, P3, "Bar"          # 1
can I0, P3, "__add"          # 1
```

## Complete Example

```
newclass P1, "Foo"
addattribute P1, "$.i"       # Foo.i

find_type I1, "Foo"
new P3, I1                   # call __init if it exists
set P3, 30                   # call __set_integer_native method

new P4, I1                   # same with P4
set P4, 12
new P5, I1                   # create a new LHS for add

add P5, P3, P4               # __add method
set I10, P5                  # __get_integer
print I10
print "\n"
print P5                     # calls __get_string prints 'fortytwo'
print "\n"

inc P3                       # __increment
add P5, P3, P4
print P5                     # calls __get_string prints '43'
print "\n"

subclass P3, P1, "Bar"

find_type I1, "Bar"
new P3, I1

set P3, 100
new P4, I1
set P4, 200
new P5, I1

add P5, P3, P4
print P5                     # prints 300
print "\n"

set P5, 42
print P5                     # prints 'fortytwo'
print "\n"

inc P5
print P5                     # prints 41 as Bar's
print "\n"                   # __increment decrements
```

```
    set S0, "_half"              # set method name
    set P2, P3                   # the object
    savetop                      # preserve registers
    callmethodcc                 # create return continuation, call
    restoretop
    print I5                     # prints 50
    print "\n"

    end

    .namespace [ "Foo" ]

.pcc_sub __init:
    classoffset I0, P2, "Foo"    # lookup first attribute position
    new P6, .PerlInt             # create a store for the attribute
    setattribute P2, I0, P6      # store the first attribute
    invoke P1                    # return

.pcc_sub __set_integer_native:
    classoffset I0, P2, "Foo"
    getattribute P10, P2, I0
    set P10, I5                  # assign passed in value
    invoke P1

.pcc_sub __get_integer:
    classoffset I0, P2, "Foo"
    getattribute P10, P2, I0
    set I5, P10                  # return value
    invoke P1

.pcc_sub __get_string:
    classoffset I0, P2, "Foo"
    getattribute P10, P2, I0
    set I5, P10
    set S5, P10                  # get stringified value
    ne I5, 42, ok
    set S5, "fortytwo"           # or return modified one
ok:
    invoke P1

.pcc_sub __increment:
    classoffset I0, P2, "Foo"
    getattribute P10, P2, I0     # as with all aggregates, this
    inc P10                      # has reference semantics - no
    invoke P1                    # setattribute needed

.pcc_sub __add:
    classoffset I0, P2, "Foo"
    getattribute P10, P2, I0     # object
    getattribute P11, P5, I0     # argument
    getattribute P12, P6, I0     # destination
    add P12, P10, P11
    invoke P1
```

```
.pcc_sub _half:                    # I5 = _half(self)
    classoffset I0, P2, "Foo"
    getattribute P10, P2, I0
    set I5, P10                    # get value
    div I5, 2
    invoke P1


    .namespace [ "Bar" ]

.pcc_sub __increment:
    classoffset I0, P2, "Foo"      # get Foo's attribute slot offset
    getattribute P10, P2, I0       # get the first Foo attribute
    dec P10                        # the evil line
    invoke P1


    # end of object example
```

This example prints out:

```
42
fortytwo
43
300
fortytwo
41
50
```

# Writing Tests

As we mentioned earlier, contributions to the Parrot project are welcome. Contributing tests is a good place to start. You don't have to understand the code behind a PASM opcode (or IMCC instruction) to test it, you only have to understand what it's supposed to do. If you're working on some code and it doesn't do what the documentation advertises, you can isolate the problem in a test or series of tests and send them to the bug tracking system. There's a good chance the problem will be fixed before the next release. Writing tests makes it a lot easier for the developer to know when they've solved your problem—it's solved when your tests pass. It also prevents that problem from appearing again, because it's checked every time anyone runs make test. As you move along, you'll want to write tests for every bug you fix or new feature you add.

The Perl 5 testing framework is at the core of Parrot tests, particularly *Test::Builder*. Parrot's *Parrot::Test* module is an interface to *Test::Builder* and implements the extra features needed for testing Parrot, like the fact that PASM code has to be compiled to bytecode before it runs.

The main Parrot tests are in the top-level *t/* directory of the Parrot source tree. *t/op* contains tests for basic opcodes and *t/pmc* has tests for PMCs. The names of the test files indicate the functionality tested, like *integer.t*, *number.t*, and *string.t*. Part of the *make test* target is the command *perl t/harness*, which runs all the *.t* files in the subdirectories under */t*. You can run individual test files by passing their names to the *harness* script:

```
$ perl t/harness t/op/string.t t/op/integer.t
```

Here's a simple example that tests the set opcode with integer registers, taken from *t/op/integer.t*:

```
output_is(<<CODE, <<OUTPUT, "set_i");
    set     I0, 42
    set     I1, I0
    print   I1
    print   "\\n"
    end
CODE
42
OUTPUT
```

The code here sets integer register I0 to the value 42, sets I1 to the value of I0, and then prints the value in I1. The test passes if the value printed was 42 and fails otherwise.

The output_is subroutine takes three strings: the code to run, the expected output, and a description of the test. The first two strings can be quite long, so the convention is to use Perl 5 here-documents. If you look into the code section, you'll see that the literal \n has to be escaped as \\n. Many tests use the noninterpolating (<<"CODE") form of here-documents to avoid that problem. The description can be any text. In this case, it's the fully qualified name of the set opcode for integer registers, but it could have been "set a native integer register."

If you look up at the top of *integer.t*, you'll see the line:

```
use Parrot::Test tests => 38;
```

(although the actual number may be larger if more tests have been added since this book went to press).

The use line for the *Parrot::Test* module imports a set of subroutines into the test file, including output_is. The end of the line gives the number of tests contained in the file.

The output_is subroutine looks for an exact match between the expected result and the actual output of the code. When the test result can't be compared exactly, you want output_like instead. It takes a Perl 5 regular expression for the expected output:

```
output_like(<<'CODE', <<'OUTPUT', "testing for text match");
...
CODE
/^Output is some \d+ number\n$/
OUTPUT
```

*Parrot::Test* also exports output_isnt, which tests that the actual output of the code *doesn't* match a particular value.

There are a few guidelines to follow when you're writing a test for a new opcode or checking that an existing opcode has full test coverage. Tests should cover the opcode's standard operation, corner cases, and illegal input. The first tests should always cover the basic functionality of an opcode. Further tests can cover more complex operations and the interactions between opcodes. If the test program is complex or obscure, it helps to add comments. Tests should be self-contained to make it easy to identify where and why a test is failing.

# CHAPTER 10

# Parrot Intermediate Representation

The Parrot intermediate representation (PIR) is an overlay on top of Parrot assembly language, designed to make the developer's life easier. It has many high-level features that ease the pain of working with PASM code, but it still isn't a high-level language.

Internally, Parrot works a little differently with PASM and PIR source code, so each has different restrictions. The default is to run in a mixed mode that allows PASM code to combine with the higher-level syntax unique to PIR.

A file with a *.pasm* extension is treated as pure PASM code, as is any file run with the -a command-line option. This mode is mainly used for running pure PASM tests. Parrot treats any extension other than *.pasm* as a PIR file. For historical reasons, files containing PIR code generally have a *.imc* extension, but this is gradually shifting to a *.pir* extension.

The documentation in *imcc/docs/* or *docs/* and the test suite in *imcc/t* are good starting points for digging deeper into the PIR syntax and functionality.

## Statements

The syntax of statements in PIR is much more flexible than PASM. All PASM opcodes are valid PIR code, so the basic syntax is the same. The statement delimiter is a newline \n, so each statement has to be on its own line. Any statement can start with a label. Comments are marked by a hash sign (#) and PIR allows POD blocks.

But unlike PASM, PIR has some higher-level constructs, including symbol operators:

```
I1 = 5                    # set I1, 5
```

named variables:

```
count = 5
```

and complex statements built from multiple keywords and symbol operators:

```
if I1 <= 5 goto LABEL      # le I1, 5, LABEL
```

We'll get into these in more detail as we go.

# Variables and Constants

Literal constants in PIR are the same as constants in PASM. Integers and floating-point numbers are numeric literals and strings are enclosed in quotes. PIR strings use the same escape sequences as PASM.

## Parrot Registers

PIR code has a variety of ways to store values while you work with them. The most basic way is to use Parrot registers directly. PASM register names always start with a single character that shows whether it is an integer, numeric, string, or PMC register, and end with the number of the register (between 0 and 31):

```
S0 = "Hello, Polly.\n"
print S0
```

When you work directly with Parrot registers, you can only have 32 registers of any one type at a time.* If you have more than that, you have to start shuffling stored values on and off the user stack. You also have to manually track when it's safe to reuse a register. This kind of low-level access to the Parrot registers is handy when you need it, but it's pretty unwieldy for large sections of code.

## Temporary Registers

PIR provides an easier way to work with Parrot registers. The temporary register variables are named like the PASM registers—with a single character for the type of register and a number—but they start with a $ character:

```
set $S42, "Hello, Polly.\n"
print $S42
```

The most obvious difference between Parrot registers and temporary register variables is that you have an unlimited number of temporaries. Parrot

---

* Only 31 for PMC registers, because P31 is reserved for spilling.

handles register allocation for you. It keeps track of how long a value in a Parrot register is needed and when that register can be reused.

The previous example used the $S42 temporary. When the code is compiled, that temporary is allocated to a Parrot register. As long as the temporary is needed, it is stored in the same register. When it's no longer needed, the Parrot register is re-allocated to some other value. This example uses two temporary string registers:

```
$S42 = "Hello, "
print $S42
$S43 = "Polly.\n"
print $S43
```

Since they don't overlap, Parrot allocates both to the S16 register. If you change the order a little so both temporaries are needed at the same time, they're allocated to different registers:

```
$S42 = "Hello, "  # allocated to S17
$S43 = "Polly.\n" # allocated to S16
print $S42
print $S43
```

In this case, $S42 is allocated to S17 and $S43 is allocated to S16.

Parrot allocates temporary variables* to Parrot registers in ascending order of their score. The score is based on a number of factors related to variable usage. Variables used in a loop have a higher score than variables outside a loop. Variables that span a long range have a lower score than ones that are used only briefly.

If you want to peek behind the curtain and see how Parrot is allocating registers, you can run it with the -d switch to turn on debugging output:

```
$ parrot -d1000 hello.imc
```

If *hello.imc* contains this code from the previous example (wrapped in a subroutine definition so it will compile):

```
.sub _main
  $S42 = "Hello, "  # allocated to S17
  $S43 = "Polly.\n" # allocated to S16
  print $S42
  print $S43
  end
.end
```

it produces this output:

```
code_size(ops) 11  oldsize 0
0 set_s_sc 17 1 set S17, "Hello, "
```

---

* As well as named variables, which we talk about next.

```
3 set_s_sc 16 0 set S16, "Polly.\n"
6 print_s 17      print S17
8 print_s 16      print S16
10 end  end
Hello, Polly.
```

That's probably a lot more information than you wanted if you're just start-ing out. You can also generate a PASM file with the -o switch and have a look at how the PIR code translates:

```
$ parrot -o hello.pasm hello.imc
```

or just:

```
$ parrot -o- hello.imc
```

to see resulting PASM on *stdout*.

You'll find more details on these options and many others in "Parrot Com-mand-Line Options" in Chapter 11.

# Named Variables

Named variables can be used anywhere a register or temporary register is used. They're declared with the `.local` statement or the equivalent `.sym` statement, which require a variable type and a name:

```
.local string hello
set hello, "Hello, Polly.\n"
print hello
```

This snippet defines a string variable named `hello`, assigns it the value "Hello, Polly.\n", and then prints the value.

The valid types are `int`, `float`, `string`, and `pmc` or any Parrot class name (like `PerlInt` or `PerlString`). It should come as no surprise that these are the same divisions as Parrot's four register types. Named variables are valid from the point of their definition to the end of the compilation unit.

The name of a variable must be a valid PIR identifier. It can contain letters, digits, and underscores, but the first character has to be a letter or under-score. Identifiers don't have any limit on length yet, but it's a safe bet they will before the production release. Parrot opcode names are normally not allowed as variable names, though there are some exceptions.

## PMC variables

PMC registers and variables act much like any integer, floating-point num-ber, or string register or variable, but you have to instantiate a new PMC object before you use it. The `new` instruction creates a new PMC. Unlike PASM, PIR doesn't use a dot in front of the class name.

```
P0 = new PerlString        # same as new P0, .PerlString
P0 = "Hello, Polly.\n"
print P0
```

This example creates a `PerlString` object, stores it in the PMC register `P0`, assigns the value "Hello, Polly.\n" to it, and prints it. The syntax is exactly the same for temporary register variables:

```
$P4711 = new PerlString
$P4711 = "Hello, Polly.\n"
print $P4711
```

With named variables, the type passed to the `.local` directive is either the generic pmc or a type compatible with the type passed to new:

```
.local PerlString hello        # or .local pmc hello
hello = new PerlString
hello = "Hello, Polly.\n"
print hello
```

# Named Constants

The `.const` directive declares a named constant. It's very similar to `.local` and requires a type and a name. The value of a constant must be assigned in the declaration statement. As with named variables, named constants are visible only within the compilation unit where they're declared. This example declares a named string constant `hello` and prints the value:

```
.const string hello = "Hello, Polly.\n"
print hello
```

Named constants function in all the same places as literal constants, but have to be declared beforehand:

```
.const int the_answer = 42        # integer constant
.const string mouse = "Mouse"     # string constant
.const float pi = 3.14159         # floating point constant
```

# Register Spilling

As we mentioned earlier, Parrot allocates all temporary register variables and named variables to Parrot registers. When Parrot runs out of registers to allocate, it has to store some of the variables elsewhere. This is known as *spilling*. Parrot spills the variables with the lowest score and stores them in a `PerlArray` object while they aren't used, then restores them to a register the next time they're needed. Consider an example that creates 33 integer variables, all containing values that are used later:

```
set $I1, 1
set $I2, 2
...
```

```
set $I33, 33
...
print $I1
print $I2
...
print $I33
```

Parrot allocates the 32 available integer registers to variables with a higher score and spills the variables with a lower score. In this example, it picks $I1 and $I2. Behind the scenes, Parrot generates code to store the values:

```
new P31, .PerlArray
...
set I0, 1          # I0 allocated to $I1
set P31[0], I0     # spill $I1
set I0, 2          # I0 reallocated to $I2
set P31[1], I0     # spill $I2
```

It creates a PerlArray object and stores it in register P31.* The set instruction is the last time $I1 is used for a while, so immediately after that, Parrot stores its value in the spill array and frees up I0 to be reallocated.

Just before $I1 and $I2 are accessed to be printed, Parrot generates code to fetch the values from the spill array:

```
...
set I0, P31[0]     # fetch $I1
print I0
```

You cannot rely on any particular register assignment for temporary variables or named variables. The register allocator does follow a set of precedence rules for allocation, but these rules may change. Also, if two variables have the same score, Parrot may assign registers based on the hashed value of the variable name. Parrot randomizes the seed to the hash function to guarantee you never get a consistent order.

# Symbol Operators

You probably noticed the = assignment operator in some of the earlier examples:

```
$S2000 = "Hello, Polly.\n"
print $S2000
```

Standing alone, it's the same as the PASM set opcode. In fact, if you run *parrot* in bytecode debugging mode (as in "Assembler Options" in Chapter 11), you'll see it really is just a set opcode underneath.

---

* P31 is reserved for register spilling in PIR code, so generally it shouldn't be accessed directly.

PIR has many other symbol operators: arithmetic, concatenation, comparison, bitwise, and logical. Many of these combine with assignment to produce the equivalent of a PASM opcode:

```
.local int sum
sum = $I42 + 5
print sum
print "\n"
```

The statement sum = $I42 + 5 translates to something like add I16, I17, 5.

PIR also provides +=, -=, >>=, ... that map to the two-argument forms like add I16, I17.

Many PASM opcodes that return a single value also have an alternate syntax in PIR with the assignment operator:

```
$I0 = length str            # length $I0, str
$I0 = isa PerlInt, "scalar" # isa $I0, PerlInt, "scalar"
$I0 = exists hash["key"]     # exists $I0, hash["key"]
$N0 = sin $N1
$N0 = atan $N1, $N2
$S0 = repeat "x", 20
$P0 = newclass "Foo"
...
```

A complete list of PIR operators is available in Chapter 11. We'll discuss the comparison operators in "Flow Control" later in this chapter.

# Labels

Like PASM, any line can start with a label definition like LABEL:, but label definitions can also stand on their own line.

PIR code has both local and global labels. Global labels start with an underscore. The name of a global label has to be unique, since it can be called at any point in the program. Local labels start with a letter. A local label is accessible only in the compilation unit where it's defined. (We'll discuss compilation units in the next section.)The name has to be unique there, but it can be reused in a different compilation unit.

```
branch L1   # local label
bsr    _L2  # global label
```

Labels are most often used in branching instructions and in subroutine calls.

## Compilation Units

Compilation units in PIR are roughly equivalent to the subroutines or methods of a high-level language. Though they will be explained in more detail later, we introduce them here because all code in a PIR source file must be defined in a compilation unit. The simplest syntax for a PIR compilation unit starts with the .sub directive and ends with the .end directive:

```
.sub _main
    print "Hello, Polly.\n"
    end
.end
```

This example defines a compilation unit named _main that prints a string. The name is actually a global label for this piece of code. If you generate a PASM file from the PIR code (see the "Temporary Registers" section earlier in this chapter), you'll see that the name translates to an ordinary label:

```
_main:
        print "Hello, Polly.\n"
        end
```

The first compilation unit in a file is normally executed first, but as in PASM, you can flag any compilation unit as the first one to execute with the @MAIN marker. The convention is to name the first compilation unit _main, but the name isn't critical.

```
.sub _first
    print "Polly want a cracker?\n"
    end
.end

.sub _main @MAIN
    print "Hello, Polly.\n"
    end
.end
```

This code prints out "Hello, Polly." but not "Polly want a cracker?".

The "Subroutines" section later in this chapter goes into much more detail about compilation units and their uses.

# Flow Control

As in PASM, flow control in PIR is done entirely with conditional and unconditional branches. This may seem simplistic, but remember that PIR is a thin overlay on the assembly language of a virtual processor. For the average assembly language, jumps are the fundamental unit of flow control.

Any PASM branch instruction is valid, but PIR has some high-level constructs of its own. The most basic is the unconditional branch: goto.

```
.sub _main
    goto L1
    print "never printed"
```

```
L1:
    print "after branch\n"
    end
.end
```

The first print statement never runs because the goto always skips over it to the label L1.

The conditional branches combine if or unless with goto:

```
.sub _main
    $I0 = 42
    if $I0 goto L1
    print "never printed"
L1: print "after branch\n"
    end
.end
```

In this example, the goto branches to the label L1 only if the value stored in $I0 is true. The unless statement is quite similar, but branches when the tested value is false. An undefined value, 0, or an empty string are all false values. The if ... goto statement translates directly to the PASM if, and unless translates to the PASM unless.

The comparison operators (<, <=, ==, !=, >, >=) can combine with if ... goto. These branch when the comparison is true:

```
.sub _main
    $I0 = 42
    $I1 = 43
    if $I0 < $I1 goto L1
    print "never printed"
L1:
    print "after branch\n"
    end
.end
```

This example compares $I0 to $I1 and branches to the label L1 if $I0 is less than $I1. The if $I0 < $I1 goto L1 statement translates directly to the PASM lt branch operation.

The rest of the comparison operators are summarized in "PIR Instructions" in Chapter 11.

PIR has no special loop constructs. A combination of conditional and unconditional branches handle iteration:

```
.sub _main
    $I0 = 1          # product
    $I1 = 5          # counter

REDO:                # start of loop
    $I0 = $I0 * $I1
```

```
      dec $I1
      if $I1 > 0 goto REDO  # end of loop

      print $I0
      print "\n"
      end
.end
```

This example calculates the factorial 5!. Each time through the loop it multiplies $I0 by the current value of the counter $I1, decrements the counter, and then branches to the start of the loop. The loop ends when $I1 counts down to 0 so that the if doesn't branch to REDO. This is a *do while*–style loop with the condition test at the end, so the code always runs the first time through.

For a *while*-style loop with the condition test at the start, use a conditional branch together with an unconditional branch:

```
.sub _main
      $I0 = 1              # product
      $I1 = 5              # counter

REDO:                      # start of loop
      if $I1 <= 0 goto LAST
      $I0 = $I0 * $I1
      dec $I1
      goto REDO
LAST:                      # end of loop

      print $I0
      print "\n"
      end
.end
```

This example tests the counter $I1 at the start of the loop. At the end of the loop, it unconditionally branches back to the start of the loop and tests the condition again. The loop ends when the counter $I1 reaches 0 and the if branches to the LAST label. If the counter isn't a positive number before the loop, the loop never executes.

Any high-level flow control construct can be built from conditional and unconditional branches.

# Subroutines

A calculation like "the factorial of a number" may be used several times in a large program. Subroutines allow this kind of functionality to be abstracted into a unit. It's a benefit for code reuse and maintainability. Even though PASM is just an assembly language for a virtual processor, it has a number of features to support high-level subroutine calls. PIR offers a smoother interface to those features.

PIR provides several different sets of syntax for subroutine calls. This is a language designed to implement other languages, and every language does subroutine calls a little differently. What's needed is a set of building blocks and tools, not a single prepackaged solution.

## Parrot-Calling Conventions

As we mentioned in Chapter 9, Parrot defines a set of calling conventions for externally visible subroutines. In these calls, the caller is responsible for preserving its own registers, and arguments and return values are passed in a predefined set of Parrot registers. The calling conventions use the Continuation Passing Style to pass control to subroutines and back again.

The fact that the Parrot-calling conventions are clearly defined also makes it possible to provide some higher-level syntax for it. Manually setting up all the registers for each subroutine call isn't just tedious, it's also prone to bugs introduced by typos. PIR's simplest subroutine call syntax looks much like a high-level language. This example calls the subroutine _fact with two arguments and assigns the result to $I0:

```
($I0, $I1) = _fact(count, product)
```

This simple statement hides a great deal of complexity. It generates a subroutine object and stores it in P0. It assigns the arguments to the appropriate registers, assigning any extra arguments to the overflow array in P3. It also sets up the other registers to mark whether this is a prototyped call and how many arguments it passes of each type. It calls the subroutine stored in P0, saving and restoring the top half of all register frames around the call. And finally, it assigns the result of the call to the given temporary register variables (for a single result you can drop the parentheses). If the one line above were written out in basic PIR it would be something like:

```
newsub P0, .Sub, _fact
I5 = count
I6 = product
I0 = 1
I1 = 2
I2 = 0
I3 = 0
I4 = 0
savetop
invokecc
restoretop
$I0 = I5
$I1 = I6
```

The PIR code actually generates an invokecc opcode internally. It not only invokes the subroutine in P0, but also generates a new return continuation in P1. The called subroutine invokes this continuation to return control to the caller.

The single-line subroutine call is incredibly convenient, but it isn't always flexible enough. So PIR also has a more verbose call syntax that is still more convenient than manual calls. This example pulls the subroutine _fact out of the global symbol table and calls it:

```
find_global $P1, "_fact"

.pcc_begin prototyped
  .arg count
  .arg product
  .pcc_call $P1
  .result $I0
.pcc_end
```

The whole chunk of code from .pcc_begin to .pcc_end acts as a single unit. The .pcc_begin directive can be marked as prototyped or unprototyped, which corresponds to the flag I0 in the calling conventions. The .arg directive sets up arguments to the call. The .pcc_call directive saves top register frames, calls the subroutine, and restores the top registers. The .result directive retrieves return values from the call.

In addition to syntax for subroutine calls, PIR provides syntax for subroutine definitions. The .param directive pulls parameters out of the registers and creates local named variables for them:

```
.param int c
```

The .pcc_begin_return and .pcc_end_return directives act as a unit much like the .pcc_begin and .pcc_end directives:

```
.pcc_begin_return
  .return p
.pcc_end_return
```

The .return directive sets up return values in the appropriate registers. After all the registers are set up, the unit invokes the return continuation in P1 to return control to the caller.

Here's a complete code example that reimplements the factorial code from the previous section as an independent subroutine. The subroutine _fact is a separate compilation unit, assembled and processed after the _main function. Parrot resolves global symbols like the _fact label between different units.

```
# factorial.imc
.sub _main
```

```
      .local int count
      .local int product
      count = 5
      product = 1

      $I0 = _fact(count, product)

      print $I0
      print "\n"
      end
.end

.sub _fact
   .param int c
   .param int p

loop:
   if c <= 1 goto fin
   p = c * p
   dec c
   branch loop
fin:
   .pcc_begin_return
   .return p
   .pcc_end_return
.end
```

This example defines two local named variables, count and product, and assigns them the values 1 and 5. It calls the _fact subroutine passing the two variables as arguments. In the call, the two arguments are assigned to consecutive integer registers, because they're stored in typed integer variables. The _fact subroutine uses .param and the return directives for retrieving parameters and returning results. The final printed result is 120.

You may want to generate a PASM source file for this example to look at the details of how the PIR code translates to PASM:

```
$ parrot -o- factorial.imc
```

## Stack-Based Subroutine Calls

The Parrot-calling conventions are PIR's default for subroutine calls, but it does also provide some syntax for stack-based calls. Stack-based calls are fast, so they're sometimes useful for purely internal code. To turn on support for stack-based calls, you have to set the fastcall pragma:

```
.pragma fastcall     # turn on stack calling conventions
```

The standard calling conventions are set by the prototyped pragma. You'll rarely need to explicitly set prototyped since it's on by default. You can mix stack-based subroutines and prototyped subroutines in the same file, but you really shouldn't—stack-based calls interfere with exception handling, and don't interoperate well with prototyped calls.

When the fastcall pragma is on, the .arg, .result, .param, and .return directives push and pop on the user stack instead of setting registers. Internally, they are just the PASM save and restore opcodes. Because of this, you have to reverse the order of your arguments. You push the final argument onto the user stack first, because it'll be the last parameter popped off the stack on the other end:

```
.arg y          # save args in reverse order
.arg x
call _foo       # (r, s) = _foo(x,y)
.result r
.result s       # restore results in order
```

Multiple return values are also passed in reverse order for the same reason. Often the first parameter or result in a stack-based call will be a count of values passed in, especially when the number of arguments can vary.

Another significant difference is that instead of the single-line call or a .pcc_ call, stack-based calls use the call instruction. This is the same as PASM's bsr opcode. It branches to a subroutine label and pushes the current location onto the control stack so it can return to it later.

This example reworks the factorial code above to use stack-based calls:

```
.pragma fastcall        # turn on stack calling conventions
.sub _main
    .local int count
    .local int product
    count = 5
    product = 1
    .arg product        # second argument
    .arg count          # first argument
    call _fact          # call the subroutine
    .result $I0         # retrieve the result
    print $I0
    print "\n"
    end
.end

.sub _fact
    saveall             # save caller's registers
    .param int c        # retrieve the parameters
    .param int p

loop:
    if c <= 1 goto fin
    p = c * p
    dec c
    branch loop
```

```
fin:
    .return p          # return the result
    restoreall         # restore caller's registers
    ret                # back to the caller
.end
```

The _main compilation unit sets up two local variables and pushes them onto the user stack in reverse order using the .arg directive. It then calls _fact with the call instruction. The .result directive pops a return value off the user stack.

This example uses the callee save convention, so the first statement in the _fact subroutine is saveall. (See "Callee saves" in Chapter 9 for more details on this convention.) With callee save in PIR, Parrot can ignore the subroutine's register usage when it allocates registers for the calling routine.

The .param directive pops a function parameter off the user stack as an integer and creates a new named local variable for the parameter. Parrot does check the types of the parameters to make sure they match what the caller passes to the subroutine, but the amount of parameters isn't checked, so both sides have to agree on the argument count.

The .return statement at the end pushes the final value of p onto the user stack, so .result can retrieve it after the subroutine ends. restoreall restores the caller's register values, and ret pops the top item off the control stack—in this case, the location of the call to _fact—and returns to it.

## Compilation Units Revisited

The previous example could have been written using simple labels instead of separate compilation units:

```
.sub _main
    $I1 = 5            # counter
    call fact          # same as bsr fact
    print $I0
    print "\n"
    $I1 = 6            # counter
    call fact
    print $I0
    print "\n"
    end

fact:
    $I0 = 1            # product
L1:
    $I0 = $I0 * $I1
    dec $I1
    if $I1 > 0 goto L1
    ret
.end
```

The unit of code from the fact label definition to ret is a reusable routine. There are several problems with this simple approach. First, the caller has to know to pass the argument to fact in $I1 and to get the result from $I0. Second, neither the caller nor the function itself preserves any registers. This is fine for the example above, because very few registers are used. But if this same bit of code were buried deeply in a math routine package, you would have a high risk of clobbering the caller's register values.

Another disadvantage of this approach is that _main and fact share the same compilation unit, so they're parsed and processed as one piece of code. When Parrot does register allocation, it calculates the data flow graph (DFG) of all symbols,* looks at their usage, calculates the interference between all possible combinations of symbols, and then assigns a Parrot register to each symbol. This process is less efficient for large compilation units than it is for several small ones, so it's better to keep the code modular. The optimizer will decide whether register usage is light enough to merit combining two compilation units, or even inlining the entire function.

## A Short Note on the Optimizer

The optimizer isn't powerful enough to inline small subroutines yet. But it already does other simpler optimizations. You may recall that the PASM opcode mul (multiply) has a two-argument version that uses the same register for the destination and the first operand. When Parrot comes across a PIR statement like $I0 = $I0 * $I1, it can optimize it to the two-argument mul $I0, $I1 instead of mul $I0, $I0, $I1. This kind of optimization is enabled by the -O1 command-line option.

So you don't need to worry about finding the shortest PASM instruction, calculating constant terms, or avoiding branches to speed up your code. Parrot does it already.

## PASM Subroutines

PIR code can include pure PASM compilation units. These are wrapped in the .emit and .eom directives instead of .sub and .end. The .emit directive doesn't take a name, it only acts as a container for the PASM code. These primitive compilation units can be useful for grouping PASM functions or

---

* The operation to calculate the DFG has a quadratic cost or better. It depends on $n\_lines * n\_symbols$.

function wrappers. Subroutine entry labels inside .emit blocks have to be global labels:

```
.emit
_substr:
    ...
    ret
_grep:
    ...
    ret
.eom
```

# Methods

PIR provides syntax to simplify writing methods and method calls. These calls follow the Parrot-calling conventions. The basic syntax is similar to the single-line subroutine call above, but instead of a subroutine label name it takes a variable for the invocant PMC and a string with the name of the method:

```
object."methodname"(arguments)
```

The invocant can be a variable or register, and the method name can be a literal string, string variable, or method object register. This tiny bit of code sets up all the registers for a method call and makes the call, saving and restoring the top half of the register frames around the call. Internally, the call is a callmethodcc opcode, so it also generates a return continuation.

This example defines two methods in the Foo class. It calls one from the main body of the subroutine and the other from within the first method:

```
.sub _main
  .local pmc class
  .local pmc obj
  newclass class, "Foo"      # create a new Foo class
  find_type $I0, "Foo"       # find its dynamic type number
  new obj, $I0               # instantiate a Foo object
  obj."_meth"()              # call obj."_meth" which is actually
  print "done\n"             # "_meth" in the "Foo" namespace
  end
.end


.namespace [ "Foo" ]         # start namespace "Foo"


.sub _meth method            # define Foo::_meth global
  print "in meth\n"
  $S0 = "_other_meth"        # method names can be in a register too
  self.$S0()                 # self is the invocant
.end
```

```
.sub _other_meth method      # define another method
    print "in other_meth\n"  # as above Parrot provides a return
.end                         # statement
```

Each method call looks up the method name in the symbol table of the object's class. Like .pcc_sub in PASM, .sub makes a symbol table entry for the subroutine in the current namespace.

When a .sub is declared as a method, it automatically creates a local variable named self and assigns it the object passed in P2.

You can pass multiple arguments to a method and retrieve multiple return values just like a single-line subroutine call:

```
(res1, res2) = obj."method"(arg1, arg2)
```

CHAPTER 11

# Parrot Reference

This chapter contains a condensed list of PASM opcodes, PIR directives and instructions, and Parrot command-line options, sorted alphabetically for easy reference. Any PASM opcode is valid in PIR code, so if you're looking up PIR syntax, you should check "PASM Opcodes," "PIR Directives," and "PIR Instructions."

## PASM Opcodes

For complete details on each opcode and the latest changes, read the documentation in *docs/ops/*, or look at all the *.ops* files in the *ops/* directory.

We've followed a few conventions. DEST is always the register where the result of the operation is stored. Sometimes the original value of DEST is one of the source values. VAL indicates that the actual value might be a literal integer, float, or string, or a register containing an integer, float, string, or PMC. See the *.ops* files for the combinations allowed with a particular operation.

### abs

```
abs DEST
abs DEST, VAL
```

Return the absolute value of a number. If VAL is left out, DEST gets the absolute value of itself.

*Arguments: IR or NR or IR, I or IR, N or NR, I or NR, N*

## acos

acos *DEST*, *VAL*

The arc cosine of *VAL* in radians.

*Arguments: NR, N or NR, I*

## add

add *DEST*, *VAL*
add *DEST*, *VAL*, *VAL*

Add two values and return the sum. If only one *VAL*, add *VAL* to *DEST*.

*Arguments: IR, I or NR, I or NR, N or P, I or P, N or P, P or IR, I, I or NR, N, I or NR, N, N or P, P, I or P, P, N or P, P, P*

## addattribute

addattribute *CLASS*, *ATTR*

Add the attribute name *ATTR* to class *CLASS*.

*Arguments: P, S*

## addparent

addparent *CLASS1*, *CLASS2*

Add class *CLASS2* to the list of parent classes for *CLASS1*.

*Arguments: P, P*

## and

and *DEST*, *VAL1*, *VAL2*

Logical AND. Return *VAL1* if it's false. Otherwise, return *VAL2*.

*Arguments: IR, I, I or P, P, P*

## asec

asec *DEST*, *VAL*

The arc secant of *VAL* in radians.

*Arguments: NR, I or NR, N*

## asin

asin `DEST, VAL`

The arc sine of `VAL` in radians.

*Arguments: NR, I or NR, N*

## assign

assign `DEST, VAL`

Assign a value to a PMC.

*Arguments: SR, S or P, I or P, N or P, S or P, P*

## atan

atan `DEST, VAL`
atan `DEST, VAL1, VAL2`

The arc tangent of `VAL1/VAL2` in radians (sign significant). If `VAL2` is omitted, then just the arc tangent of `VAL`.

*Arguments: NR, I or NR, N or NR, I, I or NR, I, N or NR, N, I or NR, N, N*

## band

band `DEST, VAL`
band `DEST, VAL, VAL`

Bitwise AND on two values. If only one `VAL`, bitwise AND on `DEST` and `VAL`.

*Arguments: IR, I or P, I or P, P or IR, I, I or P, P, I or P, P, P*

## bands

bands `DEST, VAL`
bands `DEST, VAL, VAL`

Bitwise AND on two strings. If only one `VAL`, bitwise AND on `DEST` and `VAL`.

*Arguments: SR, S or P, S or P, P or SR, S, S or P, P, S or P, P, P*

## bnot

bnot `DEST, VAL`

Bitwise NOT on `VAL`.

*Arguments: IR, I or P, P*

# bnots

bnots *DEST, VAL*

Bitwise NOT on string *VAL*.

*Arguments: SR, S or P, P*

# bor

bor *DEST, VAL, VAL*

Bitwise OR on two values. If only one *VAL*, bitwise OR on *DEST* and *VAL*.

*Arguments: IR, I or P, I or P, P or IR, I, I or P, P, I or P, P, P*

# bors

bor *DEST, VAL, VAL*

Bitwise OR on two strings. If only one *VAL*, bitwise OR on *DEST* and *VAL*.

*Arguments: SR, S or P, S or P, P or SR, S, S or P, P, S or P, P, P*

# bounds

bounds *INT*

Toggle bytecode bounds checking in the interpreter (0 for off, any other value for on).

*Argument: I*

# branch

branch *LABEL*

Branch to a label. The label is calculated as a relative offset.

*Argument: I*

# branch_cs

branch_cs *FIXUP_ENTRY*

Intersegment branch to the location of the given fixup table entry.

*Argument: S*

# bsr

bsr *LABEL*

Branch to a label, like branch, but also push the current location onto the call stack so ret can return to it.

*Argument: I*

# bxor

bxor *DEST, VAL*
bxor *DEST, VAL, VAL*

Bitwise XOR on two values. If only one *VAL*, bitwise XOR on *DEST* and *VAL*.

*Arguments: IR, I or P, I or P, P or IR, I, I or P, P, I or P, P, P*

# bxors

bxors *DEST, VAL*
bxors *DEST, VAL, VAL*

Bitwise XOR on two strings. If only one *VAL*, bitwise XOR on *DEST* and *VAL*.

*Arguments: SR, S or P, S or P, P or SR, S, S or P, P, S or P, P, P*

# callmethod

callmethod
callmethod *METHODNAME*

Call the method named *METHODNAME* on the object stored in P2 according to the Parrot-Calling Conventions. If no method name, pull the name from S0.

*Argument: S*

# callmethodcc

callmethodcc
callmethodcc *METHODNAME*

Call the method named *METHODNAME* on the object stored in P2 according to the Parrot-Calling Conventions. If no method name, pull the name from S0. Also create a return continuation and store it in P1.

*Argument: S*

## can

can *DEST, OBJECT, METHODNAME*

Return a true value if *OBJECT can* do the *METHODNAME* method. Otherwise, return a false value.

*Arguments: IR, P, S*

## ceil

ceil *DEST*
ceil *DEST, VAL*

Set *DEST* to the smallest integral value less than or equal to *VAL* (if present) or itself (if not).

*Arguments: NR or IR, N or NR, N*

## checkevents

checkevents

Check the interpreter's task queue for unhandled events and run the associated event handlers.

## chopn

chopn *DEST, VAL1*
chopn *DEST, VAL1, VAL2*

Remove *VAL2* number of characters from string *VAL1*. If no *VAL2*, remove *VAL* number of characters from string *DEST*.

*Arguments: SR, I or SR, S, I*

## chr

chr *DEST, INT*

Return the character represented by the given number.

*Arguments: SR, I*

## class

class *CLASS, OBJECT*

Return the *CLASS* of the given *OBJECT*.

*Arguments: P, P*

## classname

```
classname NAME, CLASS
```

Set *NAME* to the classname of *CLASS*.

*Arguments: SR, P*

## classoffset

```
classoffset OFFSET, OBJECT, CLASS
```

Return the offset *OFFSET* of the first attribute of class *CLASS* in object *OBJECT*.

*Arguments: IR, P, S*

## clear_eh

```
clear_eh
```

Clear the most recent exception handler.

See also: set_eh, throw

## clearX

```
cleari
clearn
clearp
clears
```

Clear all registers of the given type ("i" = integer, "n" = float, "p" = PMC, "s" = string). Integer and float registers clear to zero; string and PMC registers clear to NULL.

## clone

```
clone DEST, VAL
```

Clone (deep copy) a string or PMC and return the result.

*Arguments: SR, S or P, P*

# close

close *DEST*

Close the filehandle in the given register.

*Argument: P*

# cmod

cmod *DEST, VAL1, VAL2*

C's built-in mod operator.

*Arguments: IR, I, I or NR, N, N or P, P, I or P, P, N or P, P, P*

See also: mod

# cmp

cmp *DEST, VAL1, VAL2*

Set *DEST* to 1 if *VAL1* is greater then *VAL2*, to −1 if it's less then *VAL2* or to 0 if both are equal. If *VAL1* and *VAL2* are both PMCs, then the type of comparison depends on *VAL1*.

*Arguments: IR, I, I or IR, N, N or IR, S, S or IR, P, I or IR, P, N IR, P, S or IR, P, P*

# cmp_num

cmp_num *DEST, VAL1, VAL2*

Like cmp, but forces numeric comparison.

*Arguments: IR, P, P*

# cmp_str

cmp_str *DEST, VAL1, VAL2*

Like cmp, but forces string comparison.

*Arguments: IR, P, P*

# collect

collect

Trigger a garbage collection (GC) run.

## collectoff

```
collectoff
```

Disable garbage collection runs (nestable).

## collecton

```
collecton
```

Reenable garbage collection runs.

## compile

```
compile DEST, COMPILER, SOURCE
```

Compile a string of source code with a given compiler PMC and store the result.
*Arguments: P, P, S*

## compreg

```
compreg DEST, TYPE
```

Return a compiler PMC for a particular type of source code.
*Arguments: P, S*

```
compreg TYPE, SUB
```

Register *SUB* as a compiler for language *TYPE*.
*Arguments: S, P*

## concat

```
concat DEST, VAL
concat DEST, VAL, VAL
```

Concatenate two strings. If only one *VAL*, concatenate *VAL* onto *DEST*.

*Arguments: SR, S or SR, S, S or P, P, S or P, P, P*

## conv_*

```
conv_i1     DEST, VAL
conv_i1_ovf DEST, VAL
```

Convert value to integer or number of given type i1, i2, i4, i8, u1, u2, u4, r4, r8. i corresponds to a signed integer, u to an unsigned integer, and r to a float; the number indicates the size (in bytes) of the type. The variants with _ovf throw an exception if the conversion would overflow.

## cos

cos DEST, VAL

The cosine of VAL in radians.

*Arguments: NR, I or NR, N*

## cosh

cosh DEST, VAL

The hyperbolic cosine of VAL in radians.

*Arguments: NR, I or NR, N*

## debug

debug FLAG

Toggle debugging in the interpreter (0 for off; any other value for on).

*Arguments: I*

## dec

dec DEST

Decrement a value by 1.

*Arguments: I or N or P*

## decodelocaltime

decodelocaltime DEST, VAL

Set DEST to a new array which represents the decoded time of the given epoch-seconds value shifted to local time.

*Arguments: P, I*

# decodetime

decodetime *DEST, VAL*

Set *DEST* to a new array which represents the decoded time of the given epoch-seconds value.

*Arguments: P, I*

# defined

defined *DEST, PMC*
defined *DEST, PMC[KEY]*

Test a keyed PMC value for definedness. If no *KEY*, test a PMC for definedness.

*Arguments: IR, P*

# delete

delete *DEST[KEY]*

Delete a keyed value from an aggregate PMC.

Argument: P

# delprop

delprop *PMC, NAME*

Delete a named property from a PMC.

*Arguments: P, S*

See also: setprop, getprop

# depth

depth *DEST*

Return the depth of the user stack.

Argument: I

# deref

deref *DEST, REF*

Set *DEST* to the PMC that *REF* refers to.

*Arguments: P, P*

# die_hard

die_hard *LEVEL, ERROR*

Die at a given level of severity, and with the given error code.

*Arguments: I, I*

See also: exit

# div

div *DEST, VAL*
div *DEST, VAL1, VAL2*

Divide *VAL1* by *VAL2*. If *VAL2* is left out, divide *DEST* by *VAL*.

*Arguments: IR, I or NR, I or NR, N or P, I or P, N or P, P or IR, I, I or NR, N, I or NR, N, N or P, P, I or P, P, N or P, P, P*

# dlfunc

dlfunc *DEST, LIBRARY, SYMBOL, SIGNATURE*

Look up a symbol in a dynamic link library PMC and create a subroutine PMC for that symbol with the given signature.

*Arguments: P, P, S, S*

# dlvar

dlvar *DEST, LIBRARY, SYMBOL*

Look up a symbol in a dynamic link library PMC and create a PMC for that symbol.

*Arguments: P, P, S*

# does

does *DEST, OBJECT, VAL*

Return a true value if *OBJECT does* provide the interface *VAL*. Otherwise, return a false value.

*Arguments: I, P, S*

# downcase

downcase *DEST*
downcase *DEST, VAL*

Create a copy of the string in *VAL* with all characters converted to lowercase, and store it in *DEST*. If *VAL* is omitted, convert and replace the string in *DEST*.

*Arguments: S or S, S*

See also: upcase, titlecase

# end

end

End execution within the current code segment or halt the interpreter if in the main code segment.

# enternative

enternative

Run the run_native C function.

# entrytype

entrytype *DEST, INT*

Return the type of an entry on the user stack. *INT* specifies the position on the stack.

*Arguments: I, I*

# eq

eq *VAL, VAL, LABEL*

Jump to a label if the two values are equal.

*Arguments: I, I, IC or N, N, IC or S, S, IC or P, I, IC or P, N, IC or P, S, IC or P, P, IC*

# eq_addr

eq_addr *VAL1, VAL2, LABEL*

Jump to a label if *VAL1* and *VAL2* point to the same string or PMC. Note that this op compares the addresses of the two strings or PMCs, not simply their values.

*Arguments: S, S, IC or P, P, IC*

# eq_num

eq_num *VAL, VAL, LABEL*

Jump to a label if the two values are numerically equal.

*Arguments: P, P, IC*

# eq_str

eq_str *VAL, VAL, LABEL*

Jump to a label if the two strings are equal.

*Arguments: P, P, IC*

# err

err *DEST*
err *DEST, CODE*

Return the system error code to an integer destination or the system error message to a string destination. The two-argument version returns the system error message for a given code.

*Arguments: IR or SR or SR, I*

# errorsoff

errorsoff *VAL*

Turn off errors of type *VAL*.

*Argument: I*

# errorson

errorson *VAL*

Turn on errors of type *VAL*.

*Argument: I*

# exchange

exchange *REG, REG*

Exchange the contents of two registers.

*Arguments: IR, IR or NR, NR or SR, SR or P, P*

# exists

exists *DEST, PMC[KEY]*

Test a PMC key for existence.

*Arguments: IR, P*

# exit

exit *STATUS*

Exit the interpreter with a given *STATUS*. (For extended exit status, throw an exception with severity EXCEPT_exit.)

*Argument: I*

See also: throw, die_hard

# exp

exp *DEST, VAL*

Base of the natural logarithm, *e*, to the power of *VAL*.

*Arguments: NR, I or NR, N*

# exsec

exsec *DEST, VAL*

The exsecant of *VAL* in radians.

*Arguments: NR, N*

# fact

fact *DEST, INT*

Return the factorial of *INT*.

*Arguments: IR, I or NR, I*

# fdopen

fdopen *DEST, INT, MODE*

Get a ParrotIO object for handle *INT* with open mode *MODE*.

*Arguments: P, I, S*

# find_chartype

find_chartype *DEST, NAME*

Find the chartype named *NAME* and return its number in *DEST*.

*Arguments: IR, S*

# find_encoding

find_encoding *DEST, NAME*

Find the encoding named *NAME* and return its number in *DEST*.

*Arguments: IR, S*

# find_global

find_global *DEST, NAME*

Return a global variable with the given name.

*Arguments: P, S*

find_global *DEST, NAMESPACE, NAME*

Return a global variable with the given name from the given namespace.

*Arguments: P, S, S or P, P, S*

See also: store_global

# find_lex

find_lex *DEST, NAME*
find_lex *DEST, DEPTH, NAME*
find_lex *DEST, DEPTH, POSITION*

Return the lexical variable of the given name from a lexical scratchpad. If *DEPTH* is provided, return only a variable from the scratchpad at that depth. A find by position returns the variable at a particular position in the scratchpad.

*Arguments: P, S or P, I, S or P, I, I*

See also: store_lex

## find_method

find_method *DEST, PMC, NAME*

Look up a method by name in a PMC's vtable. Return a method PMC.

*Arguments: P, P, S*

## find_type

find_type *DEST, NAME*

Find the integer identifier for a PMC type or native Parrot datatype by name.

*Arguments: IR, S*

See also: typeof

## findclass

findclass *DEST, NAME*

Return 1 if the class *NAME* exists, and 0 otherwise.

*Arguments: IR, S*

See also: typeof

## floor

floor *DEST*
floor *DEST, VAL*

Return the largest integral value less than or equal to *VAL* (if present) or itself (if not).

*Arguments: NR or IR, N or NR, N*

## foldup

foldup *DEST*
foldup *DEST, SKIP*

Return a new array holding all passed subroutine parameters. *SKIP* defines an optional offset.

*Arguments: P or P, I*

# freeze

freeze *DEST, VAL*

Create a frozen image *DEST* from PMC *VAL*.

*Arguments: SR, P*

See also: thaw

# gc_debug

gc_debug *INT*

Toggle garbage collection debugging in the interpreter (0 for off, any other value for on).

*Argument: I*

# gcd

gcd *DEST, VAL, VAL*

Return the greatest common divisor of two values.

*Arguments: IR, I, I or IR, N, N*

# ge

ge *VAL1, VAL2, LABEL*

Jump to a label if *VAL1* is greater than or equal to *VAL2*.

*Arguments: I, I, IC or N, N, IC or S, S, IC or P, I, IC or P, N, IC or P, S, IC or P, P, IC*

# ge_num

ge_num *VAL1, VAL2, LABEL*

Jump to a label if *VAL1* is numerically greater than or equal to *VAL2*.

*Arguments: P, P, IC*

# ge_str

ge_str *VAL1, VAL2, LABEL*

Jump to a label if *VAL1* is stringwise greater than or equal to *VAL2*.

*Arguments: P, P, IC*

## get_addr

get_addr *DEST, SUB*

Get the absolute address of a subroutine PMC.

*Arguments: IR, P*

See also: set_addr

## getattribute

getattribute *DEST, OBJECT, OFFS*

Get a reference to attribute number *OFFS* from object *OBJECT*.

*Arguments: P, P, I*

See also: setattribute, classoffset

## getclass

getclass *DEST, NAME*

Return the class PMC of the given name.

*Arguments: P, S*

## getfd

getfd *DEST, PIO*

Return the file descriptor for the given ParrotIO object.

*Arguments: IR, P*

## getfile

getfile *DEST*

Return the name of the current file.

*Argument: SR*

## getinterp

getinterp *DEST*

Get a PMC representing the current interpreter.

*Argument: P*

# getline

getline *DEST*

Return the current line number.

*Argument: IR*

# getpackage

getpackage *DEST*

Return the current package name.

*Argument: SR*

# getprop

getprop *DEST, NAME, PMC*

Return the value of a named property on a PMC.

*Arguments: P, S, P*

See also: setprop, prophash

# getstd*

getstderr *DEST*
getstdin *DEST*
getstdout *DEST*

Get a ParrotIO object for the given standard handle.

*Argument: P*

# gmtime

gmtime *DEST, VAL*

Take the integer, which represents GMT epoch-seconds, and turn it into a formatted string.

*Arguments: SR, I*

See also: localtime

# gt

gt *VAL1, VAL2, LABEL*

Jump to a label if *VAL1* is greater than *VAL2*.

Arguments: I, I, IC or N, N, IC or S, S, IC or P, I, IC or P, N, IC or P, S, IC or P, P, IC

# gt_num

gt_num *VAL1, VAL2, LABEL*

Jump to a label if *VAL1* is numerically greater than *VAL2*.

Arguments: P, P, IC

# gt_str

gt_str *VAL1, VAL2, LABEL*

Jump to a label if *VAL1* is stringwise greater than *VAL2*.

Arguments: P, P, IC

# hav

hav *DEST, VAL*

The haversine of *VAL* in radians.

Arguments: NR, N

# if

if *CONDITION, LABEL*

Jump to a label if the condition is a true value.

Arguments: I, IC or N, IC or S, IC or P, IC

# inc

inc *DEST*

Increment a value by one.

Arguments: IR or NR or P

# index

index *DEST, STRING, SEARCH*
index *DEST, STRING, SEARCH, POS*

Return the position of the first occurrence of the string *SEARCH* in the string *STRING*, starting at the position *POS*. If the starting position is unspecified, start at the beginning of the string.

*Arguments: IR, S, S or IR, S, S, I*

# interpinfo

interpinfo *DEST, FLAG*

Return information about the interpreter. An integer flag selects which information to return, as listed in Table 11-1.

*Arguments: IR, I*

*Table 11-1. Interpinfo flags*

| Flag | Returns |
|------|---------|
| 1 | Allocated memory, in bytes |
| 2 | Number of DOD sweeps performed |
| 3 | Number of GC runs performed |
| 4 | Number of active PMCs |
| 5 | Number of active buffers |
| 6 | Number of allocated PMCs |
| 7 | Number of allocated buffers |
| 8 | Number of new PMC or buffer headers allocated since last DOD run |
| 9 | Number of memory blocks allocated since last GC run |
| 10 | Amount of memory copied during GC runs, in bytes |

# invoke

invoke
invoke *SUB*

Call a subroutine, coroutine, or continuation stored in a PMC. If no PMC register is specified, it calls the subroutine in P0 and uses the standard calling conventions. Otherwise, no calling convention is defined. Also yield from a coroutine.

*Argument: P*

## invokecc

```
invokecc
invokecc SUB
```

Call a subroutine like invoke, but also generate a return continuation in P1.

*Argument: P*

See also: updatecc

## isa

```
isa DEST, OBJECT, CLASS
```

Return a true value if *OBJECT* is a member of class *CLASS*, or of one of its subclasses. Otherwise, return a false value.

*Arguments: IR, P, S*

## isnull

```
isnull VAL, LABEL
```

Jump to *LABEL* if the given PMC is a NULL PMC.

*Arguments: P, IC*

## join

```
join DEST, DELIM, ARRAY
```

Create a new string by joining all elements from array with the given delimiter.

*Arguments: SR, S, P*

## jsr

```
jsr ADDRESS
```

Jump to an address, like jump, but also push the current location onto the call stack so ret can return to it.

*Argument: I*

## jump

jump *ADDRESS*

Jump to a specified absolute address.

*Argument: I*

See also: set_addr

## lcm

lcm *DEST, VAL, VAL*

Return the least common multiple of two values.

*Arguments: IR, I, I or NR, I, I*

## le

le *VAL1, VAL2, LABEL*

Jump to a label if *VAL1* is less than or equal to *VAL2*.

*Arguments: I, I, IC or N, N, IC or S, S, IC or P, I, IC or P, N, IC or P, S, IC or P, P, IC*

## le_num

le_num *VAL1, VAL2, LABEL*

Jump to a label if *VAL1* is numerically less than or equal to *VAL2*.

*Arguments: P, P, IC*

## le_str

le_str *VAL1, VAL2, LABEL*

Jump to a label if *VAL1* is stringwise less than or equal to *VAL2*.

*Arguments: P, P, IC*

## length

length *DEST, STRING*

Return the character length of a string.

*Arguments: IR, S*

# ln

ln *DEST, VAL*

The natural logarithm of *VAL*.

*Arguments: NR, I or NR, N*

# load_bytecode

load_bytecode *FILE*

Load Parrot bytecode from a file.

*Argument: S*

# loadlib

loadlib *DEST, LIBRARY*

Load a dynamic link library by name and store it in a PMC.

*Arguments: P, S*
See also: dlfunc

# localtime

localtime *DEST, VAL*

Take the integer, which represents GMT epoch-seconds, and turn it into a formatted string after adjusting to localtime.

*Arguments: SR, I*
See also: gmtime

# log10

log10 *DEST, VAL*

The base-10 logarithm of *VAL*.

*Arguments: NR, I or NR, N*

# log2

log2 *DEST, VAL*

The base-2 logarithm of *VAL*.

*Arguments: NR, I or NR, N*

# lookback

lookback *DEST, OFFSET*

Retrieve an entry from the user stack by position. A positive offset counts from the top of the stack; a negative offset counts from the bottom.

*Arguments: IR, I or NR, I or SR, I or P, I*

# lsr

lsr *DEST, BITS*
lsr *DEST, VAL, BITS*

Logically shift a value right by a given number of bits.

*Arguments: IR, I or IR, I, I*

# lt

lt *VAL1, VAL2, LABEL*

Jump to a label if *VAL1* is less than *VAL2*.

*Arguments: I, I, IC or N, N, IC or S, S, IC or P, I, IC or P, N, IC or P, S, IC or P, P, IC*

# lt_num

lt_num *VAL1, VAL2, LABEL*

Jump to a label if *VAL1* is numerically less than *VAL2*.

*Arguments: P, P, IC*

# lt_str

lt_str *VAL1, VAL2, LABEL*

Jump to a label if *VAL1* is stringwise less than *VAL2*.

*Arguments: P, P, IC*

# mmdvtfind

mmdvtfind *DEST, FUNC, LEFT, RIGHT*

Get the subroutine PMC for the multimethod vtable function *FUNC* for the two given PMC types.

*Arguments: P, I, I, I*

## mmdvtregister

mmdvtregister *FUNC, LEFT, RIGHT, SUB*

Register the subroutine *SUB* as the multimethod vtable function *FUNC* for the two given PMC types.

*Arguments: I, I, I, P*

## mod

mod *DEST, VAL*
mod *DEST, VAL1, VAL2*

Divide *VAL1* by *VAL2* and return the remainder. If *VAL2* is omitted, divide *DEST* by *VAL*. The operation is defined as:

x mod y = x - y * floor(x / y)

*Arguments: P, I or IR, I, I or NR, N, N or P, P, I or P, P, N*

See also: cmod

## mul

mul *DEST, VAL*
mul *DEST, VAL, VAL*

Multiply two values and return the result. If only one *VAL*, multiply *DEST* by *VAL*.

*Arguments: IR, I or NR, I or NR, N or P, I or P, N or P, P or IR, I, I or NR, N, I or NR, N, N or P, P, I or P, P, N or P, P, P*

## ne

ne *VAL, VAL, LABEL*

Jump to a label if the two values are not equal.

*Arguments: I, I, IC or N, N, IC or S, S, IC or P, I, IC or P, N, IC or P, S, IC or P, P, IC*

## ne_addr

ne_addr *VAL, VAL, LABEL*

Jump to a label if *VAL1* and *VAL2* do not point to the same string or PMC.

*Arguments: S, S, IC or P, P, IC*

## ne_num

ne_num *VAL, VAL, LABEL*

Jump to a label if the two values are numerically different.

*Arguments: P, P, IC*

## ne_str

ne_str *VAL, VAL, LABEL*

Jump to a label if the two strings are not equal.

*Arguments: P, P, IC*

## needs_destroy

needs_destroy *PMC*

Mark the PMC as requiring timely destruction.

*Argument: P*

See also: sweep

## neg

neg *DEST*
neg *DEST, VAL*

Return the negative of a number. If there is no *VAL*, *DEST* is the negative of itself.

*Arguments: IR or NR or P or IR, I or NR, N or P, P*

## new

new *DEST, TYPE*
new *DEST, TYPE, INITIALIZE*
new *DEST, TYPE, INITIALIZE, PROPS*

Create a new PMC of type *TYPE*. *INITIALIZE* is an array PMC containing initialization data for the new PMC. *PROPS* is a propety hash.

*Arguments: P, I or P, I, P or P, I, P, P*

new *DEST*
new *DEST, LENGTH*
new *DEST, LENGTH, ENCODING*
new *DEST, LENGTH, ENCODING, TYPE*

Allocate a new empty string with a given *LENGTH*, *ENCODING*, and *TYPE*.

*Arguments: SR or SR, I or SR, I, I or SR, I, I, I*

## new_callback

new_callback *DEST*, *SUB*, *DATA*, *SIG*

Create a callback stub *DEST* for a PASM subroutine *SUB* with user data *DATA* and function signature *SIG*.

*Arguments: P, P, P, S*

## new_pad

new_pad *DEPTH*
new_pad *DEST*, *DEPTH*

Create a new lexical scratchpad. If a destination PMC is provided, store the pad in the PMC. Otherwise, push it onto the pad stack. *DEPTH* specifies the static nesting depth for the pad (lower static depths are copied from the current static nesting).

*Arguments: I or P, I*

## newclass

newclass *DEST*, *NAME*

Create a new class with the given name.

*Arguments: P, S*

## newsub

newsub *DEST*, *CLASS*, *LABEL*

Generate a new subroutine object of the given *CLASS*, located at the given *LABEL*, and store the object in the destination PMC.

*Arguments: P, I, IC*

newsub *CLASS*, *RETCLASS*, *LABEL*, *RETADDR*

Generate a new subroutine object of the given *CLASS*, located at the given *LABEL*, and store the object in P0. Also generate a return continuation of class *RETCLASS* with the return address *RETADDR* and store it in P1.

*Arguments: I, I, IC, IC*

## noop

noop

Do nothing.

# not

not *DEST, VAL*

Logical NOT. True if *VAL* is false.

*Arguments: IR, I or P, P*

# null

null *DEST*

Set *DEST* (which must be a register) to 0, 0.0, or a NULL pointer, depending on its type.

*Arguments: IR or NR or SR or P*

# open

open *DEST, FILENAME*
open *DEST, FILENAME, MODE*

Open a file in the specified mode ("<", ">", etc.) and return a filehandle. Without the mode it defaults to read/write.

*Arguments: P, S, S or P, S*

# or

or *DEST, VAL1, VAL2*

Logical OR. Return *VAL1* if it's true. Otherwise, return *VAL2*.

*Arguments: IR, I, I or P, P, P*

# ord

ord *DEST, STRING*
ord *DEST, STRING, POS*

Return the character at position *POS* in *STRING*. If *POS* isn't specified, return the 0th character.

*Arguments: IR, S or IR, S, I*

# peek

peek *DEST*
peek *DEST, PIO*

Read the next byte from the given ParrotIO object or from stdin but don't remove it.
*Arguments: SR or SR, P*

# peek_pad

peek_pad *DEST*

Store the current lexical scope pad in a PMC.
*Argument: P*

# pin

pin *DEST*

Make the string in *DEST* immobile. This prevents the garbage collector from moving it to a different location in memory (which it otherwise may choose to do).
*Argument: SR*

See also: unpin

# pioctl

pioctl *DEST, PIO, VAL, VAL*

Perform an operation on an I/O object. This is a general purpose hook for setting various flags, modes, etc.
*Arguments: IR, P, I, I*

# pop

pop *DEST, PMC*

Pop the last entry off an aggregate PMC and return it.
*Arguments: IR, P or NR, P or SR, P or P, P*

# pop_pad

pop_pad

Pop the current lexical scope pad off the lexical scope stack.

See also: peek_pad

# popX

popi
popn
popp
pops

Restore all the registers of one type from the stack ("i" = integer, "n" = float, "p" = PMC, "s" = string).

popbottomi
popbottomn
popbottomp
popbottoms

Restore registers in the range 0..15.

poptopi
poptopn
poptopp
poptops

Restore registers in the range 16..31.

See also: pushX

# pow

pow *DEST, VAL1, VAL2*

Return *VAL1* raised to the power of *VAL2*.

*Arguments: NR, I, I or NR, I, N or NR, N, I or NR, N, N*

# print

print *VAL*
print *IO, VAL*

Print a value to an I/O object or file descriptor. If no *IO* is given, print the value to standard output.

*Arguments: I or N or S or P or P, I or P, N or P, S or P, P*

## printerr

printerr *VAL*

Print a value to stderr.

*Arguments: I or N or S or P*

## profile

profile *INT*

Toggle profiling in the interpreter (0 for off, any other value for on).

*Argument: I*

## prophash

prophash *DEST, PMC*

Return a hash containing all the properties from a PMC.

*Arguments: P, P*

See also: getprop

## push

push *PMC, VAL*

Push a value onto the end of an aggregate PMC.

*Arguments: P, I or P, N or P, S or P, P*

## push_pad

push_pad *PAD*

Push a scratchpad stored in a PMC onto the lexical scope stack.

*Argument: P*

## pushX

pushi
pushn
pushp
pushs

Save all the registers of one type to the stack ("i" = integer, "n" = float, "p" = PMC, "s" = string). Restore with popX.

```
pushbottomi
pushbottomn
pushbottomp
pushbottoms
```

Push registers 0..15.

```
pushtopi
pushtopn
pushtopp
pushtops
```

Push registers 16..31.

## read

read *DEST, BYTES*
read *DEST, IO, BYTES*

Read the specified number of bytes from a ParrotIO object. Read from stdin if no *IO* is provided.

*Arguments: SR, I or SR, P, I*

## readline

readline *DEST, IO*

Read a line from a ParrotIO object.

*Arguments: SR, P*

## register

register *PMC*

Register the given PMC in the interpreter's root set, so that it's visible during DOD.

*Argument: P*

See also: unregister

## removeparent

removeparent *CLASS1, CLASS2*

Remove *CLASS2* from class *CLASS1*'s list of parents.

*Arguments: P, P*

## repeat

repeat *DEST, VAL, REPEAT*

Repeat a string *REPEAT* number of times.

*Arguments: SR, S, I or P, P, I or P, P, P*

## restore

restore *DEST*

Restore a register from the user stack.

*Arguments: IR or NR or SR or P*

## restoreall

restoreall

Restore all the registers. Does a pop*X* for every type.

## restoretop

restoretop

Restore registers 16..31. Does a pop*X* for every type.

See also: savetop

## ret

ret

Pop a location off the top of the call stack, and go there. Often used with bsr and jsr.

## rethrow

rethrow *EXCEPTION*

Rethrow an exception. Only valid inside an exception handler.

*Argument: P*

See also: throw

## rotate_up

rotate_up *COUNT*

Rotate the top *COUNT* entries on the user stack. A positive number rotates up: the top entry becomes the *COUNT*th entry, and the others move up one (the second entry becomes first, the third becomes the second, etc.). A negative number rotates down: the *COUNT*th entry becomes the top, and the others move down (the first becomes second, etc.).

*Argument: I*

## runinterp

runinterp *INTERPRETER, OFFSET*

Use an interpreter stored in PMC to run code starting at a given offset.

*Arguments: P, I*

See also: newinterp

## save

save *VAL*

Save a value onto the user stack.

*Arguments: I or N or S or P*

## saveall

saveall

Save all the registers. Does a pushX for every type.

## savec

savec *VAL*

Save a clone of a value onto the user stack.

*Arguments: S or P*

## savetop

savetop

Save registers 16..31. Does a pushX for every type.

# sec

sec *DEST, VAL*

The secant of *VAL* in radians.

*Arguments:* NR, I or NR, N

# sech

sech *DEST, VAL*

The hyperbolic secant of *VAL* in radians.

*Arguments:* NR, I or NR, N

# seek

seek *DEST, IO, OFFSET, STARTFLAG*
seek *DEST, IO, UPPER32, LOWER32, STARTFLAG*

Set the file position of a ParrotIO object to a given offset from a starting position (STARTFLAG: 0 is the beginning of the file, 1 is current the position, 2 is the end of the file). *DEST* is the success or failure of the seek.

64-bit seek combines *UPPER32* and *LOWER32* to get one 64-bit *OFFSET*.

*Arguments:* P, I, I or P, I, I, I

# set

set *DEST, VAL*

Set a register to a value.

*Arguments:* IR, I or IR, N or IR, S or IR, P or NR, I or NR, N or NR, S or NR, P or SR, I or SR, N or SR, S or SR, P or P, I or P, N or P, S or P, P

set *DEST[KEY], VAL*

A keyed set operation on a PMC.

*Arguments:* P, I or P, N or P, S or P, P

set *DEST, PMC[KEY]*

A keyed get operation on a PMC.

*Arguments:* I, P or N, P or S, P or P, P

## setX_ind

```
seti_ind REG, VAL
setn_ind REG, VAL
sets_ind REG, VAL
setp_ind REG, VAL
```

Set register number REG of the specified type to VAL. Bypasses the register allocator, so use with care.

*Arguments: I, I or I, S or I, N or I, P*

## set_addr

```
set_addr DEST, LABEL
```

Return the current address plus the offset to LABEL. Often used to calculate absolute addresses for jump or jsr.

*Arguments: IR, IC*

```
set_addr SUB, LABEL
```

Set the subroutine address pointing to the given label.

*Arguments: P, I*

## set_chartype

```
set_chartype STRING, CHARTYPE
```

Set the chartype of a string.

*Arguments: S, I*

## set_eh

```
set_eh HANDLER
```

Push an exception handler on the control stack.

*Argument: P*

See also: clear_eh, throw

## set_encoding

```
set_encoding STRING, ENCODING
```

Set the encoding of a string.

*Arguments: S, I*

## setattribute

setattribute *OBJECT, OFFSET, ATTRIBUTE*

Set the given attribute at *OFFSET* for object *OBJECT*.

*Arguments: P, I, P*

See also: getattribute, classoffset

## setprop

setprop *PMC, NAME, VALUE*

Set the value of a named property on a PMC.

*Arguments: P, S, P*

See also: getprop and delprop

## shift

shift *DEST, PMC*

Shift a value off the front of an aggregate PMC.

*Arguments: IR, P or NR, P or SR, P or P, P*

## shl

shl *DEST, VAL, BITS*

Bitwise shift a value left by a given number of bits.

*Arguments: IR, I or P, I or P, P or IR, I, I or P, P, I or P, P, P*

## shr

shr *DEST, VAL, BITS*

Bitwise shift a value right by a given number of bits.

*Arguments: IR, I or P, I or P, P or IR, I, I or P, P, I or P, P, P*

## sin

sin *DEST, VAL*

The sine of *VAL* in radians.

*Arguments: NR, I or NR, N*

# singleton

singleton *DEST*

Take the given object and put it into its own singleton class.

*Argument: P*

# sinh

sinh *DEST, VAL*

The hyperbolic sine of *VAL* in radians.

*Arguments: NR, I or NR, N*

# sizeof

sizeof *DEST, TYPE*

Set *DEST* to the size in bytes of the given natural type.

*Arguments: IR, I*

# sleep

sleep *SECONDS*

Sleep for the given number of seconds.

*Arguments: I or N*

# spanw

spawnw *DEST, COMMAND*

Spawn a subprocess to run the given *COMMAND*, wait for it to finish, and return the result.

*Arguments: IR, S*

# splice

splice *DEST, REPLACE, OFFSET, COUNT*

Starting at *OFFSET*, replace *COUNT* number of values in the destination PMC with values provided in the *REPLACE* PMC.

*Arguments: P, P, I, I*

## sprintf

`sprintf DEST, FORMAT, ARGS`

Format arguments in an aggregate PMC, using format string *FORMAT*.

*Arguments: SR, S, P or P, P, P*

## store_global

`store_global NAME, OBJECT`
`store_global NAME, NAMESPACE, OBJECT`

Store a global variable as a named symbol.

*Arguments: S, P or S, S, P or P, S, P*

See also: `find_global`

## store_lex

`store_lex NAME, OBJECT`
`store_lex DEPTH, NAME, OBJECT`
`store_lex DEPTH, POSITION, OBJECT`

Store an object as a lexical variable with a given name. If the symbol doesn't exist, it will be created in the lexical scratchpad at the specified depth (a negative depth counts back from the current scope). If *DEPTH* isn't provided, the symbol must already exist. If a position is provided instead of a name, the symbol will be stored at the given position in the scratchpad.

*Arguments: S, P or I, I, P or I, S, P*

See also: `find_lex`

## string_chartype

`string_chartype DEST, STRING`

Return the chartype of the string.

*Arguments: IR, S*

## string_encoding

`string_encoding DEST, STRING`

Return the encoding of the string.

*Arguments: IR, S*

# stringinfo

stringinfo *DEST, STRING, FLAG*

Return information about a string. An integer flag selects which information to return, as listed in Table 11-2.

*Arguments: IR, S, I*

*Table 11-2. stringinfo arguments*

| Flag | Returns |
|------|---------|
| 1 | Location of string buffer header |
| 2 | Location of start of string memory |
| 3 | Allocated length, in bytes |
| 4 | String flags |
| 5 | Length of string buffer currently used, in bytes |
| 6 | String length, in characters |

# sub

sub *DEST, VAL*
sub *DEST, VAL1, VAL2*

Subtract *VAL2* from *VAL1*. If no *VAL2*, subtract *VAL* from *DEST*.

*Arguments: IR, I or NR, I or NR, N or P, I or P, N or P, P or IR, I, I or NR, N, I or NR, N, N or P, P, I or P, P, N or P, P, P*

# subclass

subclass *DEST, CLASS*
subclass *DEST, CLASS, NAME*

Create a sublass of *CLASS*. Without *NAME* an anonymous subclass is created.

*Arguments: P, S or P, P or P, S, S or P, P, S*

# substr

substr *DEST, STRING, OFFSET*
substr *DEST, STRING, OFFSET, LENGTH*

Return a substring of *STRING*, beginning at *OFFSET* and with length *LENGTH*.

*Arguments: SR, S, I or SR, S, I, I or SR, P, I, I*

substr *DEST, STRING, OFFSET, LENGTH, REPLACE*

If *REPLACE* is given, use it to replace the returned substring in *STRING*.
*Arguments:* SR, S, I, I, S

substr *DEST, OFFSET, LENGTH, REPLACE*

If *STRING* is omitted, operate on the string in *DEST*.
*Arguments:* SR, I, I, S

## substr_r

substr_r *DEST, STRING, OFFSET, LENGTH*

Acts like substr, but reuses the destination string instead of creating a new string.
*Arguments:* SR, S, I, I

## sweep

sweep *LAZY*

Trigger a dead object detection (DOD) sweep. If *LAZY* is set to 1, only objects that need timely destruction may be destroyed.
*Argument:* IC

## sweepoff

sweepoff

Disable DOD sweeps (nestable).

## sweepon

sweepon

Reenable DOD sweeps.

## sysinfo

sysinfo *DEST, ITEM*

Return operating-system–specific details given by ITEM.
*Arguments:* IR, I or SR, I

## tan

tan *DEST, VAL*

The tangent of *VAL* in radians.

*Arguments: NR, I or NR, N*

## tanh

tanh *DEST, VAL*

The hyperbolic tangent of *VAL* in radians.

*Arguments: NR, I or NR, N*

## tell

tell *DEST, PIO*
tell *UPPER32, LOWER32, PIO*

Return the file position of the given `ParrotIO` object.

*Arguments: IR, P or IR, I, P*

See also: seek

## thaw

thaw *DEST, STR*

Create a new PMC representing the frozen image.

*Arguments: P, S*

See also: freeze

## throw

throw *EXCEPTION*

Throw an exception.

*Argument: P*

See also: rethrow, set_eh, clear_eh

## time

time *DEST*

Return the current system time.

*Arguments: IR or NR*

## titlecase

```
titlecase DEST
titlecase DEST, VAL
```

Create a copy of the string in VAL with all characters converted to title case, and store it in DEST. If VAL is omitted, convert and replace the string in DEST.

*Arguments: SR or SR, S*

See also: upcase, downcase

## trace

```
trace INT
```

Toggle tracing in the interpreter (0 for off, any other value for on).

*Argument: I*

## transcode

```
transcode DEST, ENCODING
transcode DEST, SOURCE, ENCODING
transcode DEST, SOURCE, ENCODING, CHARTYPE
```

Transcode a string to the given CHARTYPE and ENCODING. If CHARTYPE is omitted, it is assumed to be the same as the original.

*Arguments: SR, I or SR, S, I or SR, S, I, I*

## typeof

```
typeof DEST, VAL
typeof DEST, PMC[KEY]
```

Return the type of a PMC or Parrot data type, either its class name (to a string destination) or integer identifier (to an integer destination).

*Arguments: IR, P or SR, I or SR, P*

## unless

```
unless CONDITION, LABEL
```

Jump to a label unless the condition is a true value.

*Arguments: I, IC or N, IC or S, IC or P, IC*

# unpin

unpin *DEST*

Make the string in *DEST* movable again. This is the default, so unpin is a no-op unless the string has been pinned with pin.

*Argument: SR*

See also: pin

# unregister

unregister *PMC*

Remove one reference to PMC from the root set registry.

*Argument: P*

See also: register

# unshift

unshift *DEST, VAL*

Unshift a value onto the front of an aggregate PMC.

*Arguments: P, I or P, N or P, S or P, P*

# upcase

upcase *DEST*
upcase *DEST, VAL*

Create a copy of the string in *VAL* with all characters converted to uppercase, and store it in *DEST*. If *VAL* is omitted, convert and replace the string in *DEST*.

*Arguments: SR or SR, S*

See also: downcase, titlecase

# updatecc

updatecc

Update the state of a return continuation stored in P1. Used when context information changes after the return continuation is created but before it's invoked.

See also: invokecc

## valid_type

valid_type *DEST, TYPE*

Check whether a PMC type or native Parrot datatype is a valid one.

*Arguments: IR, I*

## vers

vers *DEST, VAL*

The versine of *VAL* in radians.

*Arguments: NR, N*

## warningsoff

warningsoff *CATEGORY*

Turn off a particular category of warnings by category number. Turning off one category will not affect the status of other warnings categories. See warningson for the list of categories.

*Argument: I*

## warningson

warningson *CATEGORY*

Turn on a particular category of warnings by category number. The default is all warnings off. Turning on one category will not turn off other categories. Combine category numbers with a bitwise OR to turn on more than one at a time. If you include *warnings.pasm*, the category numbers are available by name as:

    .PARROT_WARNINGS_ALL_FLAG
    .PARROT_WARNINGS_UNDEF_FLAG
    .PARROT_WARNINGS_IO_FLAG
    .PARROT_WARNINGS_PLATFORM_FLAG

*Argument: I*

## xor

xor *DEST, VAL1, VAL2*

Logical XOR. If *VAL1* is true and *VAL2* is false, return *VAL1*. If *VAL1* is false and *VAL2* is true, return *VAL2*. Otherwise, return a false value.

*Arguments: IR, I, I or P, P, P*

# PIR Directives

This is a summary of PIR directives. Directives are preprocessed by the Parrot interpreter. Since PIR and PASM run on the same interpreter, many of the directives listed here are also valid in PASM code.

## .arg

`.arg VAL`

Push a value onto the user stack or set it according to PCC.

## .const

`.const TYPENAME = VALUE`

Define a named constant.

## .constant

`.constant NAMEVALUE`

Define a named macro that expands to a given value. Macros are called as directives—i.e., *.NAME* (PASM code only).

## .emit

`.emit`

Define a compilation unit of PASM code. Always paired with `.eom`.

## .end

`.end`

End a compilation unit. Always paired with `.sub`.

## .endm

`.endm`

End a macro definition. Always paired with `.macro`.

## .eom

```
.eom
```

End a compilation unit of PASM code. Always paired with .emit.

## .flatten_arg

```
.flatten_arg PArray
```

Flatten the passed array PMC and provide args for PCC calls.

## .globalconst

```
.globalconst TYPENAME = VALUE
```

Define a named, file visible constant.

## .include

```
.include " FILENAME "
```

Include the contents of an external file by inserting it in place.

## .invocant

```
.invocant OBJ
```

Set the invocant for a method call.

## .local

```
.local TYPENAME
```

Define a local named variable.

## .macro

```
.macro NAME (PARAMS)
```

Define a named macro with a list of parameters. The macro is called as:

```
.NAME(arg1,arg2, . . .)
```

This directive is always paired with .endm.

## .meth_call

.meth_call *SUB*
.meth_call *SUB, RETCONT*

Create a method call.

## .namespace

.namespace  [ *"namespace"* ]

Define a namespace.

## .nci_call

.nci_call *SUB*

Create an NCI call.

## .param

.param *DEST*
.param *TYPENAME*

Pop a value off the user stack into a register or typed identifier.

## .pcc_begin

Start a call sequence. Always paired with .pcc_end.

## .pcc_begin_return

Start a return sequence. Always paired with .pcc_end_return.

## .pcc_begin_yield

Start a return of a coroutine sequence. Always paired with .pcc_end_yield.

## .pcc_call

.pcc_call *SUB*
.pcc_call *SUB, RETCONT*

Create a subroutine call.

## .pcc_sub

`.pcc_sub _LABEL`

Create a symbol entry for subroutine at the _LABEL. This directive is for PASM code only.

## .pragma

`.pragma fastcall`
`.pragma prototyped`

Set default calling conventions.

## .result

`.result DEST`

Pop a value off the user stack or get it according to PCC.

## .return

`.return VAL`

Return a value to the calling subroutine by pushing it onto the user stack or set it according to PCC.

## .sub

`.sub NAME`

Define a compilation unit. Always paired with .end. Names begin with _ by convention.

## .sym

`.sym TYPE NAME`

Same as .local.

# PIR Instructions

This section is a quick reference to PIR instructions. For more details and the latest changes, see *imcc/docs/syntax.pod* or dive into the source code in *imcc/imcc.l* and *imcc/imcc.y*.

---

## =

```
DEST = VAL
```

Assign a value to a particular register, temporary register, or named variable.

---

## +, +=

```
DEST = VAL + VAL
DEST += VAL
```

Add two numbers or PMCs.

---

## -, -=

```
DEST = VAL1 - VAL2
DEST -= VAL1
DEST = - VAL
```

Subtract *VAL1* from *VAL2*. The unary - negates a number.

---

## *, *=

```
DEST = VAL * VAL
DEST *= VAL
```

Multiply two numbers or PMCs.

---

## /, /=

```
DEST = VAL1 / VAL2
DEST /= VAL1
```

Divide *VAL1* by *VAL2*.

---

## **

```
DEST = VAL1 ** VAL2
```

Raise *VAL1* to the power of *VAL2*.

---

## %, %=

```
DEST = VAL1 % VAL2
DEST %= VAL1
```

Divide *VAL1* by *VAL2* and return the (mod) remainder.

---

## ., .=

```
DEST = VAL . VAL
DEST .= VAL
```

Concatenate two strings. The concat operator must be surrounded by whitespace.

---

## <

```
if VAL1 < VAL2 goto LABEL
```

Conditionally branch to a label if *VAL1* is less than *VAL2*.

---

## <=

```
if VAL1 <= VAL2 goto LABEL
```

Conditionally branch to a label if *VAL1* is less than or equal to *VAL2*.

---

## >

```
if VAL1 > VAL2 goto LABEL
```

Conditionally branch to a label if *VAL1* is greater than *VAL2*.

---

## >=

```
if VAL1 >= VAL2 goto LABEL
```

Conditionally branch to a label if *VAL1* is greater than or equal to *VAL2*.

---

## ==

```
if VAL1 == VAL2 goto LABEL
```

Conditionally branch to a label if *VAL1* is equal to *VAL2*.

## !=

```
if VAL1 != VAL2 goto LABEL
```

Conditionally branch to a label if *VAL1* is not equal to *VAL2*.

## &&

```
DEST = VAL1 && VAL2
```

Logical AND. Return *VAL1* if it's false. Otherwise, return *VAL2*.

## ||

```
DEST = VAL1 || VAL2
```

Logical OR. Return *VAL1* if it's true. Otherwise, return *VAL2*.

## ~~

```
DEST = VAL1 ~~ VAL2
```

Logical XOR. If *VAL1* is true and *VAL2* is false, return *VAL1*. If *VAL1* is false and *VAL2* is true, return *VAL2*. Otherwise, return a false value.

## !

```
DEST = ! VAL
```

Logical NOT. Return a true value if *VAL* is false.

## &, &=

```
DEST = VAL & VAL
DEST &= VAL
```

Bitwise AND on two values.

## |, |=

```
DEST = VAL | VAL
DEST |= VAL
```

Bitwise OR on two values.

## ~, ~=

```
DEST = VAL ~ VAL
DEST ~= VAL
DEST = ~ VAL
```

Bitwise XOR on two values. The unary form is a bitwise NOT on a value.

## <<, <<=

```
DEST = VAL1 << VAL2
DEST <<= VAL2
```

Bitwise shift *VAL1* left by *VAL2* number of bits.

## >>, >>=

```
DEST = VAL1 >> VAL2
DEST >>= VAL2
```

Bitwise shift *VAL1* right by *VAL2* number of bits.

## >>>, >>>=

```
DEST = VAL1 >>> VAL2
DEST >>>= VAL2
```

Logically shift *VAL1* right by *VAL2* number of bits.

## [ ]

```
DEST = PMC [ KEY ]
PMC [ KEY ] = VAL
```

Indexed access to a PMC and indexed assignment to a PMC.

```
DEST = STRING [ OFFSET ]
STRING [ OFFSET ]  = VAL
```

Access a one-character substring on a string, starting at a particular offset, or assign to that substring.

## addr

```
DEST = addr LABEL
```

Return the address of a label.

## call

call *NAME*

Call the named subroutine (a .sub label).

## global

*DEST* = global *NAME*
global *NAME* = *VAL*

Access a global variable for read or write.

## goto

goto *NAME*

Jump to the named identifier (label or subroutine name).

## if

if *EXPR* goto *NAME*

If the value or expression evaluates as true, jump to the named identifier.

## unless

unless *VAL* goto *NAME*

Unless the value evaluates as true, jump to the named identifier.

# Parrot Command-Line Options

Since Parrot is both an assembler and a bytecode interpreter, it has options to control both behaviors. Some options may have changed by the time you read this, especially options related to debugging and optimization. The document *imcc/docs/running.pod* should have the latest details. Or just run *parrot --help*.

## General Usage

parrot [*options*] *file* [*arguments*]

The *file* is either an *.imc* (*.pir*) or *.pasm* source file or a Parrot bytecode file. Parrot creates an Array object to hold the command-line *arguments* and stores it in P5 on program start.

## Assembler Options

-a, --pasm
> Assume PASM input on stdin. When Parrot runs a source file with a *.pasm* extension, it parses the file as pure PASM code. This switch turns on PASM parsing (instead of the default PIR parsing) when a source file is read from stdin.

-c,--pbc
> Assume PBC file on stdin. When Parrot runs a bytecode file with a *.pbc* extension, it immediately executes the file. This option tells Parrot to immediately execute a bytecode file piped in on stdin.

-d,--debug [hexbits]
> Turn on debugging output. The -d switch takes an optional argument, which is a hex value of debug bits. (The individual bits are shown in Table 11-3.) When *hexbits* isn't specified, the default debugging level is 0001. If *hexbits* is separated from the -d switch by whitespace, it has to start with a number.

Table 11-3. Debug bits

| Description | Debug bit |
|---|---|
| DEBUG_PARROT | 0001 |
| DEBUG_LEXER | 0002 |
| DEBUG_PARSER | 0004 |
| DEBUG_IMC | 0008 |
| DEBUG_CFG | 0010 |
| DEBUG_OPT1 | 0020 |
| DEBUG_OPT2 | 0040 |
| DEBUG_PBC | 1000 |
| DEBUG_PBC_CONST | 2000 |
| DEBUG_PBC_FIXUP | 4000 |

To produce a huge output on stderr, turn on all the debugging bits:

```
$ parrot -d 0ffff ...
```

--help-debug
> Show debug option bits.

-h,--*help*

Print a short summary of options to stdout and exit.

-o *outputfile*

Act like an assembler. With this switch, Parrot won't run code unless it's combined with the -r switch. If the name of *outputfile* ends with a . *pbc* extension, Parrot writes a Parrot bytecode file. If *outputfile* ends with a *.pasm* extension, Parrot writes a PASM source file, even if the input file was also PASM. This can be handy to check various optimizations when you run Parrot with the -Op switch.

If the extension is *.o* or equivalent, Parrot generates an object file from the JITed program code, which can be used to create a standalone executable program. This isn't available on all platforms yet; see *PLATFORMS* for which platforms support this.

-r,--*run-pbc*

Immediately execute bytecode. This is the default unless -o is present. The combination of -r -o output.pbc writes a bytecode file and executes the generated PBC.

-v,--*verbose*

One -v switch (imcc -v) shows which files are worked on and prints a summary of register usage and optimization statistics. Two -v switches (imcc -v -v) also prints a line for each individual processing step.

-y,--*yydebug*

Turn on yydebug for *yacc/bison*.

-E,--*pre-process-only*

Show output of macro expansions and quit.

-V,--*version*

Print the program version to stdout and exit.

-Ox

Turn on optimizations. The flags currently implemented are shown in Table 11-4.

*Table 11-4. Optimizations*

| Flag | Meaning |
| --- | --- |
| -O0 | No optimization (default). |
| -O1 | Optimizations without life info (e.g., branches and constants). |
| -O2 | Optimizations with life info. |
| -Oc | Optimize function call sequence. |
| -Op | Rearrange PASM registers with the most-used first. |

# Bytecode Interpreter Options

The interpreter options are mainly for selecting which run-time core to use for interpreting bytecode. The current default is the *computed goto core* if it's available. Otherwise, the *fast core* is used.

-b,--bounds-checks
> Activate bounds checking. This also runs with the *slow core* as a side effect.

-f,--fast-core
> Run with the *fast core*.

-g,--computed-goto-core
> Run the *computed goto core* (CGoto).

-j,--jit-core
> Run with the *JIT core* if available.

-p,--profile
> Activate profiling. This prints a summary of opcode usage and execution times after the program stops. It also runs within the *slow core*.

-C,--CGP-core
> Run with the *CGoto-Prederefed* core.

-P,--predereferenced-core
> Run with the *Prederefed core*.

-S,--switched-core
> Run with the *Switched core*.

-t,--trace
> Trace execution. This also turns on the *slow core*.

-w,--warnings
> Turn on warnings.

-G,--no-gc
> Turn off DOD/GC. This is for debugging only.

-.,--wait
> Wait for a keypress before running.

--leak-test,--destroy-at-end
> Clean up allocated memory when the final interpreter is destroyed. Parrot destroys created interpreters (e.g., threads) on exit but doesn't normally free all memory for the last terminating interpreter, since the operating system will do this anyway. This can create false positives when Parrot is run with a memory leak detector. To prevent this, use this option.

# Index

## Symbols

<...> (assertion delimiters), 88
[...] (brackets), 257
- - (autodecrement) operators, 34
_ _ (double underscore), 178
+ (addition)
   opcode, 254
   operator, 34
+= (addition assignment), 254
& (ampersand), 256
= (assignment) instruction (PIR), 254
= (assignment) operator, 33
* (asterisk), 254
! (bang), 256
:= (binding) operator, 33
&= (bitwise AND assignment)
   instruction (PIR), 256
& (bitwise AND) instruction (PIR), 256
| (bitwise AND) instruction (PIR), 256
|= (bitwise AND) instruction (PIR), 256
<< (bitwise left shift), 257
<<= (bitwise left shift assignment), 257
>> (bitwise right shift), 257
>>= (bitwise right shift
   assignment), 257
~= (bitwise XOR assignment)
   instruction (PIR), 257
~ (bitwise XOR) instruction (PIR), 257
^ (caret), placeholder variables, 63
.= (concatenation assignment)
   instruction (PIR), 255
. (concatenation) instruction (PIR), 255

/ (division)
   opcode, 254
   operator, 34
/= (division assignment), 254
. (dot), 255
= (equal sign), 254, 255
== (equality) instruction (PIR), 255
** (exponentiation)
   opcode, 254
   operator, 34
> (greater than), 255
>= (greater than or equal), 255
# (hash sign), 185
- (hyphen), 254
< (left angle bracket), 255, 257
< (less than), 255
<= (less than or equal), 255
&& (logical AND)
   opcode, 256
   operator, 36
|| (logical OR)
   opcode, 256
   operator, 36
>>> (logical right shift), 257
>>>= (logical right shift
   assignment), 257
~~ (logical XOR) instruction
   (PIR), 256
%= (modulus assignment), 255
% (modulus) operator, 34, 255
* (multiplication)
   opcode, 254
   operator, 34

We'd like to hear your suggestions for improving our indexes. Send email to *index@oreilly.com*.

*= (multiplication assignment), 254
- (negation), 254
! (not), 256
!= (not equal), 256
// operator, 88
^^ operator, 36
~ operator (string concatenation), 34
% (percent sign), 255
| (pipe), 256
+ (plus sign), 254
++ (postfix autoincrement)
    operators, 34
> (right angle bracket), 255, 257
$ sigil, 29
% sigil, 31
@ sigil, 26
/ (slash), 254
~~ (smart-match) operators, 87
    syntax, 42–47
- (subtraction)
    opcode, 254
    operator, 34
-= (subtraction assignment), 254
~ (tilde), 256, 257

## A

abs opcode (PASM), 203
absolute addresses, 159
Abstract Syntax Tree (AST), 101
abstraction, 99
accessibility
    attributes, 75
    numbered capture variables, 97
acos opcode (PASM), 204
adaptability, principle of, 18
add opcode, 178, 204
addattribute opcode, 176, 204
addition (+) operator, 34
addparent opcode (PASM), 204
addr instruction (PIR), 257
addresses, 159
aggregates, PMCs, 144
alarm( ) request, 115
allocation
    garbage collection, 120
    registers, spilling, 189
alternate option syntax pairs, 27
    (see also syntax)
and opcode, 142, 204

AND relation, 36
anonymous arrayref constructor
    ([...]), 30
anonymous classes, 78
anonymous hash reference constructor
    ({...}), 31
anonymous pairs, named argument
    passing, 64
anonymous rules matching, 88
    (see also rules)
anonymous subroutines, 68
Apocalypse, 4
architecture, 23–24
    bytecode loader, 104
    compiler module, 102
    continuations, 122
    coroutines, 124
    design, 99–101
    events, 113
    garbage collection, 120
    interpreter module, 104, 105–111
    I/O, 111
    multimethod dispatching, 121
    objects, 117–119
    optimizer module, 103
    parser module, 101
    signals, 114
    threads, 115
.arg directive, 250
arguments
    floating-point operations, 133
    pairs, passing as, 58
    positional, 61
    subroutines, 64–66
    use of ^ (caret), 63
arithmetic operators, 34
    junctions, 41
arrays, 26
    assertions, 93
    list context, 29
    matching, 44
    one-element, 30
    PMCs, 144
    strings, splitting, 140
arrow operator, 68
asec opcode (PASM), 204
asin opcode (PASM), 205
assembler code, 12
assembly compiler module, 102
    (see also PASM)

assertions
    delimiters (< ... >), 88
    rules, 93
assign opcode (PASM), 205
assignment
    = operator, 33
    arrays to lists, 30
    binding, curried subroutines, 70
    PMCs, 147
    registers, 128
AST (Abstract Syntax Tree), 101
asynchronous I/O, 112
atan opcode (PASM), 205
attributes
    classes, PASM, 176
    objects, 75
    private, 83
autodecrement (- -) operators, 34
automatic referencing, 28

## B

backtracking patterns, 97
band opcode (PASM), 205
bands opcode (PASM), 205
bare blocks, 68
BASIC, 12
Befunge, 12
benchmarks, 12
Bergman, Artur, 7
binary junction operators, 40
binary logical operators, 36
binary math opcodes, 133
binding
    curried subroutines, 70
    operators, 33
bitwise operations, PASM, 142
bitwise operators, 38
blocks
    bare, 68
    class declarations, 74
    control structures, 53–57
    definitions, 75
    macros, 72
bnot opcode (PASM), 205
bnots opcode (PASM), 206
Boolean context, 37
bor opcode (PASM), 206
borrowing, principles of, 22
bors opcode (PASM), 206

bounds opcode (PASM), 206
branch opcode (PASM), 206
branch_cs opcode (PASM), 206
branches, flow control, 148–151
bsr opcode, 159, 207
bug tracking, 15
bugs, reporting, 15
BUILD method, 77
BUILDALL method, 77
built-in quantifiers, 92
built-in rules, 96
built-in types, scalars, 26
bxor opcode (PASM), 207
bxors opcode (PASM), 207
bytecode, 110
    interpreter options (Parrot), 261
    loader, 104
    PASM, 174

## C

C extensions, 100
call instruction (PIR), 258
calling
    conventions, PASM, 159–162
    fail function, 97
callmethod opcode (PASM), 207
callmethodcc opcode (PASM), 207
calls
    indirect objects, 76
    lexically scoped subroutines, 67
    Parrot-calling conventions, 195
    private attributes, 83
    stack-based subroutine, 197
    subroutines, 58
        anonymous, 68
        curried, 69
        Lvalue, 71
        multiple, 68
        wrapped, 70
can opcode (PASM), 208
caret (^), placeholder variables, 63
CATCH block, 56
ceil opcode (PASM), 208
.cglobalonst directive, 251
chained comparison operators, 35
characters, 90
    assertions, 93
    compression, Huffman coding, 17
    converting, 137

design *(continued)*
   modular, 7
   multimethod dispatching, 121
   objects, 117–119
   optimizer module, 103
   parser module, 101
   PIR, 185, 186–190, 191, 192,
      194–201
   signals, 114
   threads, 115
destination registers, 132
destruction, objects, 77
development, 11–13
   cycles, 9, 11
   internals, 5–7
   languages, 9–11
   p61 mailing list, joining, 12
   Parrot, 11–15
die_hard opcode (PASM), 214
diff -u command, 13
directories, 12
dispatches, subroutines, 121
distinction, principle of, 21
div opcode (PASM), 214
division (/) operator, 34
dlfunc opcode, 163, 214
dlvar opcode (PASM), 214
docs/ directory, 12
does opcode (PASM), 214
Dominus, Mark-Jason, 4
double underscore (_ _), 178
downcase opcode (PASM), 215
.dump method, 42
DWIM, principle of, 20
dynamic languages, 105
   (see also languages)

# E

elements
   arrays, 30
   copying, 35
.elems method, 26
.emit directive, 250
encapsulation
   objects, 74
   (see also objects)
encoding, 218, 240, 243
encoding strings, 108
.end directive, 250

end opcode, 149, 215
end weight, principle of, 19
.endm directive, 250
enternative opcode (PASM), 215
entrytype opcode (PASM), 215
enumeration, assertions, 93
.eom directive, 251
eq opcode (PASM), 215
eq_addr opcode, 150, 216
eq_num opcode (PASM), 216
eq_str opcode (PASM), 216
err opcode (PASM), 216
errors, exceptions, 56
errorsoff opcode (PASM), 216
errorson opcode (PASM), 216
escape sequences, 91
events, 113
   PASM, 169
   signals, 114
examples/ directory, 12
exceptions, 56
   PASM, 168–169
exchange opcode (PASM), 217
Exegeses, 4
Exegesis, development cycle, 10
exists opcode (PASM), 217
existsopcode, 145
exit opcode (PASM), 217
exp opcode (PASM), 217
explicit types, 32
   (see also types)
exponentiation (**) operator, 34
exsec opcode (PASM), 217
extensions
   C, 100
   .pasm, 126

# F

fact opcode (PASM), 217
fail function, 97
familiarity, 23
fast core, 261
fdopen opcode (PASM), 218
filenames, patches, 14
files
   bytecode, 111
   closing, 141
   definitions, class declarations, 75
   MANIFEST, 13

opening, 141
    reading from, 142
find_chartype opcode (PASM), 218
findclass opcode (PASM), 219
find_encoding opcode (PASM), 218
find_global opcode (PASM), 218
find_lex opcode, 157, 218
find_method opcode (PASM), 219
find_type opcode (PASM), 219
flags, formatting strings, 138
%flags hash, 61
.flatten_arg directive, 251
flattening arguments, 64
flattening-list context, 29, 37
floating-point constants, 127
floating-point numbers, scalars, 26
floating-point operations, 133
floor opcode (PASM), 219
flow control, 192
    continuations, 122
    exceptions, 56, 168–169
    PASM, 148–151
    PIR, 192
foldup opcode (PASM), 219
for loop, 51
formal parameters subroutines, 59–63
    (see also parameters)
formatting strings, 137
Forth, 12
frames, registers, 153
freedom, principles of, 22
freeze opcode (PASM), 220
functions
    fail, 97
    NCI, 163
    vtable, overriding, 177

# G

garbage collection, 120
gcd opcode (PASM), 220
gc_debug opcode (PASM), 220
ge (greater than or equal), 220
generic object interfacing, 117
ge_num opcode (PASM), 220
ge_str opcode (PASM), 220
get_addr opcode (PASM), 221
getattribute opcode (PASM), 221
getclass opcode (PASM), 221
getfd opcode (PASM), 221

getfile opcode (PASM), 221
getinterp opcode (PASM), 221
getline opcode (PASM), 222
getpackage opcode (PASM), 222
getprop opcode, 147, 222
getstderr opcode (PASM), 222
getstdin opcode (PASM), 222
getstdout opcode (PASM), 222
global instruction (PIR), 258
global labels, 191
global variables, PASM, 155
globally scoped subroutines, 68
gmtime opcode (PASM), 222
goto command (PIR), 258
grammars, 89
    yacc, 102
grouping single-character modifiers, 94
gt opcode (PASM), 223
gt_num opcode (PASM), 223
gt_str opcode (PASM), 223

# H

handles keyword, 82
handling
    exceptions, 168–169
    signals, 170
Hansen, Ask Bjørn, 8
has keyword, attribute declarations, 75
hash sign (#), 185
hashes, 27
    assertions, 93
    matching, 45
    parameters, 61
    PMCs, 145
hashlist context, 31, 38
hav opcode (PASM), 223
hierarchical data structures, value
        types, 33
Huffman coding, 17
hyper operators, 39
hypothetical variables, 97

# I

if (conditional)
    instruction (PIR), 258
    opcode (PASM), 223
if statement, 48
immediate matches, rules, 87
implicit variable types, 32

inc opcode (PASM), 178, 223
_inc subroutine, 161
.include directive, 251
include files, iterator.pasm, 145
index opcode (PASM), 224
indexed access to PMC (PIR), 257
indexes
    arrays, 26
    hashes, 27
    variables, storing, 157
indirect objects, 76
inheritance
    classes, PASM, 178
    objects, 77
    public methods, 83
_ _init method, 178
initialization, objects, 77
instance variables (see attributes)
Int value types, 32
integers
    bitwise operators, 38
    context, 37
    PASM, 127
        registers, 127–131
    registers, 132
    scalars, 26
interfaces, 79, 80
    generic objects, 117
    NCI, 162
internal modifiers, 94
internal revision (development
        cycle), 10
internals development, 5–7
interpinfo opcode (PASM), 224
interpolation, syntax rules, 93
interpreter module, 104, 105–111
.invocant directive, 251
invocants
    objects, 177
    passing, 76
invoke opcode (PASM), 224
invokecc opcode, 162, 225
I/O, PASM, 141–142
isa opcode (PASM), 225
is_null opcode, 150
isnull opcode (PASM), 225
iteration
    control structures, 50–53
    flow control, 150
iterators, PMCs, 145

## J

join opcode, 140, 225
jsr opcode (PASM), 225
jump opcode, 149, 226
jumps, flow control, 148–151
junctions
    matching, 46
    operators, 40–42

## K

.keys method, 28
keywords
    handles, 82
    has, 75
    multi, 85
    returns, 63
    role, 79
    sub, 58, 63

## L

labels, 191
languages, 9
    design, 4, 16
        architecture, 23–24
        cognitive/linguistic
            considerations, 16
        cultural influences of, 21
        Huffman coding, 17
        principle of adaptability, 18
        principle of borrowing, 22
        principle of context, 19
        principle of distinction, 21
        principle of DWIM, 20
        principle of end weight, 19
        principle of freedom, 22
        principle of prominence, 18
        principle of reuse, 20
        principle of simplicity, 17
        syntax (see syntax)
        waterbed theory of
            complexity, 17
    development, 9–11
    modular design, 7
    OO (object-oriented), 109
    optimizing, 103
    rules, 87
    yacc grammars, 102
    (see also PASM)

languages/directory, 12
LANGUAGES.STATUS file, 12
lazy list context, 38
lcm opcode (PASM), 226
le (less than or equal) opcode
        (PASM), 226
length opcode, 135, 226
le_num opcode (PASM), 226
le_str opcode (PASM), 226
let blocks, 54
lexical scope, closures, 164
lexical variables, PASM, 156, 158
lexically scoped classes, 78
lexically scoped subroutines, 67
lexing, 101
lib/ directory, 12
linguistic language design
        considerations, 16
lists
    context, 29, 37
    for loops, 51
    hyper operators, 39
    matching, 43
    operators, 35
    pairs, named argument passing, 64
    parameters, 59
ln opcode (PASM), 227
load_bytecode, 227
loading bytecode, 104, 174
loadlib opcode (PASM), 227
.local directive, 251
local labels, 191
.local statement, 188
localtime opcode (PASM), 227
log10 opcode (PASM), 227
log2 opcode (PASM), 227
logical operations, PASM, 142
logical operators, 36
long-term usability, 24
lookback opcode (PASM), 228
loops
    breaking out of, 53
    flow control, 150
    for, 51
    simple, 51
    while, 51
lsr opcode (PASM), 228
lt (less than) opcode (PASM), 228
lt_num opcode (PASM), 228
lt_str opcode (PASM), 228
Lvalue subroutines, 71

# M

m// operator, 87
.macro directive, 251
macros, 71
mailing lists
    p6l, 5, 7, 10
        joining, 10
        patch submissions, 13–15
    Ponie, 8
MANIFEST file, 13
matching
    arrays, 44
    assertions, 93
    bytecode, 111
    deferred matches, rules, 88
    hashes, 45
    hypothetical variables, 97
    immediate matches, rules, 87
    junctions, 46
    lists, 43
    objects, 46
    quantifiers, 92
    scalar values, 42
    ~~ (smart-match) operator, 87
    subroutines, 46
math operations, PASM, 131–133
memory
    bytecode, 111
    garbage collection, 120
metacharacters, 90
    backtracking, 97
    escape sequences, 91
.meth_call directive, 252
methods, 201
    BUILD, 77
    BUILDALL, 77
    classes, PASM, 177
    coroutines, 124
    CREATE, 77
    .dump, 42
    .elems, 26
    _ _init, 178
    .keys, 28
    multi keyword, 85
    multimethod dispatching, 121
    new, 75
    objects, 76
    overriding, 84
    pick, 42
    PIR, 201

methods *(continued)*
    private, 83
    public, 83
    thread3, 172
    .values, 28
    .wrap, 70
migration, Ponie, 7
mixed class-type support, 119
mixins, 79, 80
mmdvtfind opcode (PASM), 228
mmdvtregister opcode (PASM), 229
mod opcode (PASM), 229
modifiers, size, 138
modular design, 7
modules
    compiler, 102
    interpreter, 104, 105–111
    optimizer, 103
    package-scoped subroutines, 66
    parser, 101
modulus (%) operator, 34
morphing, type, 131
mul opcode (PASM), 229
multi keyword, 85
multicharacter strings, converting, 137
multimethod dispatching, 121
multiple dispatch, objects, 85
multiple subroutines, 68
multiplication (*) operator, 34
my blocks, 54

## N

named arguments, 61
    passing, 64
named constants, PIR, 189
named parameters, 60
    default values, 62
named variables, PIR, 188
names
    patches, 14
    subroutines, 66
.namespace directive, 252
namespaces, block definitions, 75
Native Call Interface (NCI), 162
NCI (Native Call Interface), 162
.nci_call directive, 252
ne (not equal) opcode (PASM), 229
ne_addr opcode (PASM), 229
needs_destroy opcode (PASM), 230
neg opcode (PASM), 230

ne_num opcode (PASM), 230
nested scope, 157
ne_str opcode (PASM), 230
.NET, 104
new features, 24
new method, 75
new opcode, 175, 230
new_callback opcode (PASM), 231
newclass opcode, 175, 231
new_pad opcode (PASM), 231
new_padopcode, 157
newsub opcode (PASM), 231
nonflattening-list context, 37
noop opcode (PASM), 231
not opcode, 143, 232
null opcode (PASM), 232
<null> rule, 96
numeric bitwise shift operators, 39
numeric context, 37
numeric quantifiers, 92

## O

object-oriented (OO) languages, 109
objects
    attributes, 75
    construction, 77
    context, 37
    declarations, 74–82
    delegation, 82
    design, 117–119
    destruction, 77
    indirect, 76
    inheritance, 77
    initialization, 77
    matching, 46
    methods, 76
    multiple dispatch, 85
    opcodes, 179
    pairs, hashlist context, 31
    Parrot, 118
    ParrotIO, 141
    ParrotThread, 172
    PerlUndef, 141
    private/public methods, 83
    scalars, 26
    submethods, 84
    subroutines, 84
    timers, 170
    TQueue, 172
one-element lists, 30

OO (object-oriented) languages, 109
opcodes, 110
  bitwise, 143
  branches, 150
  PASM, 131–133, 179
open opcode (PASM), 141, 232
opening files, 141
operators
  - - (autodecrement), 34
  + (addition), 34
  = (assignment), 33
  := (binding), 33
  / (division), 34
  ** (exponentiation), 34
  && (logical AND), 36
  || (logical OR), 36
  ^^ (logical XOR), 36
  // (match), 88
  % (modulus), 34
  * (multiplication), 34
  ++ (autoincrement), 34
  ~ (string concatenation), 34
  - (subtraction), 34
  arithmetic, 41
  arrow, 68
  m// (match), 87
  overloading, 86
  range, 35
  s/// (substitution), 87
  ~~ (smart-match), 87
  symbol, 185
    PIR, 190
  syntax, 33
    arithmetic, 34
    assignment, 33
    binding, 33
    bitwise, 38
    comparison, 35
    conditional, 39
    context forcing, 36–38
    hyper, 39
    junctions, 40–42
    lists, 35
    logical, 36
    references, 47
    smart-match (~~), 42–47
    strings, 34
    zip, 48
  unary context forcing, 88
  x (string replication), 34

xx (list replication), 35
xx= (specified number of elements
  copies), 35
optimizations (Parrot), 260
optimizer
  module, 103
  PIR, 200
option syntax, 27
  (see also syntax)
optional parameters, subroutines, 60
or opcode, 142, 232
OR relation, 36
ord opcode, 137, 232
ordering
  argument constraints, 65
  parameters, 63
our blocks, 54
output, 141
overloading operators, 86
overriding
  methods, 84
  vtable functions, 177

## P

p61 mailing list, 5, 7, 10
  joining, 10
  patch submissions, 13–15
packaged-scoped subroutines, 66
pad stack, 157
pairs, 26
  arguments, 58
  hashlist context, 31
  named argument passing, 64
.param directive, 252
parameters
  arguments, passing, 64–66
  $multiplier, 69
  subroutines, 59–63
    anonymous, 68
    curried, 69
    Lvalue, 71
    multiple, 68
    wrapped, 70
Parrot, 11–13, 15
  assembler options, 259
  bug tracking, 15
  bytecode interpreter options, 261
  command-line options, 258
  debugging bits, 259
  development, 11–15

.result directive, 253
ret opcode (PASM), 237
rethrow opcode (PASM), 237
.return directive, 253
return values, parameters, 63
returning macros, 72
returns keyword, 63
reuse, principle of, 20
RFCs (Requests For Comments), 4
roles
    classes, 79
    conflicts, 81
    delegation, 82
rotate_up opcode (PASM), 238
routines
    macros, 71
    multi keyword, 85
    multiple subroutines, 68
    (see also subroutines)
RT (Request Tracker), 15
Ruby (Cardinal), 12
rules
    assertions, 93
    backtracking, 97
    built-in, 96
    escape sequences, 91
    grammars, 89
    hypothetical variables, 97
    languages, 87
    quantifiers, 92
    syntax, 88, 89–94
runinterp opcode (PASM), 238
running.pod file, 258
runtime, attaching properties, 31
rw property, 71

## S

s/// operator, 87
save opcode, 152, 238
saveall opcode, 153, 238
savec opcode (PASM), 238
savetop opcode (PASM), 238
saving registers, 160
scalars, 26
    context, 29, 37
    values, matching, 42
Scheme, 12
scope
    lexical, closures, 164
    nested, 157
    subroutines, 66

scratchpads, nested, 157
sec opcode (PASM), 239
sech opcode (PASM), 239
seek opcode, 142, 239
selection control structures, 48–50
sequences
    escape, 91
    Huffman coding, 17
set opcode, 178, 190, 239
set_addr opcode, 159
set_addr opcode (PASM), 240
set_addrop code, 149
setattribute opcode (PASM), 241
set_chartype opcode (PASM), 240
set_eh opcode (PASM), 240
set_encoding opcode (PASM), 240
seti_ind opcode (PASM), 240
setn_ind opcode (PASM), 240
setp_ind opcode (PASM), 240
setprop opcode (PASM), 241
setpropopcode, 147
sets_ind opcode (PASM), 240
shift opcode (PASM), 241
shl opcode (PASM), 241
shortcuts
    curried subroutines, 69
    printing, 141
    typed variables, 75
shr opcode (PASM), 241
SIGALRM, 115
SIGCHLD, 115
sigils
    $, 29
    %, 31
    @, 26
SIGINT, 115
SIGKILL, 114
siglets, 63
signals, 114, 170
signatures
    multi keyword, 85
    NCI functions, 163
    subroutines, 59
SIGSEGV, 114
simple loops, 51
simplicity, principle of, 17
sin opcode (PASM), 241
single values, scalar context, 29
single-character modifiers, 94
singleton opcode (PASM), 242
sinh opcode (PASM), 242

# About the Authors

**Allison Randal** is the project manager of the Perl 6 core development team. She has been working closely with Damian Conway and Larry Wall on Perl 6 and has cowritten the "Synopses" of Perl 6. She is dedicated to the success of the project and is one of the very first to learn about anything new that's proposed for Perl 6.

**Dan Sugalski** is the chief architect of Parrot, the language-independent interpreter developed as part of the Perl 6 design strategy. He's been a Perl 5 core developer for years, writing more than a dozen modules in the process. He's been a contributor to *The Perl Journal* and *The Perl Review*, as well as the O'Reilly Network.

**Leopold Tötsch** hails from Austria, where he first started working with computers in 1976. He is an independent software developer who has been exploring and developing open source software since 1991. He is the current Parrot pumpking and spends the majority of his free time working on Parrot.

# Colophon

Our look is the result of reader comments, our own experimentation, and feedback from distribution channels. Distinctive covers complement our distinctive approach to technical topics, breathing personality and life into potentially dry subjects.

The animal on the cover of *Perl 6 and Parrot Essentials*, Second Edition, is an aoudad (*ammotragus lervia*). Commonly known as Barbary sheep, aoudads originated in the arid mountainous regions of northern Africa and have stout, sturdy bodies, standing 30–40 inches at the shoulder and weighing from 65–320 pounds. The aoudad has a bristly reddish-brown coat and is distinguished by a heavy, fringed mane covering its chest and legs. Both males and females have thick, triangular-shaped horns that curve back in a semicircle. A male aoudad's horns can grow up to 2.5 feet.

Aoudads are herbivores and are most active at dawn and dusk, avoiding the desert heat of midday. They will drink water if it is available, but can obtain sufficient moisture from dew and vegetation. Aoudads are incredible jumpers, able to clear 6 feet from a standstill. So well suited are they to their surroundings that newborns have the ability to navigate rocky slopes just hours after birth.

Despite being endangered in their native environment, aoudads are flourishing in the United States. Introduced to western Texas and southern New Mexico in the 1940s, aoudads are now so populous that it is feared that their presence may threaten the native desert bighorn sheep. Aoudads are considered native game in the desert mountains of their adopted home, where the rugged landscape is dotted with ranches catering to recreational hunters.

Matt Hutchinson was the production editor for *Perl 6 and Parrot Essentials*, Second Edition. Octal Publishing, Inc. provided production services. Darren Kelly, Genevieve d'Entremont, and Emily Quill provided quality control.

Ellie Volckhausen designed the cover of this book, based on a series design by Edie Freedman. The cover image is a 19th-century engraving from *Animate Creations, Volume II*. Maureen McMahon produced the cover layout with QuarkXPress 4.1 using Adobe's ITC Garamond font.

David Futato designed the interior layout. This book was converted by Joe Wizda to FrameMaker 5.5.6 with a format conversion tool created by Erik Ray, Jason McIntosh, Neil Walls, and Mike Sierra that uses Perl and XML technologies. The text font is Linotype Birka; the heading font is Adobe Myriad Condensed; and the code font is LucasFont's TheSans Mono Condensed. The illustrations that appear in the book were produced by Robert Romano and Jessamyn Read using Macromedia FreeHand 9 and Adobe Photoshop 6. This colophon was written by Emily Quill.

# Need in-depth answers fast?

O'REILLY NETWORK
**Safari®**
**Bookshelf.**

## Access over 2,000 of the newest and best technology books online

Safari Bookshelf is the premier electronic reference library for IT professionals and programmers—a must-have when you need to pinpoint exact answers in an instant.

Access over 2,000 of the top technical reference books by twelve leading publishers including O'Reilly, Addison-Wesley, Peachpit Press, Prentice Hall, and Microsoft Press. Safari provides the technical references and code samples you need to develop quality, timely solutions.

---

## Try it today with a FREE TRIAL
## Visit *www.oreilly.com/safari/max/*

For groups of five or more, set up a free, 30-day corporate trial
Contact: *corporate@oreilly.com*

---

What Safari Subscribers Say:

*"The online books make quick research a snap. I usually keep Safari up all day and refer to it whenever I need it."*
—Joe Bennett, Sr. Internet Developer

*"I love how Safari allows me to access new books each month depending on my needs. The search facility is excellent and the presentation is top notch. It is one heck of an online technical library."*
—Eric Winslow, Economist-System, Administrator-Web Master-Programmer

# Related Titles Available from O'Reilly

## Perl

Advanced Perl Programming

CGI Programming with Perl, *2nd Edition*

Computer Science & Perl Programming: The Best of the Perl Journal

Embedding Perl in HTML with Mason

Games, Diversions, & Perl Culture: The Best of the Perl Journal

Learning Perl, *3rd Edition*

Learning Perl Objects, References and Modules

Mastering Algorithms with Perl

Mastering Perl/Tk

Mastering Regular Expressions, *2nd Edition*

Perl & LWP

Perl & XML

ßPerl CD Bookshelf, *Version 4.0*

Perl Cookbook, *2nd Edition*

Perl Debugger Pocket Reference

Perl for System Administration

Perl Graphics Programming

Perl in a Nutshell, *2nd Edition*

Perl Pocket Reference, *4th Edition*

Perl Template Toolkit

Practical mod_perl

Programming the Perl DBI

Programming Perl, *3rd Edition*

Programming Web Services with Perl

Regular Expression Pocket Guide

Web, Graphics & Perl/Tk: The Best of the Perl Journal

# O'REILLY®

Our books are available at most retail and online bookstores.
To order direct: 1-800-998-9938 • *order@oreilly.com* • *www.oreilly.com*
Online editions of most O'Reilly titles are available by subscription at *safari.oreilly.com*

# Keep in touch with O'Reilly

## 1. Download examples from our books

To find example files for a book, go to:

*www.oreilly.com/catalog*

select the book, and follow the "Examples" link.

## 2. Register your O'Reilly books

Register your book at *register.oreilly.com*

Why register your books? Once you've registered your O'Reilly books you can:

* Win O'Reilly books, T-shirts or discount coupons in our monthly drawing.

* Get special offers available only to registered O'Reilly customers.

* Get catalogs announcing new books (US and UK only).

* Get email notification of new editions of the O'Reilly books you own.

## 3. Join our email lists

Sign up to get topic-specific email announcements of new books and conferences, special offers, and O'Reilly Network technology newsletters at:

*elists.oreilly.com*

It's easy to customize your free elists subscription so you'll get exactly the O'Reilly news you want.

## 4. Get the latest news, tips, and tools

*http://www.oreilly.com*

* "Top 100 Sites on the Web"—PC Magazine
* CIO Magazine's Web Business 50 Awards

Our web site contains a library of comprehensive product information (including book excerpts and tables of contents), downloadable software, background articles, interviews with technology leaders, links to relevant sites, book cover art, and more.

## 5. Work for O'Reilly

Check out our web site for current employment opportunities:

*jobs.oreilly.com*

## 6. Contact us

O'Reilly & Associates
1005 Gravenstein Hwy North
Sebastopol, CA 95472 USA

TEL:  707-827-7000 or 800-998-9938
    (6am to 5pm PST)

FAX:  707-829-0104

**order@oreilly.com**
For answers to problems regarding your order or our products.
To place a book order online, visit:

*www.oreilly.com/order_new*

**catalog@oreilly.com**
To request a copy of our latest catalog.

**booktech@oreilly.com**
For book content technical questions or corrections.

**corporate@oreilly.com**
For educational, library, government, and corporate sales.

**proposals@oreilly.com**
To submit new book proposals to our editors and product managers.

**international@oreilly.com**
For information about our international distributors or translation queries. For a list of our distributors outside of North America check out:

*international.oreilly.com/distributors.html*

**adoption@oreilly.com**
For information about academic use of O'Reilly books, visit:

*academic.oreilly.com*

---

# O'REILLY®

Our books are available at most retail and online bookstores.
To order direct: 1-800-998-9938 • *order@oreilly.com* • *www.oreilly.com*
Online editions of most O'Reilly titles are available by subscription at *safari.oreilly.com*